Women's Entrepreneurship and Microfinance

Chiranjib Neogi · Amit Kumar Bhandari
Sudipto Ghosh
Editors

Women's Entrepreneurship and Microfinance

Editors
Chiranjib Neogi
Indian Statistical Institute
Kolkata, West Bengal
India

Sudipto Ghosh
Government of West Bengal
Kalyani, West Bengal
India

Amit Kumar Bhandari
Rishi Bankim Chandra Evening College
Naihati, West Bengal
India

ISBN 978-981-13-3836-6   ISBN 978-981-10-4268-3   (eBook)
DOI 10.1007/978-981-10-4268-3

© Springer Nature Singapore Pte Ltd. 2017
Softcover re-print of the Hardcover 1st edition 2017
This work is subject to copyright. All rights are reserved by the Publisher, whether the whole or part
of the material is concerned, specifically the rights of translation, reprinting, reuse of illustrations,
recitation, broadcasting, reproduction on microfilms or in any other physical way, and transmission
or information storage and retrieval, electronic adaptation, computer software, or by similar or dissimilar
methodology now known or hereafter developed.
The use of general descriptive names, registered names, trademarks, service marks, etc. in this
publication does not imply, even in the absence of a specific statement, that such names are exempt from
the relevant protective laws and regulations and therefore free for general use.
The publisher, the authors and the editors are safe to assume that the advice and information in this
book are believed to be true and accurate at the date of publication. Neither the publisher nor the
authors or the editors give a warranty, express or implied, with respect to the material contained herein or
for any errors or omissions that may have been made. The publisher remains neutral with regard to
jurisdictional claims in published maps and institutional affiliations.

Printed on acid-free paper

This Springer imprint is published by Springer Nature
The registered company is Springer Nature Singapore Pte Ltd.
The registered company address is: 152 Beach Road, #21-01/04 Gateway East, Singapore 189721, Singapore

Foreword

This volume, edited by Neogi, Bhandari, and Ghosh, fills a long-standing gap in the literature on gender issues in development in terms of the impact of microfinance institutions and other public programs, such as MGNREGA (Mahatma Gandhi National Rural Employment Guarantee Act) and NRLM (National Rural Livelihood Mission) programmes, on women empowerment. The nation at large continues to suffer because women do not enjoy the freedom of choice and privileges that are supposed to be available to all citizens of the country. Several public programs and institutions, such as microfinance, explicitly and implicitly target to improve the ability of women to function in an economy that boasts of being the fastest growing in the world. Chapters in the volume apply modern techniques, rigorous empirical evidence, and well-framed hypotheses to look deeper into the policy impact for the country and specifically for West Bengal. We often forget a critical point that policy makers need to be educated and updated continuously about the outcomes of the policies, and one must use the right kind of indices to assess the true state of affairs. Anyone, from policy makers to students, who is interested in women empowerment as a tool for improving his or her role as economic functionaries of the system and feels the necessity of going beyond the rhetoric and ribbon-cutting initiatives, will learn much from this volume. It goes without saying that the lead editor and many of the contributors are seasoned campaigners and very competent economists. I am confident that this volume will be a wonderful addition to the literature on gender and development.

Sugata Marjit
RBI Professor of Industrial Economics
Centre for Studies in Social Sciences
Calcutta (CSSSC) Member
State Public Policy and Planning Board
Government of West Bengal
Former Vice Chancellor
University of Calcutta

Preface

In current times, women entrepreneurship is being regarded as an effective component of sustainable economic development. In many developing countries, where societies are male-dominated, gender discrimination is noticed with respect to income, education, property rights, and other household issues. The male-dominant social order is a major roadblock faced by women in their way towards entrepreneurial initiatives. Gender equality is an essential component of economic growth, enabling women to become more effective economic actors. Often women have not only proved to be better repayers of loans, but also better savers than men, and more willing to form effective groups to collect savings and decrease costs of many small loans. Women, who are confident, make a good livelihood and household decisions, have control over resources, and can use larger loans effectively to increase their incomes, are considered potentially very good long-term clients. They can accumulate substantial savings that could then be channeled into insurance and other financial products. Women's use of financial services can increase their income and economic security, enhance their independence, reduce the vulnerability of their families, and stimulate local economies. Making financial services available to women clients, without adapting those services to the special constraints and coping strategies that arise from women's multiple social roles, often leads to loss of opportunity to achieve both significant outreach and economic and social empowerment. Availability of such financial services might enable women to start their economic activities, acquiring assets by investing the money borrowed.

Microfinance has been accepted as a potent instrument to improve living standards of the ultra-poor women in developing and least developed countries. The basic argument, in favor of lending out to women, is that they are good credit risks, are less likely to misuse the loan and are more likely to share the benefits with others in their household, especially their children. In addition to the economic benefits, it is argued that the increasing role of women in the household economy will lead to their empowerment. During the past few decades, microcredit has enjoyed tremendous growth, and women continue to be the major beneficiaries. Impact evaluation studies routinely find that lending to women benefits their households. However, some of them also find that this may not necessarily empower the women concerned. In the impoverished settings in which microfinance projects operate, kinship ties and marriage play an important role in providing individuals with legitimate claims over household and community resources, together with vital access to insurance networks in times of crisis. It is argued that cooperation and jointness of decision making may be more desirable for women than autonomous control over resources. This perspective has important implications regarding our understanding of the empowering potential of microfinance programs. If new economic opportunities lie outside the traditional realm of the female spouse and exit options for women are severely limited, then she may be better off ignoring them to preserve her social ties within the community. For these reasons, an intervention that requires cooperation of both spouses may be more successful in achieving wider social impacts than interventions that focus on women's autonomous spheres only. In the context of microfinance, this reasoning suggests that women who receive complementary business training in an activity that ensures their husbands' cooperation are more likely to benefit from access to credit than those who receive training in an autonomous productive activity that they can undertake independently within the household. Critics of microfinance doubt whether this has a positive impact on women empowerment. Many microfinance schemes have a clear focus on women. Women use a more substantial part of their income for health and education of their children. Thus, women play a very important role in reducing poverty within households. However, critics argue that often women are forced to hand over the loan to men, who subsequently use the loan amount for their purposes, which may lead to an additional burden for women if they are held responsible for the repayment.

Women in rural areas have inherent skills and are often adept at making handmade products with easily available raw materials. With few employment choices, women often start businesses in highly saturated sectors, in the informal economy with low-productivity and low-return activities. For many rural women, entrepreneurship is part of a broader livelihood strategy, often undertaken on a part-time basis. However, financial institutions are sceptical about the entrepreneurial abilities of women. Despite evidence that loan repayment rates are higher among women than men, women still face more difficulties in obtaining credit due to the discriminatory attitude of financial institutions. It is noticed that only a minuscule percentage of women who had taken a loan for income-generating activities have autonomous control over the loan money. In maximum instances, a male member of the family enjoys the control of loan proceeds. Given this backdrop, this volume seeks to understand the influence and impact of microfinance on women's entrepreneurship and empowerment within developing countries.

The first chapter by Chaiti Sharma Biswas depicts that most Indian women have a medium-level empowerment in the family. A very small percentage of women have high level of empowerment, which is normal in a patriarchal society; the percentage of women having a low level of empowerment is also surprisingly modest in India. Majority of women have medium-level education, which is of little use because most of the respondents remain unemployed. Those who opt for a job are mainly engaged in manual or unskilled jobs, indicating that in a patriarchal

Preface

ix

society, social norms are so rigid that medium or higher education fails to involve women in the job market. To ensure high-level empowerment, women must be engaged in high-level jobs which in turn require them to be highly qualified. High qualification and high-level job simultaneously create greater confidence among women, which ultimately helps them to make choices. Moreover, if they earn as much as or more than their husband, then their level of confidence will increase to a great extent, which in turn will increase their control on household decision making.

In the second chapter, Subhendu Chakrabarti aims to develop a generalized empowerment index through an axiomatic approach taking into account the varied level of individual empowerment for each attribute within the specific context. The index has been constructed by calculating simple average of the level of empowerment along individual attributes. It is revealed from the analysis that the level of women empowerment significantly differs among states, and within and between zones. Each zone represents some degree of social and cultural homogeneity, and these social and culture systems consist of rationale norms, values, and beliefs on which there is simultaneous consensus and disagreement, and which are subject to change. Based on an application of the empowerment index, one can identify the factor dominance and then plan accordingly. However, emphasis only on these two factors will be less effective in a society where religious and/or cultural dominance is very high.

In their contribution, Arghya Kusum Mukherjee and Amit Kundu highlight the role of traditional institutions and female beneficiaries of Mahatma Gandhi National Rural Employment Guarantee Act (MGNREGA) in West Bengal. Given the similarity in the socioeconomic characteristics of household across social groups, the difference among the groups in their response to MGNREGA participation is enormous. One possibility is that MGNREGA has attracted a highly selected sample of upper caste (UC) women who were especially responsive to MGNREGA. If social restrictedness creates bottlenecks for knowledge, and participation in MGNREGA allowed UC women to challenge existing gender norms to enhance their agency, then the question arises, why Muslim women, who are most fettered by social norms, did not respond more to the MGNREGA than scheduled caste (SC) women did. One explanation of the author's result is non-monotonicity in the effect of social restrictions. Participation in MGNREGA helped women whose agency had been held down by social restrictions, but women subject to extreme oppressions had too little agency to change desire or deeds.

In the chapter titled "Empowerment of Women Through Public Programs in Rural West Bengal: A Study on National Rural Livelihood Mission in a Block of Purulia", Tithi Bose and Archita Ghosh investigated the empowerment of women through public programs adopting a village-level survey in West Bengal and found that involvement in a group can have a big impact on women empowerment. Loans from the groups can be a great source of self-employment for the women involved, which develops self-esteem among women, helps to raise their voices against any corruption, and uplifts their position in their families. Women associated with groups are comparatively more aware and, therefore, manage to get panchayat's assistance for sanitation and electrification facilities. They do not find any enhancement in expenditure as a result of group association or group loans. Nevertheless, groups and group loans have highly impacted economic empowerment. Group loans and association with groups have socially empowered women as women associated with groups can stand beside other women, influence family decisions in a better manner, participate more in public and political gatherings, and engage themselves with different sorts of social gatherings. Members of groups that are not organized properly to make the members aware of new features are losing interest in such groups. All the implementing agencies should work in a coordinated manner to develop self-help groups (SHGs) and make their members truly economically self-empowered.

In their contribution Aparajita Dhara and Biswajit Chatterjee attempt to investigate the trends and determinants of non-farm employment among women in rural India. As the share of agriculture in gross domestic product (GDP) decreases with economic growth, so does its share in employment. Over time this leads to a shift in the rural occupational structure towards different non-agricultural and non-farm activities. A vibrant rural non-farm sector has the potential of reducing disguised unemployment in agriculture, forced-migration towards urban centres, rural poverty and rural income inequality. However, the extent of its success depends on whether such livelihood diversification is driven by growth-related 'pull' factors or distress-driven 'push' factors. Based on data from the quinquennial surveys on 'Employment and Unemployment Situation in India' carried out by the National Sample Survey Office and other official sources, the chapter analyzes the determinants of non-farm employment among the female workforce in rural India, segregated by industrial subsectors and employment status, during the two post-reform decades from 1990 to 2010. The results point towards some existence of distress factors and much region-specific heterogeneity in the dynamics involved.

In the chapter "Efficiency and Mission Drift—Debate Revisited in Indian Context", Chandralekha Ghosh and Samapti Guha highlight twin objectives of microfinance institutions (MFIs), serving the poorest clients and becoming financially self-reliant. This chapter examines the technical efficiencies and cost efficiencies of MFIs in Indian context using stochastic frontier analysis to get an idea of mission drift mainly by studying the relationship of efficiencies on a percentage of woman borrowers and the average size of the loan. The authors have obtained efficiencies of 86 Indian MFIs for the period 2010 to 2014. It was observed that if the loan size increases, both technical and cost efficiencies are increased, which is a case of mission drift. The experienced MFIs and the MFIs who own the assets achieve both the efficiencies. The increase in loan size establishes the fact that MFIs who gain efficiency regarding operation are diverting their objective of serving poor clients.

In the chapter titled "Microfinance and Human Development: A Cross-Generation Study", Arijita Dutta and Sharmistha Banerjee assess the impact of microfinance on education and career choice of the second generation of microfinance users, daughters and daughters-in-law, compared to the original microfinance borrowers and non-borrowers. These strategic life choices normally include their children's schooling and education, their own healthcare options and ability to earn

Preface

and spend according to their will. This chapter aims to capture the impact of microfinance use by 1200 middle-aged women on the overall human development of women of their next generation. Using propensity score matching techniques of impact evaluation, the chapter reveals that among the second-generation women of microfinance borrowers, neither education nor income-generating activities appear to be statistically higher compared to that of non-borrowing control groups. Thus, the impact of microfinance seems to fizzle out without sustainability, representing a sure sign of mission drift.

In his chapter, Avijit Brahmachary investigates the challenges of financing women-owned businesses in India. The formal financial sector generally assumes that providing small loans and deposit services to the zero-collateral-based unbanked people would be unprofitable because of the asymmetric information about the creditworthiness of the borrowers and due to the high transaction costs associated with the delivery of small-scale financial services. In India, the supply of finance for such small businesses is very low; since these businesses mostly belong to the informal unorganized sector, they are hardly able to manage adequate suitable finance from formal sources for their small set-ups. Microfinance through SHGs may put some solution with respect to the supply of finance and protects these people from the usurious moneylenders. In this chapter, the author attempts to analyze the major problems of women-owned small businesses in India and the role of group-based microfinance to accelerate such businesses providing small finance. The study reveals that most women in India choose to set up a business as a profession just due to the necessity of the family and, therefore, are not well prepared to face different social and financial problems related to it. Although the microfinance program along with different pro-poor financial initiatives has been initiated by the government and other private agencies from time to time to overcome such problems, the supply of such initiatives is lagging far behind the total demand.

In the chapter "Going Through the New Avenue of Life: A Study on Factors Working Behind Entrepreneurship Development Through Self-Help Group", Kallol Das investigates the factors working behind entrepreneurship development through an SHG. Development of the society is directly related to the income-generation capacity of its members. Women's entrepreneurship contributes to the economic well-being of the family and communities. The number of women enterprises has grown over a period through SHGs, thus empowering women and enhancing their position in society. It is an important mechanism of grassroots programs that tries to bring positive change by working directly with poor women. This chapter discusses some important factors working behind the successful running of microentrepreneurial activities and investigates the reasons for which other SHGs are unable to run their business. The chapter also shows how SHGs help women change their life in a positive manner through microentrepreneurial activities.

In the chapter titled "Access to Finance, Entrepreneurship, and Empowerment: A Case Study", Sudipto Ghosh and Chiranjib Neogi provide a detailed investigation on the effect of women empowerment on the control of resources and decision making. Access to microcredit has led to transformation in the social recognition of women's domestic labour force. The basic objective of this chapter is to assess the impact of MFI–SHG linkage on women entrepreneurship. It was observed that there is a change in their behaviour after associating with SHGs and gaining access to credit, both of which led to their empowerment. Examining the evidence on some key indicators it was observed that a change of approach and the strategy to make women truly empowered were needed. The empirical evidence clearly indicates a general increase in women empowerment for the members of SHG, where a majority of groups are linked with the help of non-government organizations (NGOs), which provide support in financial services and specialized training. It was found that such NGOs have a greater ability to make a positive impact on women empowerment. This, however, does not imply that each and every woman who joined the SHG program got empowered to the same degree or that they all progressed at the same pace. Microfinance came across as a tool that benefitted rural women immensely to uplift economically.

Chapter "Access to Credit and Microentrepreneurship: A Gender Comparison" by Rabin Mazumder, Subham Dastidar, and Amit Kumar Bhandari highlights the evidence of gender discrimination among rural microentrepreneurs in access to formal credit. This chapter uses data from a recent primary survey of five districts of West Bengal. The factors affecting access to formal credit are categorized into socioeconomic and business-related characteristics, and investigated based on the gender of microentrepreneurs. Among business-related determinants, holding a bank account has a greater influence on access to formal credit, followed by financial literacy, household assets, and experience in the business. It is observed from the result that gender gap is wider among respondents having higher socioeconomic status. The gender gap in access to credit is also highest among respondents enjoying a better business environment. This volume helps to enable financial sector to adopt policies, programs, and initiatives that address the difficulties in access to finance faced by women.

Kolkata, India
Naihati, India
Kalyani, India
December 2016

Chiranjib Neogi
Amit Kumar Bhandari
Sudipto Ghosh

Contents

Part I Women Empowerment

Women Empowerment in India 3
Chaiti Sharma Biswas

**Measuring Women Empowerment in the Household Sector:
A Generalized Index and an Application to Indian Households** 17
Subhendu Chakrabarti

**Traditional Institutions and Female Beneficiaries of Mahatma Gandhi
National Rural Employment Guarantee in West Bengal** 41
Arghya Kusum Mukherjee and Amit Kundu

**Empowerment of Women Through Public Programs in Rural West
Bengal: A Study on National Rural Livelihood Mission in a Block
of Purulia** 57
Tithi Bose and Archita Ghosh

**Non-farm Employment Among Rural Women: Trend
and Determinants** 75
Aparajita Dhara and Biswajit Chatterjee

Part II Microfinance in India

Efficiency and Mission Drift—Debate Revisited in Indian Context 97
Chandralekha Ghosh and Samapti Guha

Microfinance and Human Development: A Cross-Generation Study 119
Arijita Dutta and Sharmistha Banerjee

**Microfinance for Women-Owned Small Business in India: Challenges
and Opportunities** 131
Avijit Brahmachary

xiii

Part III Microfinance and Women Entrepreneurship

Going Through the New Avenue of Life: A Study on Factors Working Behind Entrepreneurship Development Through Self-Help Group 157
Kallol Das

Access to Finance, Entrepreneurship, and Empowerment: A Case Study 173
Sudipto Ghosh and Chiranjib Neogi

Access to Credit and Microentrepreneurship: A Gender Comparison 191
Rabin Mazumder, Subham Dastidar and Amit Kumar Bhandari

About the Editors

Chiranjib Neogi is a retired associate scientist at the Economic Research Unit of Indian Statistical Institute, Kolkata. He has been working in the area of productivity and efficiency for many years and has published a number of research articles on this issue in national and international journals. He has also published a book titled 'India's New Economy' (Palgrave, UK), co-authored with Prof. Jati K. Sengupta of the University of California, Santa Barbara, USA. In addition, he co-edited a book titled 'Productivity and Efficiency', with Prof. Ranjan Ghosh of Indian Institute of Management Calcutta, Kolkata (Macmillan, India). Besides, he contributed chapters in many edited books on contemporary issues of the Indian economy. He was visiting Research Fellow at the Institute of Developing Economies, Tokyo, Japan, during the period 1998 to 1999 and at the Korea Institute for International Economic Policy, Seoul, in 2009.

Dr. Amit Kumar Bhandari is presently working as an assistant professor in economics at Rishi Bankim Chandra Evening College, Naihati, India. He has been a Research Fellow at IZA—Institute of Labour Economics, Bonn, Germany. He obtained his Ph.D. in economics from the University of Kalyani, India. Formerly, he was a lecturer in economics and finance at the Indian Institute of Social Welfare and Business Management (IISWBM), Kolkata. His works have been published in reputed journals and books. He has a broad interdisciplinary research interest in social, economic and financial issues. His work has been funded by Indian Council of Social Science Research (ICSSR) and University Grants Commission (UGC), India.

Sudipto Ghosh obtained a Ph.D. in sociology, and is an expert in the fields of microfinance, entrepreneurship, planning, and livelihood. As a planning expert in the government, he has ten years experience in the urban and rural sector. He is involved in the preparation of city planning and various development project reports for local government bodies. He is also a SEBI (Securities and Exchange Board of India) resource person working for the Financial Literacy Programme and has been involved in advising organization in matters related to social development.

xvi

Part I
Women Empowerment

Women Empowerment in India

Chaiti Sharma Biswas

1 Introduction

Women suffer discrimination in the society, which is an age-old problem. In the presence of patriarchy, gender inequality emerged from and within the system. In this society women are commonly constrained by the norms, beliefs, customs, and values of the society, creating separate codes of conduct for women and men (Kabeer 2000). The extent of this difference varies, even across time along with varying structure of the society on culture, caste, ethnicity, and class. The society even in this twenty-first century could not get rid of these characteristics. Being treated as a deprived section, women are still denied power indicating that they are relatively less entitled to make strategic choices.

However, from a development perspective, women's role can never be denied, as they are also a part of the society. This was mainly one of the reasons why mainstreaming of women is recommended by various scholars to entitle them the equal share of the development process. As a means empowerment of women is suggested, which signifies the expansion of freedom of choice and action (Mosedale 2003). It is assumed that empowerment generates self-confidence among women not only for making important decisions for their life but also to carry them out. In this connection it is important to mention that empowering women is not an easy task because this particular term involves multidimensionality and is latent in nature. Although proxy variables are used to capture empowerment, complexity arises in its measurement because women cannot be treated as one group or a category, such as poor and backward castes, rather they are a crosscutting category of individuals that overlaps with all those socially excluded groups (Malhotra 2003).

It is argued that disempowerment of women is generated from complex relations within the household and family, which makes assessing women empowerment

---

C.S. Biswas (✉)
Indian Statistical Institute, Kolkata, India
e-mail: csharmabiswas@gmail.com

© Springer Nature Singapore Pte Ltd. 2017
C. Neogi et al. (eds.), *Women's Entrepreneurship and Microfinance*,
DOI 10.1007/978-981-10-4268-3_1

much difficult. Commonly, empowerment of women depends on both *resources* and *agency* where *resources* are treated as the 'enabling factors' and *agency*, as the ability to formulate strategic choices, to control resources and to take decisions that affect important life outcomes. *Agency* works both at macrolevel and at microlevel. At the aggregate level, the agency acts for 'social inclusion,' whereas at the microlevel, it acts to gain 'self-efficacy' that can change the lives of women. One has to make several choices in various phases of life, but all choices cannot be transformed into desired actions because it heavily depends on the extent of power (agency) one possesses.

Gender inequality is also common in patriarchal Indian society, which deprived women of having control of their physical well-being, health, security, and so on. Being marginalized, women lose their self-confidence and self-sufficiency. Nevertheless, this gender inequality is recognized as a major issue after the publication of the report of the 'Committee on the Status of Women in India' in 1974. Since then, government and non-government organizations have been working tirelessly to eradicate gender inequality from the society including introduction of several constitutional amendments. As a measure of empowerment, national policy makers formulated many pro-women policies following the participatory approach instead of welfare one. Even, a national-level organization, namely 'National Commission for Women' was set up to protect and promote the interests of women in India.

However, the fact remains that despite earnest efforts from the government and non-government organizations, still there exists a gap between the achieved and targeted rate of women's empowerment. Even in the post-millennium period, the third Millennium Development Goal (MDG, to empower women) lags well behind the target rate. Many scholars assumed that both social and economic factors are responsible for this lag in achievement. Some believed that lack of financial power and access to the property of the female might be the root cause of denied power. This demands a minute inquiry to identify the exact causes of failure/successes that affect the achieved level of empowerment.

After the initiation of economic reform Indian economy witnessed several changes, such as increase in women employment (23–26% during 1991–2001, Census of India 2001; average yearly urban female employment increased by 2.50% between 2004–2005 and 2011–12, National Sample Survey (NSS) 68th Round Employment data) and increase in gender development index (GDI) (from 0.560 to 0.600 during 2001–2005, Human Development Report). In the context of the newly changed situation, it is important to know the effect of these positive changes on women empowerment. In this backdrop this study attempts to measure the achievement level of women empowerment and to locate the causality between women empowerment and its explanatory factors. The results may facilitate to formulate efficient policies to eradicate gender inequality and empower women.

The remainder of this chapter is organized as follows: Sect. 2 discusses the past studies; Sect. 3 presents data used in the study; Sect. 4 describes the methodology; Sects. 5 and 6 present the findings and discussion, respectively, and Sect. 7 concludes the chapter.

2 Past Studies

It is widely accepted that women are a deprived section in the society; consequently, they are denied various advantages, thereby leading to gender inequality. In fact, women are recognized as the poorest of the poor because as a poor, men often experience disadvantages and exclusion outside home, thereby generating bitterness in him which is usually meted out to the women of the family. Female of these derived families experience twofold abuse as a female and as a poor, thereby lowering their level of empowerment. Many scholars advocated that absence of economic freedom is the main reason for the low empowerment of women in the society (Mikkola and Miles 2007; Kabeer 2003). According to this school of thought, empowerment of Indian women depends on their economic freedom. In this direction, several studies examine the effect of microfinance on women empowerment (Goetz and Gupta 1996; Hashemi et al. 1996; Amin et al. 1998; Kabeer 2001, 2005b; Holvoet 2005; Pitt et al. 2006; Bali and Walletin 2009). Although economic independence is expected to empower women, it is not always found to be effective (Sharma Biswas 2008). This indicates that besides economic factors, women empowerment is determined by some other factors also. Various studies show that social factors are stronger than economic factors in a society, and it varies directly with its nature of conservativeness. Alsop et al. (2005) prove that any intervention to improve agency and enhance opportunity structures can increase people's capacity to make effective choices.

Some of the studies on empowerment show its impact on health, education, fertility, development, and so on (Kabeer 1999, 2005a; Jejeebhoy 2000; Jejeebhoy and Sathar 2001; Mason and Smith 2003; Klassen 2006; Chaudhary and Nosheen 2009). Another study (Chakrabarti and Biswas 2012) pointed out the simultaneous relationship between empowerment and the determining factors. It shows that increase in women empowerment enhances children's education, health condition, and so on. On the other hand, the factors such as higher education, better income, and health condition or better life contribute positively to enhance women empowerment, which ultimately enriches development.

Based on a study in Uttarakhand, Dighe (2008) developed a model for women empowerment. The study mainly tried to show how to alleviate poverty and secure development for women by empowering them and depicts that various policies and programs formulated to empower women cannot fetch the requisite outcome because all of them mainly focused on individual empowerment only. Such a thought detracts the prime focus of the policies to empower women as group and ensure equality to them. The reason lies in the societal attitudes, in which men secure the main role in decision making in family, at workplace, and in government. To empower women the government largely depends on setting up of self-help groups (SHGs), as there is compulsion to meet the MDGs and reduce poverty. Therefore, Dighe suggests that social issues should be given the same importance as economic empowerment of women.

3 Data

This study is based on the unit-level data extracted from National Family Health Survey third series (NFHS-3) conducted by International Institute for Population Sciences (IIPS) during 2005–2006 under the Ministry of Family and Health. The study provides information on women's background characteristics, household-level problems, activities, their economic participation, and household-level decision making. In addition to empowerment-related information, there are factors, such as caste, religion, mass media exposure, age group variation, educational qualification and occupational standard of the respondent and her husband's, relationship to household head, respondent's type of earning, amount of earning relative to the

Table 1 Explanatory variables/casual factors used in the study

Factors	Recodes	Factors	Recodes
Religion (RIL)	1. Hindu 2. Muslim 3. Others	Relationship to household head (RLHD)	1. Head 2. Wife 3. Others
Caste (CST)	1. Scheduled caste 2. Scheduled tribe 3. OBC 4. General	Respondent's type of earning (TYERN)	1. Not paid 2. Kind only 3. Cash and kind 4. Cash only
Age of respondent (in years) (RAGE)	1 = 15–25 2 = 26–40 3 = 41–49	Wife's earning compared to her husband (ERNM)	1. Husband won't bring money 2. Almost half 3. More than husband
Age of husband (in years) (HAGE)	1 = 10–25 2 = 26–45 3 = 46+	Wealth index indicating household's economic status (WI)	1. Low 2. Medium 3. High
Media (MED)	1. No exposure 2. Have exposure to newspaper, radio or television	Household structure (HHST)	1. Nuclear 2. Non-nuclear
Marital status	1. Others 2. Wife 3. Head	Empowerment (EI)	1. Low 2. Medium 3. High
Education of respondent and her husband (REDU and HEDU)	1. Illiterate 2. Primary 3. Secondary 4. Higher	Occupation of respondent and her husband (ROCU and HOCU)	1. No job 2. Production labor 3. Sales and services 4. Clerical 5. Professional, technical, or managerial

Source Data and information extracted from NFHS-3

spouse, standard of living index, and household structure, which are assumed to act as proxy for socioeconomic and cultural factors and are used as explanatory or causal factors (Table 1). All these factors influence in some way the level of women empowerment. Except few, the variables are qualitative in nature.

4 Methods

In order to measure the status of women empowerment, first an empowerment index (EI) is developed, then it is classified into low, medium, and high, and finally a regression analysis is performed to identify the determinants of empowerment.

4.1 Construction of Empowerment Index

As a measure, an EI has been constructed using all the available decision-making variables provided by NFHS-3. All these factors do not have the same level of influence on women empowerment. Therefore, their level of influence is determined by correlation analyses. According to the level of influence, these variables are classified into four broad decision-making groups (Table 2): (1) *access to money* (*AMI*), (2) *spending money decisions* (*SPI*), (3) *routine household decisions* (*RHDI*), and (4) *mobility freedom* (*MI*). Specific scores are then assigned to different responses according to the intensity of the scale. Score '3' is assigned if the response is 'Yes/Alone,' score '2,' if the response is 'Joint decision,' and score '1,' if the response is 'No.'

Table 2 Description of the indicators with their respective scores

Components of EI	Description of variables	Scores
AMI	1. Has money for her own use 2. Have bank or savings account 3. Knowledge of loan 4. Given loan	No = 1 Yes = 3
SPI	1. Spending money 2. Spending husband's earning 3. Large purchases	Other than respondent = 1 Jointly with husband = 2 Alone = 3
RHDI	1. Health care 2. Daily purchase 3. Visit to family, relatives, and friends 4. Using contraception	Other than respondent = 1 Jointly with husband = 2 Alone = 3
MI	1. Allowed to go market 2. Allowed to outside village/community 3. Allowed to go to health facility	No = 1 Yes = 3

Source Data and information extracted from NFHS-3

Based on these categories, an EI is developed and is constructed for each respondent combining all the categories mentioned earlier. Initially, for each respondent a ratio is estimated dividing the sum of the recoded responses by a total number of queries in each of the categories, namely access to and spending money decisions, routine household decisions, and freedom of mobility. Then, they are summed up to get the total value of the composite index.

Algebraically,

$$\text{EI for } k\text{th respondent} = I_k = \sum_{j=1}^{3} \left\{ \sum_{i=1}^{N_j} x_{ijk}/N_j \right\}, \quad 0 \le I_k \le 4$$

where x_{ijk} is the ith decision of jth category for kth respondent and $\sum_{i=1}^{N_j} x_{ijk} \le N_j$, where N_j is the number of decision-making variables in the jth category, and varies by j.

After computing EI, it is classified into *low*, *medium*, and *high* using the formula (maximum − minimum)/3.

Algebraically, it is done in the following way:

Let,

$$Z = (\text{EI}_{\text{Max}} - \text{EI}_{\text{Min}})/3.$$

In the last step, a multiple regression analysis is performed to identify the determinants of empowerment. In this regard, EI is regressed on various socioeconomic factors, such as respondent's religion, caste, media exposure, age, education, occupation, type of earning, earning more than husband, relationship to the household head, household structure (family is either joint or nuclear), economic condition (defined by WI), husband's age, and occupation.

The model used for multiple regression is

$$\text{EI} = \beta_0 + \sum_{i=1}^{k} \beta_i x_i + \varepsilon$$

where $x_i = x_1, x_2, \ldots, x_k$ and stands for a vector of determinants, β is a vector of corresponding regression coefficients, i stands for the number of exogenous variables, and ε is the random unobserved disturbance term with mean zero and constant variance.

4.1.1 Profile of Sample Observations

A total of 87,815 women are covered in the study, of which 74% are found to be Hindu (Table 3). Of the remaining, 13% are Muslim and 13% of women belong to other religions. By caste divisions, 36% are upper caste Hindu, 34% are Other Backward Classes (OBC), 17% are Scheduled Castes (SC), and 13% are Scheduled

Women Empowerment in India

Table 3 Profile of Indian women, 2005–2006

Respondents		Number/percentage
Surveyed	Total	87,815
Religion	Hindu	74.4
	Muslim	13.1
	Others	12.5
Castes	SC	17.33
	ST	12.78
	OBC	33.82
	Others	36.07
Media	No	19.2
	Yes	80.8
Level of education	No education	38.8
	Low/primary	15.4
	Medium/secondary	36.9
	Higher education	8.9
Employment status	Unemployed	59.74
	Employed	40.26
Level of occupation	Unemployed	60.2
	Low	33.1
	Medium	3.4
	High	3.3

Source Data extracted from NFHS-3, 2005–2006

Tribes (ST) population. Among total respondents, about 81% women have access to information in any form. Of total respondents, 39% are illiterates and 15% have primary-level education, that is, about 54% women can be considered illiterates or just literates. Of the remaining, 37% have secondary-level education and very few (9%) have higher education. Indian social structure forbids Indian women to opt for a job that is reflected in the job pattern of women. It is found that only 40% of the surveyed women are found to be employed indicating that most remain unemployed. The largest part of these employed women (33.1%) is engaged in low-level jobs, and few have medium-level (3.4%) or high-level (3.3%) jobs.

5 Findings

It is stated earlier that EI comprises four components, namely AMI, SPI, RHDI, and MI. Before starting a discussion on the main findings, this study examines the influence of these four components on EI because all of these factors do not have the same influence on EI. Besides, all of the components of EI simultaneously influence each other in determining the level of achievement of empowerment.

Levels of the influence of AMI, SPI, RHDI, and MI on EI as well as on each other are estimated through correlation analysis. It is found from the results that all the correlation coefficients, though different in magnitude, are significant at 1% level (Table 4). The results demonstrate that the influence of RHDI and SPI on EI is higher compared to that of AMI and MI.

Among AMI and MI, the latter has more significant influence on EI than that of AMI. Unlike rank correlations, AMI has positive and significant influences in determining the level of achievement of women empowerment on other three components. The findings obtained from the mentioned analysis may justify the use of EI as a measure of the level of achievement of women empowerment in India.

On average, the value of EI for Indian women is found to be 7.42. It is found that by components of EI, the average value of AMI, SPI, RHDI, and MI is 1.58, 1.52, 1.84, and 2.48, respectively (Table 5). A noticeable fact is that the value is lowest for SPI and highest for MI. According to the value of the index, MI acquires the highest value among the four EI components, and it is 2.48 at India level.

It is also found from the study that although India level average value of EI is 7.42, there exists a wide level of variation in the value of EI at the respondent level. Hence, to estimate the degree of achieved level of women empowerment, respondents are classified into three categories, low, medium, and high, based on the value of EI scored by them.

As expected, in the conservative Indian society, only about 14% of women have a high level of empowerment (Table 6). However, it is surprising that the

Table 4 Degree of association between the components of EI and EI, 2005–2006

Pearson correlation coefficient (r)	Components of EI				EI
	AMI	SPI	RHDI	MI	
AMI	**1.000**	0.232*	0.211*	0.218*	0.630*
SPI	0.232*	**1.000**	0.473**	0.279**	0.710*
RHDI	0.211*	0.473*	**1.000**	0.331**	0.731*
MI	0.218*	0.279*	0.331*	**1.000**	0.665*
EI	0.630*	0.710*	0.731*	0.665**	**1.000**

Source NFHS-3 extracted data, total number of observation is 87,815
*Correlation is significant at the 0.01 level (2-tailed)
**Correlation is significant at the 0.05 level (2-tailed)

Table 5 Components of EI of women in India

Components of EI	Score
AMI	1.58
SPI	1.52
RHDI	1.84
MI	2.48
EI	7.42

Source Data extracted from NFHS-3, 2005–2006

Women Empowerment in India

Table 6 Distribution of women by level of empowerment in India, 2005–2006

Category of empowerment	Number of women	Percent
Low	8042	9.16
Medium	67,586	76.96
High	12,187	13.88
Total	87,815	100

percentage of women having low-level empowerment ($\sim 9\%$) is also significantly low. Most of the Indian women (about 77%) have medium-level empowerment. Hence, the results indicate that although women in Indian society are generally debarred from having a high level of empowerment, they are not allowed to remain powerless because of the social environment and household needs.

This study also depicts that very few women have a high level of empowerment, leaving most of them in the medium level. Moreover, for those belonging to a medium category, a few have much say in financial matters. Hence, it is necessary to explore the reasons that restrict women to attain the right to influence or take part in financial decisions or to achieve a high level of empowerment. There are various factors influencing the decision-making power of women. Some of these factors may facilitate to enhance women's empowerment and some stand in the way to empowerment. Hence, it is necessary to identify the regulatory factors having a positive influence on enhancing women's empowerment along with their functions, as this information may help to adopt appropriate as well as efficient steps to empower women.

Multiple regression analysis is carried out to identify the causal factors (socioeconomic) that influence empowerment of women. In this regard, constructed EI is regressed on various socioeconomic factors, such as religion (RIL), caste (CST), media exposure (MED), age of the respondent (RAGE) and her husband (HAGE), level of education of the respondent (REDU) and her husband (HEDU), occupational (ROCU) and marital status (MST) of the respondent, her husband's occupation (HOCU), respondent's type of earning (TYERN) and earning more than her husband (ERNM), household structure (HHST), her relationship to the household head (RLHD), and household's economic status represented by wealth index (WI).

However, it is observed from the estimation that the marital status of the respondent and her husband's education do not have any significant contribution, hence excluded from the finally estimated relation. The regression equation containing 13 factors that contribute significantly to determining the level of empowerment of Indian women is presented in this study. Among the selected factors, caste, relationship to household head, and household structure influence significantly, but negatively, to achieve a certain level of empowerment (Table 7). Negative significant regression coefficient with respect to CST indicates that women belonging to general castes are less empowered than that of the women in backward castes. Similarly, empowerment of women reduces in the family, as their positional status (RLHD) on household head shifts from head to wife to others (such as daughter, sister, sister-in-law, and daughter-in-law). The results also

Table 7 Factors influencing women's empowerment in India, 2005–2006

Variables	B	SE	t	R^2
Constant	4.403	0.029	151.817*	0.347*
Religion (RIL)	0.023	0.006	3.835*	
Caste (CST)	−0.026	0.004	−7.264*	
Media (MED)	0.376	0.012	31.666*	
Respondent's education (REDU)	0.211	0.005	38.895*	
Respondent's occupation (ROCU)	0.163	0.009	17.291*	
Husband's occupation (HOCU)	0.045	0.007	6.763*	
Respondent's age (RAGE)	0.469	0.009	54.670*	
Husband's age (HAGE)	0.179	0.010	17.181*	
Relationship to household head (RLHD)	−0.196	0.007	−29.358*	
Household structure (HHST)	−0.125	0.008	−15.765*	
Respondent's type of earning (TYERN)	0.037	0.006	6.213*	
Earns more than husband (ERNM)	0.437	0.005	80.232*	
Wealth index (WI)	0.202	0.006	32.234*	

Source Author's calculation from NFHS-3 extracted data

Note EI is the dependent variable. *Significant at 0.01% level

indicate that women lose their control on decision making as their family structure (HHST) changes from nuclear to joint family. Moreover, empowerment of women varies directly and significantly with their religion (RIL), media exposure (MED), education (REDU), occupation (ROCU), age (RAGE), type of earning (TYERN), higher earnings than their husband (ERNM), and household's economic status (WI). In addition, empowerment of women is influenced by their husband's age (HAGE) and occupation (HOCU).

6 Discussion

The majority of the Indian women are Hindu, and they mostly belong to backward classes. Due to poverty and backwardness, many of them cannot afford the required time and expenses for education. Consequently, most of them have low-level/ medium-level literacy. As regards media exposure, television plays a popular role in majority of the population. The incidence of unemployment is high because, within patriarchy, women are supposed to manage household chores, reproduce both legal heir and labor instead of earning outside. Therefore, disobeying the social norms, women who are available in the job market are mainly manual and unskilled or semiskilled labor. They are forced to do such jobs due to their poverty and poor level of education.

Indian society is characterized by the harmony of different cultures, religions, and languages. Still, men being instigated by patriarchy always try to retain the control over women. As a result, autonomy of women becomes a debatable issue.

However, the point to note is that majority of women are endowed with medium-level empowerment. It is the uniqueness of Indian social fabric. On the one hand, it does not allow women to be too much powerful, and on the other, it does not even encourage women's low empowerment. Probably, women are discouraged from having no/low empowerment to protect the family interest and to carry on the routine household activities. In search of the casual factors, *self-confidence-* and *awareness-generating* factors are found to be mainly responsible for determining the level of women empowerment in India. Some of these confidence-generating factors are women's education, exposure to media, job, earning in cash, higher income than their husband, their stay in the nuclear family instead of joint families, economic class, and husband's good job.

Respondent's level of education can bring about changes in cognitive ability, which is essential to women's capacity to question, to reflect on, to act on the conditions of their lives, and to gain access to knowledge, information, and new ideas that will help them to do so. This may also influence the level of freedom indirectly by getting employment and contributing in the family expenditure. The results indicate that respondent's education becomes significant in every region and all states.

Women's exposure to media plays a fairly significant role in their empowerment because it enhances one's awareness of self and surrounding, thereby generating self-confidence among them. Although this study includes reading newspaper, listening to radio, and watching television to define respondent's exposure to media, majority of women are found to watch television. Media exposure is found to be a significant contributory factor of EI.

Women's participation in economic activities with remuneration, either at home or outside, acts as a 'catalyst' for enhancement of autonomy in decision making at the household level through the contribution of money. If women are placed in higher-level jobs, their level of confidence is enhanced further. Moreover, if she earns more than her husband, then her level of confidence increases to a great extent, which in turn increases her control on household decision making. All these increase their self-confidence and awareness about social issues. It enhances the access to credit by increasing the assets, which leads to some positive changes in women's perceptions of themselves and their role in household decision making. Like media, this factor contributes significantly to EI. Women's economic participation, however, influences EI significantly.

Besides, family structure (nuclear or joint family) is found to be an important factor for women empowerment because women living in the nuclear family have more control on household decision making than those who live in joint families and sharing many things with other family members.

Higher economic classes and husband's higher-level job create self-confidence among women. Probably, husband's higher-level job makes him much busier with his job, which compels him to lend his wife more freedom of decision making in some issues compared to that of in low- or middle-order jobs. This responsibility further boosts up their confidence and self-awareness; this enables them to enhance their agency. This ability of women ultimately helps them to achieve empowerment.

Study validates that besides the self-confidence-generating factors mentioned earlier, there exist other factors, such as their own and husband's age, and the relationship to household head which also regulate the empowerment of women. It is observed that with age, women achieve relatively higher empowerment. Probable reason may be that with age, they appropriate the patriarchal norms, try to give priority to family, and, above all, their status change from a newly married wife to the wife of the head or they act as the head of the family or get the position of mother-in-law. All of these transformations ultimately endow them additional power. With age, Indian women become powerful within the family. Similarly, empowerment of woman seems to be enhanced with an increase in her husband's age, may be, with an increase in age, the male member (husband) gradually becomes busy with his job, familial and social assignments, so he is compelled to allow his wife to take some decisions in the family. As a head of the family, women get more control on decision making, if she is allowed to. Usually, Indian social norm relies on showing respect to the seniors. Hence, if a senior person is present in the family, he or she is generally accepted as the head of the family. If senior women of the family get the position of head, seldom they get the opportunity to be functional head. Most of the time this responsibility is taken by the able male member of the household. Thus, women who can exercise their functional power of headship in the family, their power of agency enhances to a greater extent which in turn make them more empowered. Religion and caste also act as a significant determinant of women empowerment. Moreover, upper castes women are always found to be less empowered than the backward castes women. Probably, due to economic reason, backward castes women have to contribute more to the family expenditure, which in turn enhances their say in family decision making compared to their upper castes counterpart.

7 Conclusion

This study depicts that Indian women have a medium-level empowerment in the family. Very small percentage of women have a high-level of empowerment, which is normal in a patriarchal society, but surprisingly the percentage of women having a low level of empowerment is also modest in India. Despite earnest efforts, a gap is still observed between the achieved and targeted level of women empowerment (EI). This happens probably due to a lag in confidence-generating factors, such as education and employment. To cope with the problem, pro-women policies changed over time from the beneficiary to participatory to get more effective solutions of the problem from the sufferers. Among several factors, education is found as the most important factor for building confidence; it also brings about changes in the cognitive ability of women, which in turn helps them to be empowered.

Medium-level education of majority of the Indian women failed to instigate them to join the job market. Only few percent of women who opt for job are mainly engaged in mannual or unskilled jobs. This indicates that within patriarchy, social

Women Empowerment in India

norms are so rigid that medium or higher education failed to involve women in the job market. Thus, to ensure high-level empowerment women must be engaged in high-level jobs, which in turn requires high qualification. High qualification and high-level job simultaneously create greater confidence among women, which ultimately help them to make choices for desired action and outcome. Moreover, if they earn more than their husband, then their level of confidence increases to a great extent, which in turn increases their control on household decision making. Still, the existence of a good-enough percentage of illiterate and unemployed women indicates the inappropriateness in implementing the Government of India's two most vital policies linked to education and employment of women.

Government of India adopted several policies to promote education and employment among women. Education policies like "Sakshar bharat mission for female literacy" aims to provide education among adult women, "Right to Education" provide free and compulsory education to every child aged between 6 to 14, "Kasturba Balika Vidyalaya" scheme provides residential upper primary schools for girls etc. Employment policies for women, like "Swawlamban Programme" provide training and skills among poor and needy women to obtain employment or self-employment on sustained basis, "Support to Training and Employment Programme (STEP)" provide skills and new knowledge to poor and asset less women in the traditional sectors and "DWCRA" scheme aims to strengthen the economic base for rural women by providing them credit, subsidies and help to enhance their productive skills and capabilities.

Therefore, it can be suggested that policies must aim to increase the scope of higher studies and opportunities for higher-level jobs for women. Besides, attempts should be made to enhance women's self-esteem and awareness about self and surrounding. All these increase their self-confidence and awareness about social issues. It enhances the access to credit by increasing the assets, which leads to some positive changes in women's perceptions about themselves and their role in household decision making.

References

Alsop, Ruth, Mette Frost Bertelsen and Jeremy Holland 2005. *Empowerment in practice: From analysis to implementation*. World Bank Publications, ISBN 10 0821364502.

Amin, Ruhul, Stan Becker and Abdul Byes. 1998. NGO-promoted micro-credit program and women's empowerment in rural Bangladesh: quantitative and qualitative evidence. *The Journal of Developing Areas*, 221–236.

Bali, Ranjubala Swain, and Fan Yang Wallentin. 2009. Does microfinance empower women? *International Review of Applied Economics* 23 (5): 541–556.

Chakrabarti, Snigdha, and Chaiti Sharma Biswas. 2012. An exploratory analysis of women empowerment in India: A structural equation modelling approach. *Journal of Development Studies* 48 (1): 164–180.

Chaudhary, Imran Sharif, and Farhana Nosheen. 2009. The determinants of women empowerment in Southern Punjab (Pakistan): An empirical analysis. *European Journal of Social Sciences* 10 (2): 216–229.

Census of India. 2001. Registrar General of India.

Goetz, Anne M., and Rina Sen Gupta. 1996. Who takes the credit? Gender, power and control over loan use in rural credit programs in Bangladesh. *World Development* 24 (1): 45–63.

Dighe, Anita. 2008. Women's empowerment at the local level (WELL)—A study undertaken in Uttarakhand. Available at http://dspace.col.org/bitstream/123456789/.../WELL-scan-Uttarakhand. pdf on 22nd September, 2008.

Hashemi, M.Syed, Sidney Ruth Schuler, and Ann P. Riley. 1996. Rural credit programs and women's empowerment in Bangladesh. *World Development* 24 (4): 635–653.

Holvoet, Nathalie. 2005. The impact of microfinance on decision–making agency: Evidence from South India. *Development and Change* 36 (1): 75–102.

Jejeebhoy, Shireen. 2000. Women's autonomy in rural India: Its dimension, determinants and the influence on context. In *Women and demographic processes-moving beyond Cairo*, ed. H.B. Presser, and G. Sen, 204–238. New York: Oxford University Press.

Jejeebhoy, Shireen Jejeebhoy and Zeba A. Sathar. 2001. Women's autonomy in India and Pakistan: The influence of religion and region. *Population and Development Review*, 27(4), 687–712.

Kabeer, Naila. 1999. Resources, agency, achievements: Reflections on the measurement of women's empowerment. *Development and Change* 30 (3): 435–464.

Kabeer, Naila. 2000. *The Power to Choose: Bangladeshi Women and Labour Market Decisions in London and Dhaka*. London: Verso.

Kabeer, Naila. 2001. Reflections on the measurement of women's empowerment. *Discussing women's empowerment-theory and practice*. SIDA: Swedish International Cooperation Agency.

Kabeer, Naila. 2003. Gender equality, poverty eradication and the millennium development goals: Promoting women's capabilities and participation. Available at http://www.unescap.org/esid/committee2003/genderequality.pdf.

Kabeer, Naila. 2005a. Gender equality and women's empowerment: A critical analysis of the third millennium development goal. *Gender and Development* 13 (1): 13–24.

Kabeer, Naila. 2005b. Is microfinance a 'magic bullet' for women's empowerment? Analysis of findings from South Asia. *Economic and Political Weekly* 40 (44 & 45): 4709–4718.

Klasen, Stephan. 2006. UNDP's gender related measures: some conceptual problems and possible solutions. *Journal of Human Development* 7 (2): 243–274.

Malhotra, A. 2003. Conceptualizing and Measuring Women's Empowerment as a Variable in International Development. Paper presented at the Workshop on "Measuring Empowerment: Cross-Disciplinary Perspectives" held at the World Bank in Washington, DC on February 4 and 5, 2003.

Mason, Karen Oppenheim, and Herbert L. Smith. 2003. *Women's empowerment and social context: Results from five Asian countries*. World Bank Washington, DC.: Gender Development Group.

Mikkola. Anne and Carrie A. Miles. 2007. Development and gender equality: consequences, causes, challenges and cures. Discussion Paper No. 159, Institute for the Studies of Religion at Baylor University.

Mosedale, S. 2003. Towards a framework for assessing empowerment. Paper Presented at the International Conference on "New Direction in Impact Assessment for Development: Methods and Practice", Manchester, pp. 24-25, November 2003.

Pitt, Mark M., Shahidur Rahman Khandker and Jennifer Cartwright. 2006. Empowering women with micro finance: evidence from Bangladesh. *Economic Development and Cultural Change* 54 (4): 791–831.

Sharma, Biswas Chaiti. 2008. Can employment empower women more at the household level in India? *The International Journal of Interdisciplinary, Social Sciences* 3 (7): 43–51.

Weber, Max. 1978. *Economy and society: An outline of interpretive sociology*, trans. Ephraim Fischoff et al. Berkeley, CA: University of California Press.

Measuring Women Empowerment in the Household Sector: A Generalized Index and an Application to Indian Households

Subhendu Chakrabarti

1 Introduction

When the development practitioners realized that the top-down approaches failed to achieve the desired goal of poverty eradication, they began advocating the bottom-up approaches to achieve that goal. The evidence of such an effort is the World Development Report 2000/2001: *Attacking Poverty*, which brought the enhanced concept of poverty into the policy sphere by proposing a poverty reduction strategy based on promoting opportunities, facilitating empowerment, and enhancing the security of the poor (World Bank 2000). Earlier, the concept of poverty was narrowly defined and confined to only income and expenditure (Kolm 1969; Atkinson 1970; Sen 1973, 1976; Kakwani 1980). However, over the past more than two decades, the concept has been broadening to include health, literacy, and life expectancy at birth. The development economists argue that it is inappropriate to consider income as the sole attribute of well-being and advocated the basic need approach by considering development as an improvement in an array of human needs, not just as a growth of income (Streeten 1981). It has also been argued that 'people do not just want to be alive. They want to be knowledgeable; and they certainly may want a decent life, one that is not considerably undermined by extreme poverty and constant worry about sheer physical survival' (UNDP 1991, p. 88).

Development economists incorporated enhancement of well-being of the deprived section of the population by expanding their choices, enhancing their capabilities, and promoting their freedoms in the process of economic growth and poverty reduction. Studies reveal that women belong to the more deprived among the deprived section of the society. As a result, empowerment of women has been considered by the World Bank as an important means to eradicate poverty, and

---

S. Chakrabarti (✉)
Economic Research Unit, Indian Statistical Institute, Kolkata, India
e-mail: chakrabartisubhendu@gmail.com

© Springer Nature Singapore Pte Ltd. 2017
C. Neogi et al. (eds.), *Women's Entrepreneurship and Microfinance*,
DOI 10.1007/978-981-10-4268-3_2

emphasis has been given by setting empowerment of women as one of the millennium development goals (MDGs). The World Bank's *Empowerment and Poverty: A Sourcebook* (Narayan 2002) provided a specific definition of empowerment as follows: *Empowerment is the expansion of assets and capabilities of the poor people to participate in, negotiate with, influence, control and hold accountable institutions that affect their lives.* This definition, however, had several limitations: (i) it was narrower and more specific than what one could understand from the common parlance of use of the term 'power' and (ii) it associated empowerment with poverty (implying that non poor have adequate power and do not need to be empowered) and limited the range of action to those that involve an interaction with institutions (Grootaert 2006). Nevertheless, the source book clarified that 'empowering poor men and women requires the removal of formal and informal institutional barriers.'

Nowadays, the term 'empowerment' is defined in different ways by scholars of various disciplines, but it broadly refers to the proliferation of freedom of choice and action to shape one's life. It implies more control over resources and decisions. Three important ideas are inherent in the concept of empowerment. First, empowerment is context specific. Second, empowerment is not power over others (i.e., domination), but the power to achieve goals and ends. Third, the concept of empowerment applies to the powerless, irrespective of gender, class, and caste. Hence, there is nothing about the concept of empowerment per se, which applies to women alone. It, therefore, becomes imperative to know why we are interested in introducing women's empowerment in the study of poverty and development. As a bottom-up approach, empowering the disadvantaged groups is considered as a means to enhance the well-being of those groups. Emphasis is given to women's empowerment because women are not just a subset of socially disadvantaged groups, but they are a crosscutting category that overlaps with all other disadvantaged groups. At the same time, women empowerment has some additional unique features, such as (i) women's disempowerment is ingrained in the household and interfamilial relations, which is not true for other disadvantaged groups and (ii) general empowerment requires institutional transformation, but women's empowerment requires social reform.

One important aspect of the integration of empowerment in the poverty analysis is how to measure levels of empowerment and its progress. Regarding capability functioning achievement framework, functioning of empowerment is an achievement of an individual that would reflect, as it were, a part of the state of that individual. The capability of an individual, on the other hand, is a derived notion that reflects an individual's freedom of choice through his or her decision making and action.

Most of the earlier studies on women empowerment are based on percentage distribution of various indicators that focus on the circumstances of women's lives and reflect the available opportunities for them vis-à-vis their counterpart, men. Mason (1986) focuses on the negative effect of women's early marriage on empowerment by way of denying access to formal education. Studies by Dyson and Moore (1983) and Dixon-Mueller (1989) revealed that residence in nonnuclear families is likely to have a negative effect on women's ability to access resources directly as well as control in the decision making. One should acknowledge the fact

Measuring Women Empowerment in the Household Sector ...

that within given circumstances, the degree of empowerment varies among the concerned women. However, the degree of empowerment can never be captured by any of the earlier studies.

In this chapter, I propose a women empowerment index using an arbitrary number of attributes related to household affairs. In fact, first I try to formulate individual woman empowerment index based on individual woman's role regarding degrees of freedom of decision making on different attributes in the domain of household affairs. Then, the individual woman's empowerment indices composed of different household attributes are aggregated to arrive at a group or social women empowerment. The index is constructed taking into account the variation in the degree of control over decision making on different household attributes.

The next section proposes an index of women's empowerment at the household level based on the degree of freedom of decision making on household's attributes, while the third section provides the empirical illustration of women's empowerment in the household affairs using India's third National Family Health Survey (NFHS-3, 2005–2006) data and the fourth section presents conclusions.

2 Women Empowerment Index at the Household Level

Suppose that there are a number of attributes of decision making and each of them represents a particular dimension in the domain of household affairs. These attributes can be related to health care; major household purchase; purchase of daily household needs; freedom to go alone to market, health facility and outside community or village; freedom of visit friends and relatives; control over husband's earnings; and control over her own earnings. Here, the women empowerment is viewed regarding her role in the decision-making process of each attribute.

Let $x_i \geq 0$ be the extent of women empowerment associated with attributes i. There are various alternative responses to each attribute that reflect a woman's role (i.e., the level of empowerment) on each attribute. The alternative responses are as follows. The decision on a particular household attribute is usually taken (i) by others in the household, (ii) by husband, (iii) jointly with others in the household, (iv) jointly with husband, (v) by respondent herself. Depending on her role in the decision-making process, we assign empowerment score to each response. If she is not at all a party to the decision making regarding an attribute, then her empowerment score for that attribute will be 0. For example, when others take a decision on an attribute in the household or her husband alone, and she has no role in that decision making, then she will be assigned 0 empowerment score for that attribute. Again, if she takes a decision on a household attribute jointly with others in the household, then her empowerment score will be 1 and when she takes a decision with her husband, empowerment score will be 2. On the other hand, if she is the sole decision maker, then she will obtain the highest score assigned to that attribute, that is, 3. Now, we define a characteristic function that takes the values in the set $\{0, 1, 2, 3\}$ in increasing order of empowerment. Therefore, $x_i \in \{0, 1, 2, 3\}$ represents the set of nonnegative real numbers lying between 0 and 3.

An empowerment index for attribute i is a nonnegative real-valued function F: $\{0, 1, 2, 3\} \to R_+$, which associates a value $F(x_i)$ to each $x_i \in \{0, 1, 2, 3\}$, where R is the nonnegative part of the real line. More precisely, $F(x_i)$ determines the extent of empowerment corresponding to x_i. We assume that F is twice differentiable, a technical assumption that makes the analysis simple. It also implies continuity of F, which ensures that F will not be oversensitive to minor observational errors on the role of decision making of attribute i.

Following Chakravarty and Ambrosis (2003), we impose the following properties on the empowerment function F.

Normalization (NM): $F(x_i) = 0$ if $x_i = 0$
The normalization axiom indicates that if the role of a woman in the decision making for an attribute is 0, then her empowerment on that attribute is also 0.

Monotonicity (MN): An increase in x_i increases F; that is, for $x_i \in \{0, 1, 2, 3\}$,

$$F(x_i + c) > F(x_i), \quad \text{where } c > 0 \text{ is arbitrary and } x_i + c \in \{1, 2, 3\}$$

The monotonicity axiom demands that an increase in the extent of control over decision of an attribute makes one more empowered in that attribute.

Diminishing Marginal Empowerment (DME): For any $x_i \in \{0, 1, 2, 3\}$ and any $\delta > 0$, the magnitude of empowerment $F(x_i + \delta) - F(x_i)$ is monotonically decreasing in x_i, where $x_i + \delta \in \{1, 2, 3\}$. $F(x_i)$ is concave, that is,

$$\text{if } g(x_i) = F(x_i + \delta) - F(x_i), \text{ then } g(x_i + h) \leq g(x_i)$$

According to DME, the extent of control over the attribute represents a lesser degree of empowerment at higher levels than an identical case at the lower level. For example, in a society or a state, an increase in the fraction of women population with freedom of movement from 0.7 to 0.8 shows a lesser degree of empowerment increase than an increase in the fraction from 0.1 to 0.2.

Normalization and monotonicity jointly imply that the degree of women empowerment index is bounded from below by 0, and the lower bound is attained in the case when she does not have any role in decision making of household affairs.

Let us now consider the following functional form of empowerment index (EI) for j arbitrary attributes:

$$\text{EI} = \frac{1}{J} \sum_{i=1}^{j} x_i^\alpha, \quad \alpha \leq 1 \tag{1}$$

As x_i values are unit free, averaging $x_i^\alpha, i = 1, 2, \ldots, j$ is well defined in Eq. (1). Now consider an arbitrary component of the empowerment index:

$$x_i^\alpha \tag{2}$$

It satisfies NM, MN, and DME. Therefore, the function $F_\alpha(x_i) = x_i^\alpha, \alpha \leq 1$ can be regarded as women empowerment index for attribute i. If there are N women in a society or state, then the women empowerment index for attribute i becomes

$$\frac{1}{N}\sum_{l=1}^{N} F_\alpha(x_{il}) = \frac{1}{N}\sum_{l=1}^{N} x_{il}^\alpha, \quad \alpha \leq 1 \tag{3}$$

The parameter α is the empowerment aversion parameter because an increase in the value of α decreases $F_\alpha(x_i)$ for a given x_i.

3 The Generalized Empowerment Index

The index F summarizes empowerment for one attribute. The overall women empowerment at the household level, which is a generalization of the index, involving all the attributes associated with the household affairs has to be constructed.

Now consider $F(x_i)$ by a_i, where $i = 1, 2, \ldots, j$. We can write $a = (a_1, a_2, \ldots, a_j)$. The relationship can be stated as:

There exists a function $I: R_+^j \rightarrow R$, such that for all $(x_1, x_2, \ldots, x_j)$, the empowerment index $G(x_1, x_2, \ldots, x_j)$ can be written as $I(a_1, a_2, \ldots, a_j)$. This assumption ignores all other features of the household other than women's role on decision making on the household affairs.

Under this assumption, we can state certain postulates for an arbitrary index I:

Normalization (NOM): For any $z \geq 0, I(z_1, z_2, z_3, \ldots, z_n) = z$.
Additivity (ADD): For any $a, b \in R_+^j$,

$$\begin{aligned} &I(a_1 + b_1, a_2 + b_2, \ldots, a_i + b_j) \\ &= I(a_1, a_2, \ldots, a_i) + I(b_1, b_2, \ldots, b_j) \end{aligned} \tag{4}$$

Symmetry (SYM): For all $a \in R_+^j$, $I(a) = I(ap)$,
where p is any $j \times j$ permutation matrix.

According to NOM, if the empowerment levels for different attributes are the same, then the general social women empowerment index takes on this common value. It implies that the social women's empowerment index at the household level is an average of individual women's empowerment at the household affairs. ADD can be interpreted as follow. Suppose that attribute i has two components. For example, if the attribute i is freedom of movement, then its two components can be 'allowed to go alone outside the home' and 'allowed to visit friends and relatives outside community'. Let $a_i(b_i)$ be the empowerment level of attribute i based on the first (second) component. If it is not possible to split attribute i, we can attach zero empowerment to $b_i(a_i)$, so that the first (second) component represents the degree of empowerment for this attribute. Thus, ADD implies that the sum of empowerments based on the vectors $(a_1, a_2, \ldots, a_j)$ and $(b_1, b_2, \ldots, b_j)$ is the same as the empowerment based on the vector $(a_1 + b_1, a_2 + b_2, \ldots, a_i + b_j)$. SYM requires that the intensity of I is to be based on permutation of its arguments. That is, the index I remains invariant under any reordering of individual empowerment levels.

An overall empowerment index I satisfies NOM, ADD, and SYM, if and only if, it can be written in the form:

$$I(a_1, a_2, \ldots a_j) = \frac{1}{J} \sum_{i=1}^{J} a_i = \frac{1}{N} \sum_{i=1}^{N} \left\{ \frac{1}{J} \sum_{i=1}^{j} x_i^\alpha \right\} = \frac{1}{JN} \sum_{l=1}^{N} \sum_{i=1}^{J} x_{il}^\alpha \tag{5}$$

To illustrate the formula in Eq. (5), supposing that F is of the form of Eq. (3), we have the corresponding general women empowerment index (WEI) at the household level as

$$\text{WEI} = I_E = \left(\frac{1}{JN} \sum_{l=1}^{N} \sum_{i=1}^{J} x_{il}^\alpha \right), \quad \alpha \le 1$$

where parameter α captures the sensitivity of I_E to changes in individual empowerment. That is, $\alpha \le 1$ implies an equal increase in individual empowerment (x_i), and the effect on group index will be higher at a higher level of individual empowerment. Again, when the value of α increases, then the value of group index will increase at an increasing rate with the increase of individual's empowerment (x_i).

4   An Empirical Application

An empirical application of the women's empowerment index (I_E) has been made in this study using five basic dimensions of household affairs. The I_E is calculated here on the basis of the data available from the NFHS-3 2005–2006 of India. NFHS-3 is the third in a series of national surveys; earlier, NFHS surveys were carried out in 1992–93 (NFHS-1) and 1998–99 (NFHS-2). All three surveys were conducted under the stewardship of the Ministry of Health and Family Welfare, Government of India, with the International Institute for Population Sciences, Mumbai, serving as the nodal agency. ORC Macro, Calverton, Maryland, USA, provided technical assistance for all three NFHSs.

In all the NFHSs, along with intensive information on health and nutrition status of mother and child, information on the aspects of women's empowerment had also been collected. However, the nature of information regarding attributes of household affairs varies among the three NFHSs. As a result, with few common attributes of household affairs, any comparison of women's empowerment among different periods would not be technically possible, and thus, this study is based on the NHFS-3 (2005–2006) data for the empirical application. In NFHS-3, information regarding empowerment on household affairs of the ever-married women aged 15–49 years has been collected from 124,385 ever-married women respondents. Based on their responses on five household attributes (i.e., the degree of freedom of choice enjoyed by them on the affairs of (i) respondent's own health care, (ii) major household purchase, (iii) purchase of daily household needs, (iv) visit to friends and relatives, and (v) how husband's earnings will be used), the empowerment index is constructed. Of the total women respondents, only 87,925 respondents were in the category of current marital status 'married'. However, among the 'married' women, only 85,942 respondents have given complete information on the five attributes of household affairs mentioned earlier. Therefore, in this study, we are concerned only with those married women respondents who had given complete information on the five attributes of the household affairs mentioned earlier.

The selected five attributes of household affairs represent five dimensions of the household, and each dimension represents a part of the state of her domestic life. Freedom of choice or the level of empowerment is reflected by the role played by her in decision making on each of those dimensions. Therefore, women empowerment is judged here regarding women's role in the decision making on household affairs. If she is the sole decision maker of a particular attribute, then she will be assigned the highest empowerment score of 3 for that attribute. On the other hand, if she does not play any role in the decision making of any attribute, then she will be assigned 0 score for that attribute.

There are altogether 29 states in India, and according to their location and to some extent sociocultural similarities, the states are classified into six zones, namely north zone, central zone, east zone, north-east zone, west zone, and south zone. Empowerment index I_E for $\alpha = 0.2$, 0.5, and 0.8 has been calculated for individual attributes of household affairs at the state and zonal levels.

According to the poverty estimation for 2004–2005 (Press Information Bureau, Government of India), the overall percentage of population below poverty line remains very high in the states of eastern and central regions compared to other regions of India. Women's empowerment on household attributes is also found to be very low in each state of these regions (Table 1). It is evident that the women of the north-east region enjoy a much higher level of empowerment in the household affairs than any other region in India. Delhi (DL), Punjab (PJ), and Haryana (HR) are comparatively advanced states in various aspects, but on women's empowerment, their ranks among the 29 Indian states are miserably low. In this respect, one interesting finding is that Jammu and Kashmir (JK) has the lowest percentage of population below poverty line (5.4%, according to poverty estimation 2004–2005), but there, the women's empowerment is the lowest in India.

Regarding respondent's own health care, in Jammu and Kashmir (JM), Rajasthan (RJ), and Uttaranchal (UC) in the north zone; Chhattisgarh (CH) and

Table 1 Women's empowerment on five attributes of the household affairs at different states, zones, and all of India

Zone	State	Women empowerment at five attributes of household affairs														
		Own health			Household's large purchase			Purchase of household's daily needs			Visit to friends and relatives			Use of husband's money		
		$\alpha = 0.2$	$\alpha = 0.5$	$\alpha = 0.8$	$\alpha = 0.2$	$\alpha = 0.5$	$\alpha = 0.8$	$\alpha = 0.2$	$\alpha = 0.5$	$\alpha = 0.8$	$\alpha = 0.2$	$\alpha = 0.5$	$\alpha = 0.8$	$\alpha = 0.2$	$\alpha = 0.5$	$\alpha = 0.8$
(1)	(2)	(3)	(4)	(5)	(6)	(7)	(8)	(9)	(10)	(11)	(12)	(13)	(14)	(15)	(16)	(17)
North	DL	0.88	1.15	1.51	0.78	0.98	1.22	0.92	1.22	1.63	0.87	1.09	1.37	0.95	1.18	1.47
	HP	0.81	1.07	1.40	0.68	0.85	1.08.	0.77	1.01	1.34	0.71	0.90	1.16	0.93	1.15	1.42
	HR	0.86	1.14	1.51	0.63	0.78	0.98	0.73	0.90	1.26	0.80	1.01	1.27	0.83	1.03	1.27
	JM	0.52	0.67	0.88	0.52	0.66	0.83	0.57	0.74	0.97	0.51	0.64	0.80	0.70	0.88	1.10
	PJ	0.93	1.03	1.65	0.56	0.70	0.88	0.68	0.89	1.18	0.80	1.02	1.29	0.81	1.01	1.25
	RJ	0.63	0.83	1.09	0.49	0.61	0.76	0.61	0.81	1.07	0.53	0.67	0.85	0.69	0.86	1.07
	UC	0.73	0.94	1.23	0.58	0.73	0.92	0.69	0.90	1.19	0.66	0.85	1.08	0.78	0.97	1.21
North overall		**0.77**	**0.98**	**1.32**	**0.61**	**0.76**	**0.80**	**0.71**	**0.92**	**1.23**	**0.70**	**0.88**	**1.12**	**0.81**	**1.01**	**1.26**
Central	CH	0.59	0.76	0.99	0.60	0.75	0.94	0.78	1.03	1.38	0.72	0.89	1.11	0.89	1.10	1.36
	MP	0.68	0.88	1.16	0.63	0.79	0.98	0.73	0.97	1.28	0.65	0.82	1.03	0.84	1.05	1.30
	UP	0.81	1.05	1.36	0.67	0.84	1.05	0.73	0.97	1.28	0.66	0.83	1.04	0.85	1.06	1.32
Central overall		**0.69**	**0.90**	**1.17**	**0.63**	**0.79**	**0.99**	**0.75**	**0.99**	**1.31**	**0.68**	**0.85**	**1.06**	**0.86**	**1.07**	**1.33**
East	BH	0.65	0.84	1.10	0.61	0.77	0.98	0.72	0.95	1.25	0.66	0.83	1.04	0.75	0.95	1.20
	JH	0.73	0.93	1.18	0.72	0.89	1.11	0.79	1.02	1.33	0.78	0.97	1.22	0.91	1.13	1.41
	OR	0.79	1.05	1.39	0.68	0.85	1.06	0.73	0.95	1.24	0.75	0.93	1.16	0.80	0.99	1.23
	WB	0.74	0.98	1.29	0.50	0.64	0.82	0.60	0.80	1.06	0.63	0.81	1.04	0.68	0.86	1.08

(continued)

Table 1 (continued)

| Zone | State | Women empowerment at five attributes of household affairs | | | | | | | | | | | | | | |
| | | Own health | | | Household's large purchase | | | Purchase of household's daily needs | | | Visit to friends and relatives | | | Use of husband's money | | |
		$\alpha = 0.2$	$\alpha = 0.5$	$\alpha = 0.8$	$\alpha = 0.2$	$\alpha = 0.5$	$\alpha = 0.8$	$\alpha = 0.2$	$\alpha = 0.5$	$\alpha = 0.8$	$\alpha = 0.2$	$\alpha = 0.5$	$\alpha = 0.8$	$\alpha = 0.2$	$\alpha = 0.5$	$\alpha = 0.8$
East overall		**0.73**	**0.95**	**1.24**	**0.63**	**0.79**	**0.99**	**0.71**	**0.93**	**1.22**	**0.71**	**0.89**	**1.12**	**0.79**	**0.98**	**1.23**
North-east	AR	0.81	1.06	1.38	0.87	1.11	1.41	1.05	1.41	1.90	1.06	1.37	1.77	0.99	1.24	1.56
	AS	0.94	1.19	1.51	0.85	1.05	1.31	0.83	1.05	1.34	0.95	1.19	1.49	0.86	1.07	1.33
	MN	1.03	1.30	1.64	0.94	1.16	1.44	1.03	1.38	1.85	1.01	1.27	1.60	1.05	1.31	1.62
	MG	1.03	1.32	1.70	0.96	1.21	1.54	1.01	1.31	1.72	1.01	1.26	1.58	0.92	1.15	1.43
	MZ	1.09	1.41	1.82	0.95	1.19	1.51	1.06	1.41	1.90	1.06	1.33	1.69	1.03	1.27	1.57
	NA	1.06	1.34	1.71	0.95	1.19	1.49	1.04	1.40	1.89	1.08	1.35	1.69	1.07	1.33	1.65
	SK	0.97	1.29	1.71	0.89	1.11	1.38	0.95	1.26	1.67	0.99	1.26	1.61	0.97	1.21	1.53
	TR	0.72	0.94	1.22	0.57	0.72	0.92	0.70	0.93	1.23	0.73	0.95	1.24	0.59	0.74	0.92
North-east overall		**0.96**	**1.23**	**1.59**	**0.87**	**1.09**	**1.38**	**0.96**	**1.27**	**1.69**	**0.99**	**1.25**	**1.58**	**0.94**	**1.17**	**1.45**
West	GO	0.81	1.06	1.39	0.79	1.00	1.27	0.90	1.20	1.60	1.00	1.29	1.67	0.86	1.08	1.36
	GJ	0.76	1.00	1.32	0.63	0.78	0.99	0.82	1.11	1.51	0.82	1.03	1.29	0.77	0.97	1.21
	MH	0.86	1.13	1.49	0.76	0.95	1.19	0.90	1.20	1.60	0.91	1.14	1.44	0.90	1.11	1.39
West overall		**0.81**	**1.06**	**1.40**	**0.73**	**0.91**	**1.15**	**0.87**	**1.17**	**1.57**	**0.91**	**1.15**	**1.47**	**0.84**	**1.05**	**1.32**
South	AP	0.79	1.03	1.33	0.65	0.83	1.07	0.75	0.98	1.29	0.79	0.99	1.25	0.69	0.86	1.09
	KA	0.62	0.81	1.05	0.59	0.75	0.95	0.67	0.90	1.19	0.65	0.83	1.06	0.71	0.88	1.10
	KE	0.89	1.16	1.50	0.72	0.92	1.16	0.78	1.03	1.34	0.91	1.15	1.45	0.75	0.93	1.16
	TN	0.87	1.14	1.49	0.78	1.01	1.30	0.97	1.31	1.78	0.90	1.15	1.48	0.94	1.19	1.49
South overall		**0.79**	**1.04**	**1.34**	**0.69**	**0.88**	**1.12**	**0.79**	**1.06**	**1.40**	**0.81**	**1.03**	**1.31**	**0.77**	**0.97**	**1.21**
All India		**0.80**	**1.04**	**1.35**	**0.69**	**0.86**	**1.09**	**0.79**	**1.04**	**1.38**	**0.78**	**0.99**	**1.25**	**0.83**	**1.04**	**1.29**

Delhi (DL), Himachal Pradesh (HP), Haryana (HR), Jammu and Kashmir (JK), Punjab (PJ), Rajasthan (RJ), Uttaranchal (UC), Chhattisgarh (CH), Madhya Pradesh (MD), Uttar Pradesh (UP), Bihar (BH), Jharkhand (JH), Orissa (OR),West Bengal (WB), Arunachal Pradesh (AR), Assam (AS), Manipur (MN), Meghalaya (MG), Mizoram (MZ), Nagaland (NA), Sikkim (SK), Tripura (TR), Goa (GO), Gujarat (GJ), Maharashtra (MH), Andhra Pradesh (AP), Karnataka (KA), Kerala (KE), Tamil Nadu (TN)

Madhya Pradesh (MD) in the central zone; Bihar (BH) and Jharkhand (JH) in the east zone; Tripura (TR) in the north-east zone; and Andhra Pradesh (AP) and Kerala (KA) in the south zone greater percentage of women are not taking decision on their own health care neither by herself nor jointly with husbands, and this is reflected by the respective state values of I_E for $\alpha = 0.5$. In the case of 'households' large purchase' (which may be considered as control over household resources), a very meager percentage of women are enjoying the absolute power of decision making in almost every state. A significant percentage of women take a decision on household's large purchase either jointly with their husband or do not have any role. However, in the decision making of the large household purchase, women of the north-east states, except TR, are enjoying a comparatively higher level of empowerment than any other state in India.

Most of the Indian women are comparatively more aware and concerned about their household's daily needs than the male members. This phenomenon has also been reflected in the decision making on household's daily needs. A significant percentage of women are observed to take a decision on household's daily needs either solely or jointly with their husband or partner in most of the states in India. However, such similar picture is not found in the case of JM, RJ, UC, OR, WB, AS, and TR.

Two most important attributes of household's affairs are 'visit to friends and relatives' (which is considered as freedom of movement) and 'use of husband's money' (which is considered as financial autonomy). It has been observed that nearly 55% of the Indian women take a decision on the 'visit to friends and relatives' in consultation with their husbands or partners. In this regard, all the states in the north-east region enjoy much higher level of empowerment than any other state in India, and more than 30% of women respondents in Arunachal Pradesh (AR), highest among the states in India, take decision by herself to visit friends and relatives, followed by Goa (GO) 28%, TR 26%, and Sikkim (SK) 20%.

On the other hand, more than 69% of Indian women take a decision on the 'use of husband's money' jointly with their husbands. Among the states, only in BH and AR, it is just above 10% of the women respondents who enjoy the highest empowerment on this attribute as they themselves take a decision regarding how to use their husband's money.

Table 2 provides a comparative picture of empowerment between rural and urban women over the five household attributes. In general, rural women are found to be less empowered than their urban counterpart. One interesting feature observed here is that in AR, MN, NA, and GO, rural women enjoy higher empowerment than their urban counterpart. Both for urban and rural women, the overall empowerment of women in the north-eastern states is much higher than the other states and any other zone. With respect to overall empowerment, women of the western states come next to north-eastern states, followed by the southern states.

Caste and religion are the two most sensitive issues in India and on many occasions become important determining factors of India's sociopolitical matters. Therefore, the extent of variation in the level of women empowerment due to differences in caste and religion is examined here. In this regard, one of our hypotheses is that irrespective of caste and religion, empowerment of the newly

Table 2 Women's overall empowerment on five attributes of the household affairs by sectors of different states, zones, and all India

Zone	State	Women empowerment by sector								
		$\alpha = 0.2$			$\alpha = 0.5$			$\alpha = 0.8$		
		Urban	Rural	Combined	Urban	Rural	Combined	Urban	Rural	Combined
(1)	(2)	(4)	(5)	(6)	(7)	(8)	(9)	(10)	(11)	(13)
North	DL	0.88	0.85	0.88	1.13	1.08	1.12	1.44	1.38	1.44
	HP	0.86	0.75	0.78	1.10	0.96	1.00	1.41	1.23	1.28
	HR	0.85	0.74	0.77	1.08	0.95	0.98	1.38	1.21	1.26
	JM	0.62	0.53	0.56	0.80	0.68	0.72	1.02	0.87	0.92
	PJ	0.80	0.73	0.75	1.02	0.94	0.97	1.32	1.21	1.25
	RJ	0.76	0.51	0.59	0.97	0.65	0.75	1.25	0.84	0.97
	UC	0.82	0.64	0.69	1.05	0.81	0.88	1.35	1.04	1.13
North overall		**0.80**	**0.68**	**0.72**	**1.02**	**0.87**	**0.92**	**1.31**	**1.11**	**1.18**
Central	CH	0.78	0.68	0.72	1.00	0.86	0.91	1.28	1.10	1.15
	MP	0.80	0.61	0.71	1.02	0.78	0.90	1.31	0.99	1.15
	UP	0.87	0.66	0.74	1.10	0.85	0.95	1.41	1.08	1.21
Central overall		**0.82**	**0.65**	**0.72**	**1.04**	**0.83**	**0.92**	**1.33**	**1.06**	**1.17**
East	BH	0.71	0.66	0.68	0.91	0.85	0.87	1.16	1.09	1.11
	JH	0.83	0.76	0.78	1.04	0.96	0.99	1.32	1.21	1.25
	OR	0.79	0.73	0.75	1.01	0.93	0.95	1.28	1.19	1.22
	WB	0.70	0.56	0.63	0.91	0.72	0.81	1.18	0.94	1.06

(continued)

Table 2 (continued)

Zone	State	Women empowerment by sector								
		α = 0.2			α = 0.5			α = 0.8		
		Urban	Rural	Combined	Urban	Rural	Combined	Urban	Rural	Combined
East overall		**0.76**	**0.68**	**0.71**	**0.97**	**0.87**	**0.91**	**1.23**	**1.11**	**1.16**
North-east	AR	0.93	0.97	0.96	1.20	1.25	1.24	1.55	1.62	1.60
	AS	0.93	0.87	0.89	1.17	1.09	1.11	1.47	1.36	1.40
	MN	1.00	1.02	1.01	1.27	1.29	1.28	1.61	1.65	1.63
	MG	0.97	1.00	0.99	1.24	1.26	1.25	1.59	1.60	1.59
	MZ	1.04	1.03	1.04	1.33	1.31	1.32	1.71	1.68	1.70
	NA	1.03	1.05	1.04	1.31	1.33	1.32	1.68	1.69	1.69
	SK	0.99	0.94	0.96	1.27	1.20	1.23	1.64	1.54	1.58
	TR	0.75	0.63	0.66	0.97	0.82	0.85	1.26	1.06	1.11
North-east overall		**0.96**	**0.94**	**0.94**	**1.22**	**1.19**	**1.20**	**1.56**	**1.53**	**1.54**
West	GO	0.85	0.90	0.87	1.09	1.16	1.12	1.41	1.51	1.46
	GJ	0.82	0.71	0.76	1.06	0.92	0.98	1.38	1.19	1.27
	MH	0.92	0.75	0.86	1.18	0.96	1.11	1.51	1.23	1.42
West overall		**0.86**	**0.79**	**0.83**	**1.11**	**1.01**	**1.07**	**1.43**	**1.31**	**1.38**
South	AP	0.76	0.69	0.73	0.98	0.88	0.94	1.26	1.13	1.21
	KA	0.76	0.58	0.65	0.97	0.75	0.83	1.24	0.97	1.07
	KE	0.84	0.80	0.81	1.08	1.02	1.04	1.38	1.30	1.33
	TN	0.93	0.85	0.89	1.21	1.10	1.16	1.58	1.43	1.51
South overall		**0.82**	**0.73**	**0.77**	**1.06**	**0.94**	**0.99**	**1.36**	**1.21**	**1.28**
All India		**0.84**	**0.73**	**0.78**	**1.08**	**0.92**	**0.99**	**1.39**	**1.18**	**1.27**

married women is expected to be less than the women having long marital duration. The reason behind this may be the existing social customs. The general social custom is that after marriage, the bride will go to the groom's house for living. Initially, the bride tries to adjust herself in a new environment and with the in-laws and new family customs and values. As a result, during the initial phase, her role in the groom's family is like a guest member; but as time passes, she adjusts herself in the groom's family, becomes a part of the family and then she can exercise a positive role in household affairs. To test this hypothesis, we also classified our married women respondents according to their marital duration.

Table 3 shows a comprehensive, all of-India, picture of the level of empowerment enjoyed by the women of different castes and religions, as well as their marital duration over the five attributes of household affairs. It is evidenced that in both rural and urban scheduled tribe (ST) women enjoy a much higher level of empowerment than among other castes in each of the five household attributes. Except for 'household large purchase' and 'visit to friends and relatives,' the scheduled caste (SC) women come next to ST women, and the women of the other backward communities (OBC) rank the lowest over the five household affairs. Nevertheless, the state-level decomposition gives an altogether different picture (Table 4). Only ST women in the states of east and north-east regions are enjoying a much higher level of empowerment than the other castes of those regions. Virtually, in the states of the north, central, and western regions, overall rank of the ST women regarding empowerment level becomes the lowest.

Again, when the women respondents are classified according to their religion, we observed that the Christian women are enjoying a much higher level of empowerment in the household affairs in each of the five household attributes both in the rural and the urban areas than the women belonging to other religions. Next to the Christian women come the women belonging to Sikh, Buddhist, Jain, and Jewish religions. Muslim women both in rural and urban areas enjoy the least level of empowerment as compared to women of the other religions. The overall region-wise and individual state-wise pictures are almost similar to that of all India (Table 5). It is worthwhile to mention here that the women belonging to 'Others' religion category, which consists of 'Donyipolo,' 'no religion,' and 'others,' enjoy a higher level of empowerment than Hindu and Muslim women.

The empowerment of the married women on their household affairs increases with longer marital duration. The estimated average level of empowerment of each category shows that irrespective of their caste, religion, and rural–urban divisions, the overall level of empowerment increases significantly with greater marital duration. This is also true for each of the five attributes of the household affairs.

Table 6 provides us a picture of the differentials of the level of women empowerment according to male- and female-headed household across different regions and states. The overall Indian scenario is that the women of the female-headed household enjoy a much higher level of empowerment than that of male-headed household, and this is true for the women of both rural and urban areas. Of the 29 Indian states, only in three states, namely, DL, RJ, and MZ, urban male-headed women enjoy a slightly higher level of empowerment than their

Table 3 Women's empowerment on five attributes of the household affairs in India by caste, religion, and marital duration

Household classification		Women's empowerment on different household affairs across social characteristics ($\alpha = 0.5$)								
		Own health			Household's large purchase			Purchase of household's daily needs		
		Urban	Rural	Combined	Urban	Rural	Combined	Urban	Rural	Combined
(1)	(2)	(3)	(4)	(5)	(6)	(7)	(8)	(9)	(10)	(11)
Caste	SC	1.11	0.98	**1.03**	0.95	0.76	**0.84**	1.14	0.94	**1.02**
	ST	1.28	1.04	**1.10**	1.16	0.93	**0.99**	1.38	1.12	**1.18**
	OBC	1.09	0.90	**0.98**	0.95	0.73	**0.82**	1.14	0.91	**1.01**
	Others	1.12	1.01	**1.07**	0.95	0.77	**0.87**	1.13	0.91	**1.03**
	Overall	**1.12**	**0.97**	**1.04**	**0.96**	**0.78**	**0.86**	**1.15**	**0.96**	**1.04**
Religion	Hindu	1.12	0.94	**1.01**	0.96	0.76	**0.84**	1.14	0.93	**1.02**
	Muslim	1.02	0.89	**0.96**	0.87	0.68	**0.78**	1.05	0.83	**0.95**
	Christian	1.32	1.28	**1.30**	1.20	1.14	**1.17**	1.41	1.36	**1.38**
	Sikh, Buddhist, Jain, and Jewish	1.22	1.18	**1.19**	1.01	0.78	**0.87**	1.24	0.96	**1.08**
	Others	1.18	1.16	**1.16**	1.21	1.07	**1.11**	1.44	1.33	**1.36**
	Overall	**1.12**	**0.96**	**1.04**	**0.96**	**0.78**	**0.86**	**1.15**	**0.96**	**1.04**
Marital duration (in years)	≤4	0.97	0.80	**0.87**	0.74	0.55	**0.63**	0.84	0.64	**0.73**
	5–14	1.12	0.97	**1.04**	0.94	0.77	**0.85**	1.14	0.94	**1.03**
	15–24	1.18	1.05	**1.11**	1.08	0.89	**0.97**	1.29	1.10	**1.18**
	25+	1.19	1.03	**1.10**	1.08	0.89	**0.97**	1.28	1.08	**1.16**
	Overall	**1.12**	**0.97**	**1.04**	**0.96**	**0.78**	**0.86**	**1.15**	**0.96**	**1.04**

Household classification		Women's empowerment on different household affairs across social characteristics ($\alpha = 0.5$)					
		Visit to friends and relatives			Use of husband's money		
		Urban	Rural	Combined	Urban	Rural	Combined
		(12)	(13)	(14)	(15)	(16)	(17)
Caste	SC	1.05	0.89	**0.96**	1.08	1.00	**1.03**
	ST	1.29	1.06	**1.12**	1.24	1.11	**1.14**

(continued)

Table 3 (continued)

Household classification		Women's empowerment on different household affairs across social characteristics ($\alpha = 0.5$)					
		Visit to friends and relatives			Use of husband's money		
		Urban	Rural	Combined	Urban	Rural	Combined
	OBC	1.06	0.85	**0.94**	1.08	0.96	**1.01**
	Others	1.07	0.92	**1.00**	1.07	0.97	**1.02**
	Overall	**1.08**	**0.91**	**0.99**	**1.09**	**1.00**	**1.04**
Religion	Hindu	1.07	0.88	**0.96**	1.09	0.98	**1.03**
	Muslim	0.96	0.76	**0.87**	0.98	0.89	**0.94**
	Christian	1.32	1.31	**1.31**	1.25	1.24	**1.25**
	Sikh, Buddhist, Jain, and Jewish	1.18	1.05	**1.10**	1.15	1.04	**1.09**
	Others	1.33	1.25	**1.27**	1.28	1.22	**1.24**
	Overall	**1.08**	**0.91**	**0.99**	**1.09**	**1.00**	**1.04**
Marital duration (in years)	≤ 4	0.89	0.69	**0.78**	0.93	0.82	**0.87**
	5–14	1.07	0.90	**0.97**	1.09	0.99	**1.04**
	15–24	1.17	1.01	**1.08**	1.15	1.07	**1.11**
	25+	1.17	1.03	**1.09**	1.14	1.07	**1.10**
	Overall	**1.08**	**0.91**	**0.99**	**1.09**	**1.00**	**1.04**

Table 4 Women's overall empowerment on the five attributes of the household affairs according to caste by states and zones and all India

Zone	State	Women empowerment by caste											
		$\alpha = 0.2$				$\alpha = 0.5$				$\alpha = 0.8$			
		SC	ST	OBC	Others	SC	ST	OBC	Others	SC	ST	OBC	Others
(1)	(2)	(3)	(4)	(5)	(6)	(7)	(8)	(9)	(10)	(11)	(12)	(13)	(14)
North	DL	0.85	0.95	0.89	0.89	1.08	1.20	1.14	1.13	1.38	1.53	1.47	1.45
	HP	0.75	0.69	0.75	0.80	0.96	0.87	0.97	1.02	1.23	1.11	1.26	1.31
	HR	0.78	0.93	0.75	0.77	0.99	1.16	0.95	0.99	1.27	1.45	1.20	1.27
	JM	0.72	0.46	0.52	0.56	0.91	0.59*	0.65	0.71	1.17	0.76	0.83	0.91
	PJ	0.73	0.58	0.81	0.76	0.95	0.74	1.04	0.97	1.22	0.94	1.33	1.25
	RJ	0.59	0.52	0.54	0.72	0.76	0.67	0.69	0.92	0.97	0.86	0.89	1.19
	UC	0.66	0.63	0.69	0.70	0.83	0.80	0.88	0.90	1.06	1.01	1.12	1.16
North overall		**0.72**	**0.68**	**0.71**	**0.74**	**0.93**	**0.86**	**0.90**	**0.95**	**1.19**	**1.10**	**1.16**	**1.22**
Central	CH	0.72	0.70	0.70	0.79	0.91	0.89	0.89	1.00	1.16	1.12	1.14	1.27
	MP	0.70	0.64	0.68	0.79	0.90	0.82	0.86	1.00	1.15	1.04	1.10	1.28
	UP	0.77	0.94	0.71	0.78	0.98	1.17	0.90	1.00	1.25	1.47	1.15	1.27
Central overall		**0.73**	**0.76**	**0.70**	**0.79**	**0.93**	**0.96**	**0.88**	**1.00**	**1.19**	**1.21**	**1.13**	**1.28**
East	BH	0.70	1.01	0.65	0.74	0.89	1.26	0.83	0.94	1.14	1.58	1.07	1.20
	JH	0.81	0.81	0.76	0.79	1.01	1.02	0.96	1.00	1.27	1.29	1.22	1.27
	OR	0.79	0.77	0.72	0.74	1.01	0.98	0.91	0.94	1.29	1.25	1.16	1.20
	WB	0.60	0.59	0.55	0.65	0.78	0.75	0.71	0.83	1.01	0.97	0.91	1.08

(continued)

Table 4 (continued)

Zone	State	Women empowerment by caste											
		$\alpha = 0.2$				$\alpha = 0.5$				$\alpha = 0.8$			
		SC	ST	OBC	Others	SC	ST	OBC	Others	SC	ST	OBC	Others
East overall		**0.72**	**0.79**	**0.67**	**0.73**	**0.92**	**1.00**	**0.85**	**0.93**	**1.18**	**1.27**	**1.09**	**1.19**
North-east	AR	0.87	0.99	0.89	0.92	1.11	1.28	1.14	1.18	1.41	1.67	1.48	1.52
	AS	0.93	0.96	0.92	0.85	1.16	1.21	1.15	1.07	1.46	1.53	1.45	1.34
	MN	1.00	1.00	1.02	1.02	1.27	1.27	1.29	1.29	1.62	1.62	1.63	1.64
	MG	0.99	1.03	0.76	0.73	1.25	1.31	0.96	0.92	1.59	1.66	1.21	1.18
	MZ	0.50	1.04	1.01	1.02	0.63	1.33	1.29	1.30	0.80	1.70	1.64	1.66
	NA	0.91	1.09	1.01	0.92	1.15	1.38	1.28	1.16	1.45	1.77	1.63	1.47
	SK	0.98	0.98	0.99	0.80	1.27	1.25	1.28	1.03	1.65	1.61	1.64	1.32
	TR	0.67	0.62	0.68	0.66	0.87	080	0.88	0.86	1.12	1.03	1.14	1.11
North-east overall		**0.86**	**0.96**	**0.91**	**0.87**	**1.09**	**1.23**	**1.16**	**1.10**	**1.39**	**1.58**	**1.48**	**1.40**
West	GO	0.84	0.82	0.85	0.88	1.09	1.05	1.09	1.14	1.41	1.34	1.41	1.47
	GJ	0.76	0.77	0.71	0.81	0.98	0.99	0.92	1.04	1.27	1.28	1.19	1.34
	MH	0.88	0.80	0.85	0.88	1.13	1.02	1.09	1.12	1.46	1.30	1.40	1.44
West overall		**0.83**	**0.80**	**0.80**	**0.86**	**1.07**	**1.02**	**1.03**	**1.10**	**1.38**	**1.30**	**1.33**	**1.42**
South	AP	0.76	0.79	0.73	0.71	0.98	1.01	0.94	0.92	1.25	1.30	1.20	1.18
	KA	0.62	0.63	0.64	0.69	0.81	0.82	0.82	0.98	1.05	1.06	1.05	1.14
	KE	0.80	0.75	0.82	0.81	1.03	0.96	1.04	1.04	1.32	1.23	1.34	1.32
	TN	0.92	0.84	0.89	0.93	1.20	1.08	1.15	1.18	1.57	1.40	1.49	1.052
South overall		**0.78**	**0.75**	**0.77**	**0.78**	**1.00**	**0.97**	**0.99**	**1.01**	**1.30**	**1.25**	**1.27**	**1.29**
All India		**0.76**	**0.87**	**0.74**	**0.78**	**0.98**	**1.11**	**0.95**	**1.00**	**1.25**	**1.41**	**1.22**	**1.28**

Table 5 Women's overall empowerment on the five attributes of household affairs according to religions by states and zones and all India

Zone	State	Women's empowerment by religion														
		$\alpha = 0.2$					$\alpha = 0.5$					$\alpha = 0.8$				
		Hin	Mus	Chr	Sikh, Buddhist, Jain, and Jewish	Others	Hin	Mus	Chr	Sikh, Buddhist, Jain, and Jewish	Others	Hin	Mus	Chr	Sikh, Buddhist, Jain, and Jewish	Others
(1)	(2)	(3)	(4)	(5)	(6)	(7)	(8)	(9)	(10)	(11)	(12)	(13)	(14)	(15)	(16)	(17)
North	DL	0.88	0.88	0.92	0.92	–	1.12	1.12	1.18	1.18	–	1.44	1.42	1.53	1.51	–
	HP	0.78	0.74	1.03	0.67	0.57	1.00	0.96	1.35	0.86	0.77	1.28	1.23	1.78	1.11	1.03
	HR	0.77	0.82	0.69	0.80	–	0.98	1.03	0.85	1.03	–	1.25	1.30	1.04	1.32	–
	JM	0.70	0.48	0.77	0.87	–	0.89	0.60	0.96	1.12	–	1.15	0.76	1.21	1.44	–
	PJ	0.77	0.75	0.73	0.74	0.93	0.98	0.96	0.94	0.96	1.18	1.27	1.23	1.20	1.24	1.50
	RJ	0.59	0.58	1.03	0.79	–	0.75	0.75	1.35	1.00	–	0.96	0.96	1.76	1.27	–
	UC	0.68	0.68	1.10	0.78	–	0.87	0.87	1.43	0.99	–	1.12	1.13	1.85	1.25	–
North overall		**0.74**	**0.70**	**0.90**	**0.80**	**0.75**	**0.94**	**0.90**	**1.15**	**1.02**	**0.97**	**1.21**	**1.15**	**1.48**	**1.31**	**1.27**
Central	CH	0.71	0.72	0.88	0.75	–	0.90	0.92	1.12	0.95	–	1.15	1.18	1.42	1.21	–
	MP	0.69	0.76	0.88	0.91	–	0.88	0.97	1.14	1.17	–	1.13	1.24	1.48	1.50	–
	UP	0.74	0.77	0.91	0.79	–	0.94	0.98	1.16	1.00	–	1.20	1.26	1.47	1.27	–
Central overall		**0.72**	**0.75**	**0.89**	**0.82**	**–**	**0.91**	**0.96**	**1.14**	**1.04**	**–**	**1.16**	**1.23**	**1.46**	**1.33**	**–**
East	BH	0.66	0.75	–	0.88	–	0.85	0.96	–	1.08	–	1.09	1.23	–	1.33	–
	JH	0.78	0.77	0.83	0.84	0.85	0.98	0.98	1.07	1.06	1.07	1.24	1.24	1.37	1.35	1.35
	OR	0.75	0.74	0.83	0.89	0.93	0.95	0.94	1.05	1.14	1.16	1.21	1.19	1.33	1.46	1.45
	WB	0.65	0.57	0.79	0.69	0.70	0.84	0.74	1.04	0.89	0.88	1.09	0.96	1.36	1.14	1.11

(continued)

Table 5 (continued)

Zone	State	Women's empowerment by religion														
		α = 0.2					α = 0.5					α = 0.8				
		Hin	Mus	Chr	Sikh, Buddhist, Jain, and Jewish	Others	Hin	Mus	Chr	Sikh, Buddhist, Jain, and Jewish	Others	Hin	Mus	Chr	Sikh, Buddhist, Jain, and Jewish	Others
East overall		**0.71**	**0.71**	**0.61**	**0.83**	**0.83**	**0.90**	**0.90**	**1.05**	**1.04**	**1.04**	**1.16**	**1.15**	**1.35**	**1.32**	**1.30**
North-east	AR	0.91	0.77	0.98	1.03	0.99	1.17	0.97	1.27	1.33	1.28	1.51	1.23	1.66	1.73	1.67
	AS	0.93	0.77	0.91	0.90	0.92	1.16	0.97	1.15	1.14	1.13	1.46	1.21	1.45	1.43	1.39
	MN	1.02	1.00	1.00	1.07	1.00	1.29	1.06	1.28	1.36	1.27	1.64	1.59	1.63	1.72	1.62
	MG	0.85	0.65	1.04	1.04	1.05	1.08	0.82	1.32	1.33	1.35	1.37	1.04	1.67	1.72	1.73
	MZ	0.92	1.08	1.04	10.3	–	1.16	1.43	1.33	1.34	–	1.48	1.90	1.70	1.74	–
	NA	0.93	0.88	1.08	1.00	0.78	1.17	1.11	1.38	1.27	0.99	1.48	1.40	1.76	1.61	1.25
	SK	0.94	0.65	1.02	0.99	0.71	1.21	0.83	1.31	1.27	0.90	1.56	1.06	1.68	1.64	1.16
	TR	0.67	0.61	0.79	0.63	–	0.86	0.79	1.02	0.83	–	1.12	1.04	1.31	1.09	–
North-east overall		**0.90**	**0.80**	**0.98**	**0.96**	**0.91**	**1.14**	**1.02**	**1.26**	**1.23**	**1.15**	**1.45**	**1.31**	**1.61**	**1.59**	**1.47**
West	GO	0.85	0.78	0.98	0.92	0.71	1.09	1.01	1.28	1.13	0.91	1.40	1.31	1.68	1.39	1.18
	GJ	0.76	0.73	0.88	0.80	–	0.98	0.95	1.12	1.03	–	1.27	1.24	1.43	1.32	–
	MH	0.86	0.85	1.07	0.91	0.88	1.10	1.08	1.36	1.17	1.14	1.41	1.40	1.73	1.51	1.47
West overall		**0.82**	**0.78**	**0.98**	**0.87**	**0.8/0**	**1.06**	**1.01**	**1.25**	**1.11**	**1.02**	**1.36**	**1.31**	**1.61**	**1.41**	**1.32**
South	AP	0.75	0.65	0.79	0.66	0.96	0.96	0.82	1.02	0.86	1.26	1.23	1.07	1.31	1.12	1.66
	KA	0.65	0.66	0.78	0.75	0.66	0.82	0.85	1.01	0.95	0.87	1.06	1.09	1.32	1.20	1.15
	KE	0.84	0.72	0.89	–	0.54	1.08	0.92	1.13	–	0.68	1.37	1.18	1.44	–	0.86
	TN	0.89	0.93	0.93	0.87	–	1.15	1.22	1.21	1.10	–	1.50	1.59	1.57	1.39	–
South overall		**0.78**	**0.74**	**0.85**	**0.57**	**0.72**	**1.00**	**0.95**	**1.09**	**0.97**	**0.94**	**1.29**	**1.23**	**1.41**	**1.24**	**1.22**
All India		**0.76**	**0.70**	**1.00**	**0.83**	**0.96**	**0.97**	**0.90**	**1.28**	**1.07**	**1.23**	**1.25**	**1.15**	**1.64**	**1.38**	**1.58**

Note Hin Hindu; *Mus* Muslim; *Chr* Christian; *Others* 'no religion,' 'Donyipolo,' and 'others'; '–' no sample

Table 6 Differentials of the level of women empowerment between male- and female-headed households across states, zones, and sectors

Zone	State	Women's empowerment according to male- and female-headed households ($\alpha = 0.5$)								
		Urban			Rural			Combined		
		Male-headed household	Female-headed household	Overall	Male-headed household	Female-headed household	Overall	Male-headed household	Female-headed household	Overall
(1)	(2)	(3)	(4)	(5)	(6)	(7)	(8)	(9)	(10)	(11)
North	DL	1.13	1.11	**1.13**	1.09	0.53	**1.08**	1.13	1.10	**1.12**
	HP	1.10	1.14	**1.10**	0.92	1.11	**0.96**	0.97	1.12	**1.00**
	HR	1.10	0.96	**1.08**	0.95	0.97	**0.95**	0.98	0.97	**0.98**
	JM	0.78	1.01	**0.80**	0.65	1.15	**0.68**	0.69	1.11	**0.72**
	PJ	1.03	1.00	**1.02**	0.93	1.05	**0.94**	0.96	1.04	**0.97**
	RJ	0.98	0.88	**0.97**	0.63	0.91	**0.65**	0.75	0.90	**0.75**
	UC	1.04	1.12	**1.05**	0.79	0.98	**0.81**	0.75	1.02	**0.88**
North overall		**1.02**	**1.03**	**1.0**	**0.85**	**0.96**	**0.87**	**0.89**	**1.04**	**0.92**
Central	CH	1.00	0.96	**1.00**	0.87	0.80	**0.86**	0.91	0.87	**0.91**
	MP	1.02	0.96	**1.02**	0.78	0.91	**0.78**	0.90	0.94	**0.90**
	UP	1.09	1.20	**1.10**	0.82	1.01	**0.85**	0.93	1.07	**0.95**
Central overall		**1.04**	**1.04**	**1.04**	**0.82**	**0.91**	**0.83**	**0.91**	**0.96**	**0.92**
East	BH	0.91	0.86	**0.91**	0.77	1.08	**0.85**	0.83	1.03	**0.87**
	JH	1.04	1.03	**1.04**	0.95	1.11	**0.96**	0.98	1.09	**0.99**
	OR	1.00	1.04	**1.01**	0.92	1.07	**0.93**	0.94	1.07	**0.95**
	WB	0.91	0.90	**0.91**	0.71	0.87	**0.72**	0.81	0.89	**0.81**

(continued)

Table 6 (continued)

| Zone | State | Women's empowerment according to male- and female-headed households ($\alpha = 0.5$) | | | | | | | | |
| | | Urban | | | Rural | | | Combined | | |
		Male-headed household	Female-headed household	Overall	Male-headed household	Female-headed household	Overall	Male-headed household	Female-headed household	Overall
East overall		**0.97**	**0.96**	**0.97**	**0.84**	**1.03**	**0.87**	**0.89**	**1.02**	**0.91**
North-east	AP	1.18	1.36	**1.20**	1.25	1.32	**1.25**	1.23	1.34	**1.24**
	AS	1.16	1.28	**1.17**	1.08	1.22	**1.09**	1.10	1.23	**1.11**
	MN	1.28	1.25	**1.27**	1.29	1.27	**1.29**	1.29	1.26	**1.28**
	MG	1.21	1.43	**1.24**	1.25	1.36	**1.26**	1.23	1.39	**1.25**
	MZ	1.34	1.28	**1.33**	1.32	1.23	**1.31**	1.33	1.27	**1.32**
	NA	1.31	1.42	**1.31**	1.33	1.33	**1.33**	1.32	1.39	**1.32**
	SK	1.26	1.39	**1.27**	1.20	1.17	**1.20**	1.23	1.24	**1.23**
	TR	0.96	1.03	**0.97**	0.81	0.96	**0.82**	0.85	0.99	**0.85**
North-east overall		**1.21**	**1.31**	**1.22**	**1.19**	**1.23**	**1.19**	**1.20**	**1.26**	**1.20**
West	GO	1.06	1.22	**1.09**	1.14	1.25	**1.16**	1.10	1.23	**1.12**
	GJ	1.06	1.04	**1.06**	0.92	0.98	**0.92**	0.98	1.01	**0.98**
	MH	1.18	1.09	**1.18**	0.96	1.01	**0.96**	1.11	1.07	**1.11**
West overall		**1.10**	**1.12**	**1.11**	**1.01**	**1.08**	**1.01**	**1.06**	**1.10**	**1.07**
South	AP	0.98	0.94	**0.98**	0.87	1.06	**0.88**	0.93	0.98	**0.94**
	KA	0.96	1.04	**0.97**	0.75	0.73	**0.75**	0.83	0.84	**0.83**
	KE	1.07	1.10	**1.08**	1.00	1.07	**1.02**	1.02	1.08	**1.04**
	TN	1.21	1.23	**1.21**	1.08	1.33	**1.10**	1.15	1.29	**1.16**
South overall		**1.06**	**1.08**	**1.06**	**0.93**	**1.05**	**0.94**	**0.98**	**1.05**	**0.99**
All India		**1.08**	**1.10**	**1.08**	**0.91**	**1.07**	**0.92**	**0.98**	**1.08**	**0.99**

female-headed counterpart. However, in DL, CH, and MZ the women of the rural male-headed household enjoy a significantly higher level of empowerment, and slightly higher in SK and KA than the female-headed counterpart.

5 Conclusion

Empowerment is a process of entrusting power to an individual in a specific context for the expansion of freedom of choice and action to shape one's life, implying control over resources and decisions. Every context is sensitive to its surrounding interactive social, cultural, economic, and political factors, and the final result will be the outcome governed by the dominant factor. This chapter aimed to develop a generalized empowerment index through an axiomatic approach taking into account the varied level of individual empowerment for each attribute within the specific context. The index can be conceived as the simple average of the level of empowerment along individual attributes. Here, the application of the empowerment index is made to household affairs due to data availability on women's decision making with respect to some household affairs. The index can be used to find out the level of empowerment to any other context, and the average of empowerment indices of different contexts will give the global empowerment.

It is revealed from the empirical analysis that the level of women empowerment significantly differs among states of within and between zones. Each zone represents some degree of social and cultural homogeneity, and these social and culture systems consist of rationale norms, values, and beliefs on which there is simultaneously consensus and disagreement and are subject to change. It has been observed that in India a large percentage of women take a decision on household affairs either in consultation with their husband or do not have any say otherwise. This reaffirms the phenomenon that empowerment is a property of social and cultural system rather than of individual experiences and traits (Smith 1989; Masson 2005). Social and cultural dominance is also evidenced by large variation in the degree of empowerment when the women of each state or zone are grouped according to their caste, religion, and so on.

Finally, some policy suggestions on empowering women of the disadvantaged group could be worth mentioning. Based on the application of the empowerment index, one can identify the factor dominance and then plan accordingly. For example, formal education and financial independence are the two most important factors of empowerment. However, emphasis only on these two factors will be less effective in a society where religious or cultural dominance is very high. In such a situation, along with formal education, emphasis should also be given to religious and cultural values, educate both male and female to cease the persisting orthodox norms and beliefs, which otherwise come in the way of any rational human behavior and only then can one expect to achieve the required goal.

References

Atkinson, A.B. 1970. On the measurement of Inequality. *Journal of Economic Theory* 2 (3): 244–263.

Chakravarty, S.R., and C. D'Ambrosio. 2003. *The measurement of social exclusion.* GermanInstitute for Economic Research, Berlin.

Dixon-Mueller, Ruth. 1989. Patriarchy, fertility and women's work in rural societies. In *International Union for the Scientific Study of Population, International Population Conference*, New Delhi, 1989, Vol. 2, 291–304. IUSSP, Liege, Belgium.

Dyson, Tim, and Mick Moore. 1983. On kinship structure, female autonomy and demographic behaviour in India. *Population and Development Review* 9 (1): 35–60.

Grootaert, C. 2006. Assessing empowerment at the national level in eastern europe and central Asia. In *Measuring empowerment: Cross-disciplinary perspectives*, ed. Deepa Narayan. Washington, D.C.: The World Bank, Oxford University Press.

Kakwani, N.C. 1980. *Income inequality and poverty. Methods of estimation and policy applications*. Oxford: Oxford University Press.

Kolm, S.C. 1969. The optimal production of social justice. In *Public economics*, ed. J. Margolis, and H. Guitton, 145–200. London: Macmillan.

Mason, Karen Oppenheim. 1986. The status of women: conceptual and methodological issues in demographic studies. *Sociological Forum* 1 (2): 284–300.

Masson, Karen Oppenheim. 2005. Measuring women's empowerment: Learning from cross-national research. In *Measuring empowerment: Cross-disciplinary perspectives*, ed. Deepa Narayan, 89–102. Washington D.C.: The World Bank, Oxford University Press.

Narayan, D. (ed.). 2002. *Empowerment and poverty reduction: A sourcebook*. Washington, DC: World.

Sen, A.K. 1973. *On economic inequality*. Oxford: Clarendon Press.

Sen, A.K. 1976. Poverty: On ordinal approach to measurement. *Econometrica* 44 (2): 219–231.

Smith, Herbert L. 1989. Integrating theory and research on the institutional determinants of fertility. *Demography* 26 (2): 171–184.

Streeten, P. 1981. *First things first: Meeting basic human needs in developing countries*. Oxford: Oxford University Press.

United Nations Development Programme (UNDP). 1991. *Human Development Report*. New York: Oxford University Press.

World Bank. 2000. *World development report 2000/2001: Attacking poverty*. New York: Oxford University Press.

Traditional Institutions and Female Beneficiaries of Mahatma Gandhi National Rural Employment Guarantee in West Bengal

Arghya Kusum Mukherjee and Amit Kundu

1 Introduction

The Mahatma Gandhi National Rural Employment Guarantee Act (MGNREGA) strives to enhance the income security of rural poor through entitlement of 100-day employment in a financial year. This act ensures 100-day employment for any adult from a household residing in rural areas and willing to work in manual-labor-intensive public works at statutory minimum wage. The scheme was rolled out all over India in three phases that started in February 2006, September 2007, and April 2008 (Deininger and Liu 2013). Elected local authorities play instrumental role in allocation and supervision of works. Any intended participant of MGNREGA has to apply first for registration in the Gram Panchayat (GP). GP officials will verify eligibility of the applicant and issue a job card for the household. Job card is a prerequisite for accessing MGNREGA (Dey 2010). Under MGNREGA, an eligible applicant is entitled to get job within 15 days of application. Otherwise, he or she will be paid an unemployment allowance. To ensure the participation of women, the MGNREGA has stipulated a quota of 33% for women and equal wage across gender.

In Indian social fabric, women of scheduled caste (SC) community are least restrained by social norms compared to women of upper caste (UC) community and Muslim community. In general, the return from participation in MGNREGA will be highest for those women whose mobility and conservative social norms least impede social interaction. However, the story will be altogether different if any intervention changes existing paradigm of male hierarchy. Therefore, National Rural Employment

---

A.K. Mukherjee (✉)
Department of Economics, Srikrishna College, Bagula, West Bengal, India
e-mail: arghya97@rediffmail.com

A. Kundu
Department of Economics, Jadavpur University, Kolkata, West Bengal, India

© Springer Nature Singapore Pte Ltd. 2017
C. Neogi et al. (eds.), *Women's Entrepreneurship and Microfinance*,
DOI 10.1007/978-981-10-4268-3_3

Guarantee Scheme (NREGS) may enhance the female labor force participation by exploring new avenues of employment opportunities in their own locality, and reduced gender disparity in wage rate (Afridi et al. 2012). A rise in women's earning can increase women's say in the intra-household distribution of resources.

Now, opportunity cost of time is very high for women. Increased earning of women put greater weight to their preference in household decision making. However, in a society sharply divided across caste and religion, the benefits of participation in the labor force for women might not be even across caste and religion. Women belonging to UC face more taboos on mobility and social restrictions than women belonging to SC community. A poor household has to depend profoundly on female earning (Kapadia 1997). Most SC households are poor, and women share a significant portion of financial burden of the family. As a result, SC women have more physical mobility and greater say in household financial decision compared to UC women (Mencher 1988). However, UC women of wealthy class are not restrained by social norms or lack of autonomy in different spheres of decision making (Eswaran et al. 2009). Muslim women face more social restrictions regarding contact beyond kinship sphere compared to UC women (Field et al. 2010).

In general, the return from participation in MGNREGA will be highest for those women whose mobility and conservative social norms least impede social interaction. Field et al. (2010) have challenged this notion. The return from an intervention may be highest for the treated who are restrained most by constrained social norms, if that intervention expands awareness or defies the male domination of the society.

Using primary data, the chapter attempts to investigate whether there exists any non-monotonic effect of restrictedness on household's expenditure on consumption, temptation good, women's health, children's education, and health across castes and religion. The sample is relatively homogeneous regarding socioeconomic status, but differs in affiliation to castes and religion. In this backdrop, the chapter has been organized as follows: Section 2 discusses the economics of discrimination in Indian society and Sect. 3 describes the performance of MGNREGA in West Bengal. Section 4 deals with data and methodology. Section 5 discusses the results and Sect. 6 concludes the whole study.

2 Economics of Discrimination, Indian Social Fabric, and Women

The first statement of the neoclassical theory of discrimination was apparently proposed by F.Y. Edgeworth in 1922, but most of the work in America follows Gary Becker's 'The Economics of Discrimination' (1971). Many economists have revised Becker's model, but Arrow (1972) has contributed significantly in formulating neoclassical theory. Many theorists have agreed only on the form of neoclassical tradition, but they have varied opinions on detail or on major conclusions.

Akerlof and Kranton (2000) have shown how a person's identity affects economic consequences. They frame a model of economic behavior and incorporate the psychology and sociology of identity. Using game theory they have shown how identity can alter mutual interactions among players.

Persistent and pervasive intergroup inequality exists in economic life of Indian society. Caste system has been developed on the division of population into a hierarchical order of social groups. This social hierarchy also determines the economic right that is hereditary in nature. Entitlement of economic right gets contracted on the downward movement of caste ladder. Intervention is required to safeguard the interest of the untouchable existing at the lowest tier of the society (Akerlof 1976; Ambedkar 1936, 1987; Thorat and Newman 2010).

In extremely hierarchical Hindu caste system, the condition of UC women of lower economic strata is not very different from Dalits. The man is assumed as source of pollution. Therefore, women are restrained to come into contact with the people other than the husband. All these factors hinder the labor force participation of the women of UC community. As per Islamic law, men and women both enjoy equal rights. It contradicts the prevailing beliefs that Islamic laws are derogatory for women. Muslim clerics advocate for restrained movement of women. In UC Hindu and Muslim communities, there may be a stigma attached to women working outside the home, especially if it involves work considered menial. On the contrary, women of SC community face fewer social restrictions and mostly engage in caste-based age-old trades. Being independent earner, SC women have greater say in the financial decision making of the households compared to UC or Muslim women.

3 MGNREGA

3.1 MGNREGA in West Bengal

As per Section 4(1) of the National Rural Employment Guarantee Act (NREGA), September 2005, Government of West Bengal introduced 'the West Bengal Rural Employment Guarantee Scheme' in 2006 for providing employment to rural people. This scheme was rolled out in different districts of the state in three phases.

The number of job cards issued in West Bengal by the middle of the year 2015–16 was 120.41 lakh. The total number of workers employed is 265.71 lakh, of which 26.34% are SC and 7.79% are ST. However, 71.46 lakh are active job card holders. It implies that a significant number of job card holders are not participating in MGNREGA. Person-days generated in the state were 1697.51 lakh, 2296.34 lakh, and 2018.42 lakh, respectively, during the financial years 2014–15, 2013–14, and 2012–13. SC person-days as a percentage of total person-days were 32.29, 33.49, and 32.53 during the financial years 2014–15, 2013–14, and 2012–13, respectively.

For ST, these figures are 8.45%, 9.65%, and 9.96%, respectively. Women are also well represented in the MGNREGA. For women program participants these figures are 1.34%, 35.7%, and 33.71% during the financial years 2014–15, 2013–14, and 2012–13, respectively. Although there is a provision of 100-day employment in the Act, the average days of work provided to the households in West Bengal is 33.15, 37.44, and 34.7, respectively, during the financial years 2014–15, 2013–14, and 2012–13. In these three consecutive years Government of West Bengal was able to provide 100 days of employment to 158,290, 280,627, and 253,088 jobs, respectively. Therefore, there are clear mismatches across job card holders, active job card holders, and the number of days of employment provided. Total expenditures in MGNREGA were INR 401,614.71, 372,517.24, and 385,087.42 lakh respectively during the financial years 2014–15, 2013–14, and 2012–13. Therefore, in 2013–14 the MGNREGA did better in West Bengal compared to other two financial years (Government of India, Ministry of Rural Development 2015).

Demand for employment under MGNREGA is lower in Kolkata and other urban parts of the state. As per MGNREGA, GP can initiate a work based on the demand of 10 persons. Demand for employment was increased during 2014–15 in Murshidabad, Malda, and North 24 Parganas districts. The performance of West Bengal is not satisfactory in the implementation of the program.

3.2 Existing Work on MGNREGA

Impact studies on NREGS put forward mixed results on different welfare indicators of the households. Ravi and Engler (2009) conducted a study in Medak district of Andhra Pradesh. They observed that households participating in the NREGS spend more on food and some nonfood consumables than nonparticipating households. Participant households also have higher likelihood of savings than that of nonparticipants. Deininger and Liu (2013) using data from Andhra Pradesh showed that interventions like MGNREGA have increased per capita consumption expenditure, aggregate calorie, and protein intake for the treated households. Azam (2011) using National Sample Survey Organization (NSSO) data has shown that NREGS has increased real wage for both women and men. However, the wage hike is larger for women.

Dreze et al. (2008) observed that MGNREGA is creating more employment than other employment programs in Chhattisgarh. They observe that corruption incurred in the implementation of MGNREGA is not very significant. It has been corroborated by the verification of muster roll. Bhatia and Dreze et al. (2006) have shown in another study the loopholes in the execution of the program in Jharkhand.

Afridi (2008) discussed community control mechanism for monitoring the implementation of MGNREGA and found that civil society took a crucial role in Rajasthan to make rural people aware with a bottom-up approach. On the contrary, government took lead responsibility for introduction of this process with a top-down approach. The study proposes blending of both the models for better scrutiny of MGNREGA works.

Khera (2008) found that the farmer's organization played a major role in making MGNREGA perform better. Khera and Nayak (2009) conducted an investigation in six states on how much importance women put in MGNREGA works. The study reveals that 79% women workers think that the program is important. They unearth anomalies of MGNREGA, such as nonpayment of unemployment allowances for inability of the local administration to allot work within 15 days of application for work and delayed payment.

Gaiha et al. (2009) has analyzed two propositions: (a) excess demand of work for existence of poverty and (b) increased wage in MGNREGA fueling inflation. The study corroborates both propositions.

Dey (2010) has conducted a study in Birbhum district of West Bengal to assess the targeting efficiency of the program, role of Panchayati Raj Institution (PRI) in implementing MGNREGA, and impact on different household welfare indicators. The study finds that MGNREGA does not have any major impact on household welfare indicators, but has significant impact on the reduction of stress due to joblessness.

Using data from Karnataka, Harish et al. (2011) have analyzed whether MGNREGA has increased income and supply of labor at agriculture. The study finds that consumption expenditure has been increased and debt burden has been reduced due to participation in MGNREGA.

Anderson et al. (2013) investigated how unique identification (UID) can be used to bring better transparency in the execution of MGNREGA. They further proposed use of control group methodology to assess the efficacy of UID system for enhancing performance of MGNREGA.

Narayanan and Das (2014) made a study on MGNREGA. They found that there are several incentives in MGNERGA guideline to enhance the participation of women. Different government reports show that 47% of MGNREGA beneficiaries are female. Using data from National Sample Survey, the study tried to evaluate the extent to which the program is accessible to widows and lactating mothers who face apathy of employer in the formal labor market.

Ranaware et al. (2015) conducted a study in Maharashtra to assess the quality of works created under MGNREGA. Their study reveals that most of the program beneficiaries think that works are very beneficial. Assets created from MGNREGA are well maintained and kept in a better condition. This study has disagreed with the existing observation that the MGNREGA has not created any quality asset. The study further concludes that there is opportunity for getting better work choice, design, and implementation. However, there is hardly any study evaluating the nonmonotonicity of social restrictedness for female workers in MGNREGA.

4 Data and Methodology

4.1 Field Selection

West Bengal has been chosen for the following reasons: (a) a sizable section of the total population is Muslim; (b) erstwhile Left Front Coalition Government and present Trinamul Congress Government are committed for the upliftment of marginalized; and (c) due to political stability, the state has been able to pursue the goal of social justice (Chatterjee and Hussain 2009). All districts of West Bengal have been clubbed in three strata using district-level human development index (HDI) score: (1) high-HDI districts; (2) medium-HDI districts; and (3) low-HDI districts. From each stratum, one district has been chosen randomly. The selected districts are Burdwan, Nadia, and Murshidabad. First, we have chosen two blocks from each district, and then five villages from each block. At the village level, to identify women beneficiary households[1] of the MGNREGA, we first conducted a survey of all households using a brief questionnaire. From this survey, we identified women beneficiaries of the MGNREGA program. In every village, participating households are chosen randomly among program participants, and nonparticipating households were chosen randomly from nonparticipating households using probability proportional to size (PPS) method. In PPS method, number of households to be selected from each village depends on a total number of program participants and nonparticipants. Thus, our sample comprised of 180 program participating households and 120 nonparticipating households. The women have been categorized into three broad social groups: Hindu SCs, Hindu UCs, and Muslim (Table 1).

We gathered pre-intervention data, that is, the data of 2010, on a number of characteristics of caste and religion. Differences in background characteristics are not significant. The sample is homogeneous with respect to observable characteristics, such as age, education, and occupation. Respondent was asked whether she had never gone alone to five places: market, bank, health clinic, movie, and outside the village. The respondent was given one point if her response is affirmative. Therefore, the index runs from 0 to 5. All respondents are women and they differ in their affiliation to caste and religion. Therefore, restrictions on mobility and social interaction vary with affiliation to caste and religion. This is evident from Table 2 that shows mean values of different variables. Subsamples have significant differences across an index of restrictedness. This value is significantly higher for Muslim community compared to SC community.

---

[1]Only those households have been chosen as treatment households from where at least one woman has participated in MGNREGA programmes in the past four years.

Traditional Institutions and Female Beneficiaries ... 47

Table 1 Overview of sample households across caste and religion

	Participant MGNREGA	Nonparticipant MGNREGA
UCs	64	42
SCs	70	15
Muslim	46	63
Total	180	120

Table 2 Descriptive statistics of variables used in the regression

	UCs	SCs	Muslims	Control
Mean age of female members (years)	20.73	20.16	19.2	21.02
Mean female education (years)	5.73	5.57	6.03	7.1
Difference of age between husband and wife (years)	5.38	4.87	5.6	4.34
Household size	5.05	5.25	4.84	4.96
Household heads (HH) attend political meeting or rally (%)	61.8	58.4	58.4	60.6
Whether HH is literate (%)	25.28	25.23	25.36	25.46
Female-headed household (%)	11.3	11.7	11.21	11.21
Main occupation—agriculture (%)	45.28	46.9	44.2	45.24
Restricted	1.85	1.53	2.8	1.45

Source Calculated from field survey data

5 Access to MGNREGA for Rural Women

5.1 MGNREGA and Poverty Status of the Household

MGNREGA is a self-targeted, low-waged, and toil-intensive work. In some states, wage in MGNREGA is lower than the statutory minimum wage of the unskilled labors. A poor household depends on the earning of the female members. In the absence of any fruitful employment scopes, women are mostly engaged in a household chore or do some odd jobs, such as collecting firewood and cow dung. MGNREGA opens the opportunity of earning for the rural women. Table 3 shows that most of the participants of MGNREGA belong to poor economic strata. About one-quarter of the participants belongs to 'marginal' households. However, there is no participant from high- or middle-income strata. As income rises, it is expected that female member's likelihood of participation in MGNREGA will decline.

Table 3 Distribution of MGNREGA participation of female by poverty status

Poverty status	Participation (%)
Poor	64.7
Marginal	26.72
Vulnerable	8.58
Middle income	0
High income	0
Total	100

Source Calculated from field investigation

5.2 MGNREGA and Affiliation to Caste and Religion

The mobility of women is governed by different norms in a society, divided across castes and religions. About 28.33% of households in total sample belong to SC category, whereas 38.85% of beneficiaries are from SC community. About 36.33% of households in total sample belong to the Muslim community, whereas 25.65% female beneficiaries of the program are from the Muslim community. Women of SC community have a significant higher likelihood of participating in MGNREGA compared with women of UC and Muslim community. In survey area, Muslim women are allowed to be engaged in a household business, such as paddy husking, processing of hair, and animal husbandry. However, there are restrictions in participating MGNREGA for Muslim women where they have to work or interact with those outside the sphere of kinship. Sometimes being veiled signals social status. These limit the chance of labor force participation of Muslim women.

5.3 Accessing the Program: Probit Estimate

$D_i = Z\gamma + \theta S_1 + \lambda S_2 + \mu_i$; $D_i = 1$ for the program participants and $D_i = 0$ otherwise.

$S_1 = 1$ for SC, 0 otherwise; $S_2 = 1$ for Muslim, 0 otherwise.

Caste and religion: Among UC, SC, and Muslim, SC women are least restrained by social norms. Therefore, it is expected that women of SC community have a greater likelihood of participation in the MGNREGA. On the contrary, women of the Muslim community have a lower probability of participating in the program.

Z comprises following variables:

Monthly per capita consumption expenditure (mpce): It is evident from Table 4 that as the economic status of a household rises, the likelihood of participating women in MGNREGA decreases. Our a priori expectation is negative between these two variables.

Mean age of female in the household: We anticipate a negative relationship between age and probability of participation in MGNREGA (Table 5).

Traditional Institutions and Female Beneficiaries ...

Table 4 Distribution of MGNREGA female participation across caste and religion

SRCs	% of households in total sample (HH = 300)	% of households accessing MGNREGA (HH = 180)
UC	35.34	35.5
SC	28.33	38.85
Muslim	36.33	25.65
Total	100	100

Source Calculated from field investigation

Table 5 Factors determining participation of women in MGNREGA

Variables		Coefficients
Caste and religion (Ref: UC)	SC	0.209^{*} (0.137)
	Muslim	-0.176 (0. 093)
mpce		-0.053^{**} (0.03)
Age of female		-0.011 (0.9)
Education of female		-0.022^{***} (0.013)
Difference of age between husband and wife		-0.410 (0.380)
Household size		0.330^{**} (0.170)
Household head (HH) attended political meeting/rally		0.100^{***} (0.530)
Education of HH (Ref: literate)		0.590 (0.480)
Main occupation of HH (Ref: nonagriculture)		1.108^{***} (0.460)
Gender of the household head (Ref: female)		0.460 (0.360)
Index of restrictedness		-0.540^{**} (0.310)

***, **, * Significance at 1%, 5%, and 10% level, respectively
$n = 300$, McFadden's $R^2 = 0.1765$, LR statistics = 49.7361

Mean education of the female in the household: Education increases the opportunity cost of time. The wage of MGNREGA in some states is lower than the statutory minimum wage of the unskilled labor. Therefore, education might act as a disincentive in determining participation decision in MGNREGA.

The difference of age between husband and wife: If the difference of age between husband and wife is less, then the wife has higher decision-making agency. Hence we anticipate a positive relationship between the difference of age and participation in MGNREGA.

Household size: Generally, bigger households are poor. Therefore, our a priori expectation is that members of large households have a higher chance of participation.

Occupation of the household head: If the occupation of the household head is agriculture, then it is expected that female members have a higher chance of participation.

Education of the household head: We anticipate that if the household head is literate, then female members have a lower chance of participating in NREGA.

Participation in a political meeting or campaign: MGNREGA is not accessible to all in reality. There is patron clientele relationship between politician and their supporters. Therefore, participation in a political campaign may enhance the chance of participation in MGNREGA.

Gender of the household head: Women-headed households are resource poor in nature, and taboos on women are less. Therefore, we can anticipate that households having a woman head have a fair chance of joining MGNREGA.

Index of restrictedness: Households having less restrictions on the movement of women have greater chance of participation of women in MGNREGA. Therefore, a priori expectation is negative between score of restrictedness and likelihood of participation in MGNREGA.

From the probit estimate we can observe that even after controlling other variables, women of SC community have a significantly higher likelihood of participating in MGNREGA compared to the women of UC community. However, women of the Muslim community have a lower likelihood of participating in the program. Therefore, we can conclude that access to MGNREGA varies across caste and religion. Women of SC community are least fettered by social norms, and they have the highest chance of participating MGNREGA. Common sense says that return from MGNREGA will be highest for women of SC community. In this backdrop, next section tries to examine whether an intervention like MGNREGA benefited most to least socially restrained women. The variable 'mpce' reflects economic status of the households. Therefore, significant 'mpce' implies that affluent households are not willing to participate in the program. Among other variables, 'mpce' has significant negative impact on the participation of female in MGNREGA. If education of female member increases, then likelihood of participating in MGNREGA decreases. Household head's participation in political meeting or rally significantly increases the likelihood of participating in MGNREGA. Index of restrictedness has significant unfavorable effect on the likelihood of participation of women in MGNREGA. The value of likelihood ratio (LR) statistics shows that the model has got the overall significance. Index of restrictedness has significant negative impact on the likelihood of participation of women in MGNREGA. Value of LR statistics shows that the model has got overall significance.

Traditional Institutions and Female Beneficiaries ...

6 Examining Non-monotonicity of Social Restrictedness

6.1 *Impact Analysis*

MGNREGA is a self-targeted program. It might happen that women having higher decision-making agency participated in the program. Therefore, using simple nonparticipant households as control might yield a biased result.

In nonexperimental studies, one has to invoke some identifying assumptions to solve the selection problem. There are several methodologies. We have used Heckman's treatment effect.[2] D_i of participation equation indicates the treatment condition, where $D_i = 1$ for the program participants and $D_i = 0$ otherwise. This D_i directly enters into the outcome equation. We can write the model using the following two equations:

Participation equation

$$D_i = Z\gamma + \theta S_{i1} + \lambda S_{i2} + \mu_i \tag{1}$$

Outcome equation

$$Y_i = X_i\beta + \alpha_1 D_i + \sum_{j=1}^{2} \alpha_{2j} S_{ij} + \sum_{j=1}^{2} S_{ij} D_i \delta_j + \varepsilon_i \tag{2}$$

Y is the outcome variable, such as 'consumption expenditure,'[3] 'expenditure on temptation good,'[4] expenditure on women health,' and 'expenditure on children's health and education.' X is the vector of explanatory variables, such as education, participation in social security measures, the social capital of the households, and the gender of the household head.

Here, $S_{i1} = 1$ for SC category and 0 otherwise.

$S_{i2} = 1$ for Muslim and 0 otherwise. Therefore, 'UC' is the reference category.

Coefficient δ represents the differential impact of program participation across castes and religions. If δ is significant, then we can say that the differences are

---

[2]The difference between Heckman's two-step or sample selection method and Heckman's treatment effect model is that in the latter model a dummy variable indicating treatment condition directly enters into the regression equation; and outcome variable of the regression equation is observed for both treated and untreated.

[3]Here we calculate monetary expenditure on the following items: (1) food, fuel, and lighting items; (2) clothing and footwear; and (3) miscellaneous goods and services and durable articles. The value of consumption for a period of 30 days is obtained for a surveyed household.

[4]'Temptation good' comprises the following items: (i) betel leaves including supari (areca nut), lime, and katthha (Catechu); (ii) tobacco and its products; (iii) liquor; (iv) intoxicants like 'mahua' and 'ganza'; (iv) meals or snacks consumed outside the home; and (v) lottery tickets and gambling. In surveyed household respondents were asked expenditure on these items during the last 30 days.

significant for SC and Muslim participants compared to UC participants. The coefficient α shows the impact of the intervention of MGNREGA for women of UC community, which is the omitted category. This coefficient also shows the impact of the intervention MGNREGA.

Here, ε and μ are bivariate normal with mean 0 and covariate matrix $\begin{bmatrix} \delta & \rho \\ \rho & 1 \end{bmatrix}$

Eqs. (1) and (2) are estimated jointly.

7 Result and Implications

If women do not participate in MGNREGA, they would have been engaged in the household chore. Therefore, the opportunity cost of labor is not very significant. However, participating in MGNREGA women share the financial burden of the households. There are two approaches regarding empowerment of women: instrumentalist and minimalist. The minimalist approach advocates that access to money empowers women both within and outside households. It is said that women empowerment generates series of positive impacts within households. It reduces wasteful consumption and enhances saving, spending on children's schooling and so on.

From Table 6, we can observe that due to participation in MGNREGA, the consumption expenditure has been increased significantly for households of Muslim and SC communities compared to households of UC community. However, expenditure on temptation good, a wasteful expenditure for the household, has been increased for the households of SC and Muslim communities compared to the UC community. Participation of women of UC community in MGNREGA has

Table 6 Impact of MGNREGA participation on outcome variables across social groups

Variables	Consumption expenditure	Expenditure on temptation good	Expenditure on women health	Expenditure on children's health and education
MGNREGA	197.21 (186.37)	262.39*** (98.24)	0.17** (0.073)	0.18** (0.09)
MGNREGA × SC	341.24*** (112.7)	293.82*** (102.7)	−0.11 (0.08)	−0.13 (0.1)
MGNREGA × Muslim	318.3*** (127.3)	308.84** (139.38)	−0.09 (0.08)	−0.17 (0.15)
SC	198.72 (168.5)	179.4 (165.63)	0.068 (0.088)	0.093 (0.076)
Muslim	107.8 (140.38)	150.6 (141.5)	0.046 (0.039)	0.056 (0.07)

***, ** Imply significance at 1% and 5%, respectively

significantly reduced expenditure on temptation good. The net impact of participation on the expenditure of temptation good is lower for the households of Muslim community compared to households of SC community. Participation in MGNREGA has significantly increased expenditure on women's health, that is, participation of female in MGNREGA has increased expenditure on women's health significantly for the household of UC community. However, this expenditure has been decreased for the treatment households of SC and Muslim communities compared to UC community. The net impact of participation in MGNREGA on expenditure of women health is positive across all castes and religions. Similarly, participation of females in MGNREGA has increased expenditure on children's health and education significantly for the omitted category, that is, the UC community. The net impact of participation in MGNREGA is positive for the households of SC and Muslim communities, but insignificant.

Employment in MGNREGA has enabled women to share the financial burden of the family. As a result, their say is likely to increase in household decisions regarding allocation of resources for women and children. Results from Table 6 reiterate this claim. The conventional notion is that women who are least fettered by social norms should get maximum benefits of participation in MGNREGA. However, our analysis shows that women of UC community have been able to exercise the highest level of agency in allocating household resources compared to the women of SC community. It substantiates the non-monotonicity of restrictedness of social norms across castes and religions. Agency of Muslim women has not increased significantly compared to the UC women.

8 Conclusions

The return from participation in MGNREGA should be highest for those women whose mobility and conservative social norms least impede social interaction. However, women of that community extract highest benefits from MGNREGA who are most constrained by social norms. It may be interpreted as the non-monotonic effect of restrictedness across caste and religion. Using primary data from three districts of West Bengal, this chapter has tried to examine whether there exists any non-monotonic effect of restrictedness on household's 'expenditure on consumption,' 'expenditure on temptation good,' 'expenditure on women's health,' and 'expenditure on children's education and health' across social groups. Given the similarity in the household's socioeconomic characteristics across social groups, the benefit accrued from MGNREGA differs significantly across castes and religions. One possibility is that MGNREGA women participants of UC community are more receptive to MGNREGA. If social restrictedness creates bottlenecks for knowledge, and participation in MGNREGA allowed UC women to challenge existing gender norms to enhance their agency, then why Muslim women, who are most fettered by social norms, did not respond more to the MGNREGA than SC women did. It may be explained as non-monotonic effect of social restrictions.

References

Afridi, Farzana. 2008. Can community monitoring improve the accountability of public officials. *Economic and Political Weekly*, October 18, 2008.

Afridi, Farzana, A. Mukhopadhaya, and S. Sahoo. 2012. Female labour force participation and child education in India: The effect of national rural employment guarantee scheme, IZA, DP No. 6593.

Akerlof, George. 1976. The economics of caste and of rat race and other woeful tales'. *Quarterly Journal of Economics*, X, C, 4, November, 1976.

Akerlof, George and R.E. Kranton. 2000. Economics and identity. *Journal of Quarterly Economics* CXV: 715–753.

Ambedkar, B.R. 1987. (first published 1936) Philosophy of Hinduism. In *Dr Babasaheb Ambedkar writings and speeches*, Vol. 3, ed. Vasant Moon, 1–94. Department of Education, Government of Maharashtra Bombay.

Ambedkar, B.R. 1987. (first published 1936) The Hindu social order: Its essential features. In *Dr Babasaheb Ambedkar Writings and Speeches*, Vol. 3, ed. Vasant Moon, 95–115.

Anderson, Siwan, Ashok Kotwal, Ashwini Kulkarni, and Bharat Ramaswami. 2013. *Measuring the impacts of linking NREGA payments to UID*. Working Paper, International Growth Centre, London School of Economics and Political Science, London.

Arrow, K.J. 1972. "Models of job discrimination" and Some models of race in the labor market. In *Racial discrimination in economic life*, ed. H. Pascala (Chaps. II and VI). Lexington, Massachusetts: D.C. Heath-Lexington Books.

Becker, S. 1971. *The economics of discrimination*, 2nd ed. Chicago: University of Chicago Press.

Chatterjee, Amrita and Jakir Hussain. 2009. Primary completion rates across socio religious communities in West Bengal. *Economic Political Weekly*, 44 (15).

Deininger, K., and Y. Liu. 2013. Welfare and poverty impact of India's national rural employment guarantee schemes. IFPRI Discussion Paper, 01289.

Dey, Subhasish. 2010. Evaluating India's national rural employment guarantee scheme: The case of Birbhum District, West Bengal. Working Paper No 490, International Institute of Social Studies, the Netherlands.

Dreze, Jean, Nikhil Dev, and Reetika Khera. 2006. *Employment guarantee: A primer*. NBT: New Delhi.

Dreze, Jean, Nikhil Dev, and Reetika Khera. 2008. Corruption in NREGA: Myths and reality. The Hindu dated January 22, 2008.

Eswaran, Mukesh, Bharat Ramaswami, and Wilima Wadhwa. 2009. *Status, caste, and the time allocation of women in rural India*. Mimeo, University of British Columbia.

Field, Erica, Seema Jayachandran, and Rohini Pande. 2010. Do traditional institutions constrain female entrepreneurship? A field experiment on business training in India. Working Paper Series No. 36, IFMR Research, Centre for Micro Finance.

Gaiha, Raghav, Vani S. Kulkarni, Manoj K. Pandey, and Katsushi S. Imai. 2009. *National rural employment guarantee scheme, poverty and prices in rural India*. ASARC working paper 2009/03.

Government of India, Ministry of Rural Development. 2015. Data on MGNREGA availed from nrega.nic.in on 11/12/2015.

Harish, B.G., N. Nagaraj., M.G. Chandrakanth., P.S. Srikantha Murthy., P.G. Chengappa, and G. Basavaraj. 2011. Impacts and implications of MGNREGA on labour supply and income generation for agriculture in central dry zone of Karnataka. *Agricultural Economics Research Review*, 24: 485–494.

Kapadia, Karin. 1997. Mediating the meaning of market opportunities: Gender, class and caste in rural South India. *Economic and Political Weekly*, 35 (52): 3329–3335.

Khera, Reetika. 2008. Employment Guarantee Act. *Economic and Political Weekly*, August 30, 2008.

Khera, R., and N. Nayak. 2009. Women workers and perceptions of the NREGA. *Economic and Political Weekly*, February 12, 2009.

Mencher, Joan P. 1988. Women's work and poverty: Women's contribution to household maintenance in South India. In *A home divided*, ed. Daisy Dwyer and Judith Bruce. Stanford, CA: Stanford University Press.

Narayanan, Sudha, and Upasak Das. 2014. Women participation and rationing in the employment guarantee scheme. *Economic and political Weekly*, 31 (46).

Ranaware, Krushna, Upasak Das, Ashwini Kulkarni, and Sudha Narayanan. 2015. Blocked by caste: Economic discrimination and social exclusion in modern India. New Delhi: Oxford University Press.

Ravi, Shamika, and Monika Engler. 2009. Workfare as an effective way to fight poverty: The case of India's NREGA, available at SSRN:http://ssrn.com/abstract=1336837.

Thorat, Sukhadeo, and Katherine Newman (eds.). 2010. *Blocked by caste: Economic discrimination and social exclusion in modern India*. New Delhi: Oxford University Press.

Empowerment of Women Through Public Programs in Rural West Bengal: A Study on National Rural Livelihood Mission in a Block of Purulia

Tithi Bose and Archita Ghosh

1 Introduction

Empowerment can be described as a process to delegate weaker or marginalized people the power so that more choices are opened before them to live a better life in every respect. This multidimensional process of empowerment provides greater access to knowledge and resources, more autonomy in decision making, greater ability to plan lives, and more control over the circumstances to influence lives, as well as freedom from customs, beliefs, and practices of one's choice. As the marginalized section of the society is devoid of the choices of life, be it social, economic, or political, through empowerment it is possible to develop their abilities that help them create different opportunities for themselves and also to choose the suitable alternative.

Women for a long time have remained marginalized in a sense that they have remained deprived of the opportunities that men used to enjoy. It has subsequently been realized that unless women are equally equipped, half of the human resources remain unexploited, which is not affordable for any nation. One of the foremost goals of the new millennium is to uplift the overall conditions of women, which is possible only by empowering them. Empowerment, thus, will enable women to realize their identity and power in all spheres of life (Narang 2012).

Development of women got focused worldwide especially after the observance of United Nations Decade for Women, 1976 to 1985. Empowerment of women became a major concern of every nation, particularly in the developing world where the question of capabilities of women remained unattended to a large extent.

T. Bose
Department of Economics, Haldia Government College, Haldia, West Bengal, India

A. Ghosh (✉)
Department of Economics, University of Kalyani, Kalyani, West Bengal, India
e-mail: archita@klyuniv.ac.in

© Springer Nature Singapore Pte Ltd. 2017
C. Neogi et al. (eds.), *Women's Entrepreneurship and Microfinance*,
DOI 10.1007/978-981-10-4268-3_4

Since the 1990s, development strategies of the developing countries are being focused on alleviation of poverty in a participatory mode and through social inclusion. One such strategy was a generation of microcredit for the vulnerable section of the society. This was attempted through the formation of self-help groups (SHGs) with marginalized people so that an organizing attitude could be developed among this section. These groups were supposed to function for self-employment through a new process of saving and borrowing, termed 'microcredit practice'. Primarily, saving habit was promoted to enhance thrift practice of the group members. Later, they are trained to go through a process of borrowing for productive investment and repayment of the loans. Thus, a group can function as an economic agency. In this process of organizing themselves for economic activities group members get aware of their rights/facts, start raising their voice for their rights, and accumulate bargaining power, and power to fight any economic and social exploitation. Therefore, to generate a process of economic and social empowerment was the main motive behind the agency development among the vulnerable people. This practice of microenterprise credit among women became a popular and one of the most common government interventions to eradicate poverty of women in the developing world (Hashemi et al. 1996) from the 1990s, as it could be used as an effective instrument for women empowerment besides generating income for them.

India started experimentation with SHGs through NABARD (National Bank for Agriculture and Rural Development) SHG–bank linkage during the 1990s. Despite the phenomenal expansion of the organized banking system in India, a very large number of poor continued to remain excluded from the formal banking system. Hence, the need for an alternative credit delivery mechanism, which would meet the requirements of the poor, was acutely felt during the late 1980s. It was NABARD that came forward by initiating alternative policies for generating loan products that would fulfill the requirements of the poorest, especially of the women family members. The emphasis was on improving the access of the rural poor to an integrated microfinance service.

The success of the SHG–bank linkage program of NABARD encouraged the state to initiate microcredit process to empower women on a larger scale through rural development department and panchayats (village-level government bodies in India). Thus, the experimentation with SHGs and microcredit is carried forward as an independent program under the Union Ministry of Rural Development that was to be executed by panchayats and rural development cells. This Swarnajayanti Gram Swarozgar Yojana (SGSY) can be cited as an initial attempt of the State in alleviating poverty through capability enhancement and agency development. It is a microcredit program that works through SHGs, formed especially with women members at the village panchayat level. The Swarozgar scheme was planned to promote group loans and encourage small-scale savings and group enterprise to develop agency in some predetermined stages. The District Rural Development Cell (DRDC) is the prime implementing agency in the district, and panchayats were the associating organization at the local level. The district cells and the panchayats work in cooperation with the local-level banks to execute the whole process.

This study tries to investigate the impact of SGSY, more recently known as National Rural Livelihood Mission (NRLM), on the socioeconomic and political status of women at the household level and at the village level. We have chosen Purulia district for the village survey. The choice of the district is purposive, as Purulia is one of the most backward districts in West Bengal on human development index and in number of backward villages. It lies on the plateau of Chota Nagpur, in the extreme west of West Bengal. Geographical conditions are quite unfavorable for agriculture in this mostly forest-covered region. A major proportion of the inhabitants is of tribal origin depending upon the forest products. As the district is completely rural, villagers mostly depend on casual labor. The purpose of the study is to examine the socioeconomic and political impacts of SGSY or NRLM on the lives of women as well as on their lives at the household level in a poor, completely rural-based, backward, and tribal-habitat area of West Bengal, far from the State capital where literacy level is very low. The study also tries to judge whether the prescribed factors, such as, poverty level, caste, and so on decide the beneficiaries or the other sociopolitical, economic, and the cultural factors decide group involvement. Especially, analyzing the impact of group bonding and group activities on socioeconomic and political empowerment of women at the village level is the aim of this study.

1.1 Progress of SGSY (NRLM)

Since the inception of SGSY 1.06 crore swarojgaris at the national level have been assisted under it. As per the mandate, the program in practice tried to work in favor of the most vulnerable groups, such as scheduled tribes (STs) and scheduled castes (SCs), and women. The SC and ST swarojgaris accounted for about 47.46% of the total swarojgaris, and minorities accounted for 10.6% of total swarojgaris. In 2011–12, 16.77 lakh swarojgaris were involved in SGSY, of which 11.03 lakh (65.80%) were women (Ministry of Rural Development, Annual Report 2012–13).

From April 1999 to 2012, 43 lakh SHGs were formed under the scheme at the national level. From June 2011, SGSY was restructured as NRLM program with a wider vision and universal approach to overcome the shortcomings of SGSY. NRLM performs comparatively well for universal mobilization. Up to December 2014, 20 lakh SHGs have been formed, and 2.4 crore households have been mobilized under NRLM in 316 districts.

However, if we assess the progress of SGSY by maturity level of the groups, the success of the program is far from satisfactory. As revealed from the available secondary information, of the 43 lakh of SHGs, only 30 lakh obtained the status of Grade I and 14.63 lakh Grade II. Only 22% of the SHGs were matured enough to take up economic activities financed by bank credit and supported by subsidy (Ministry of Rural Development, Annual Report 2011–12). Even under NRLM, only 31% of total targeted SHGs have been linked to the bank, and only 39% of total targeted loan amount has been released (Annual Report 2014–15, Ministry of Rural Development).

As our study focuses on the progress of SGSY at the microlevel in a district of West Bengal, we tried to take a look at the financial and physical progress of SGSY in West Bengal. We see that though West Bengal manages to utilize 60% of the total fund, higher than the national average of 58%, only 26% of available credit is disbursed. Credit subsidy ratio is far below the national target of 3:1 showing the inefficiency of the groups and malfunctioning of the credit linkage process. However, in the case of physical performance, West Bengal performs a little better than the national average regarding coverage of beneficiaries and involvement of SCs. The state manages to involve SC swarojgaris up to 38%, which is marginally above the national average (35%). Women participation is also encouraging. About 90% of the swarojgaris are women. However, as far as the ST coverage in the state is concerned, the picture is appalling.

As in this study, we have tried to present a village-level investigation about the impact of SHGs on women under SGSY in the district of Purulia, let us take a look at the progress of SGSY in different blocks of Purulia. From the secondary data, we can have an idea about the group formation and their efficiency, which will give us an overall idea of the involvement of rural women with the groups and the impetus of these groups in mobilizing women toward forming of economic agency among them.

Table 1 demonstrates the physical progress of the SHGs, both under SGSY and NRLM in all the blocks of Purulia. As we note from the table, the percentage of SHGs that passed Grade I is too low on every block. Again all the groups, which passed Grade I were sanctioned for the first revolving fund. In most of the blocks with some exceptions, the percentage of groups, which passed Grade II is lower than the proportion of groups passing Grade I. The trend shows that percentage of group formation is getting lower.

When SGSY was transformed into NRLM, policies at the grassroots level and involvement of DRDC have changed to a large extent. Although NRLM was launched in 2011, it started to be implemented at the block level only since 2013. This resulted in slow progress of group formation and sanction of a revolving fund to the groups. Again all the blocks are not included in the selection of intensive blocks for implementation of NRLM in the primary phase. Therefore, we can see a complete pause in group formation in some backward blocks, except Arsha.

Table 1 Advancement of the SHGs under SGSY in the blocks of Purulia

Name of the block	Number of SHG formed since inception	SHGs formed in 2011–12 (%)	SHGs passed Grade I in 2011–12 (%)	Percentage of SHGs passed Grade II in 2011–12	SHGs for which RF sanctioned in 2011–12 (%)	SHGs for which second installment of RF sanctioned in 2011–12 (%)	SHGs economically assisted in 2011–12 (%)	SHGs formed from 2012 to February 2015 (%)	Pre-NRLM SHGs provided for revolving fund (RF) (2013 to 15 February 2015) (%)
Puncha	1050	4.38	7.43	5.90	7.43	8.95	6	2.61	0.09
Bundwa	982	3.56	3.97	1.43	3.97	8.25	2.14	0.00	0.00
Hura	1377	0.65	1.02	0.36	1.02	2.90	0.36	1.29	1.15
Manbazar-I	1624	8.50	7.88	0.06	7.88	7.08	0.00	2.74	3.20
Manbazar-II	1172	0.94	4.01	9.39	4.01	4.01	9.22	0.00	0.00
Bagmundi	1239	0.89	3.55	0.08	3.55	2.82	0.08	0.00	0.00
Purulia-I	1208	2.90	6.79	1.49	6.79	7.70	1.41	5.40	0.00
Purulia-II	1507	1.79	3.45	2.12	3.45	7.43	2.06	3.14	3.14
Balarampur	1270	6.06	6.22	0.79	6.22	8.50	1.50	2.49	4.18
Jhalda-I	1377	2.32	7.33	4.58	7.33	4.07	4.72	3.84	5.17
Jhalda-II	1233	0.89	8.84	4.14	8.84	5.68	4.79	5.35	1.22
Santuri	563	3.02	7.82	4.09	7.82	2.84	6.39	2.05	0.00
Kashipur	1437	4.80	5.98	2.37	5.98	1.88	2.51	2.49	8.42
Joypur	979	3.17	4.80	2.04	4.80	2.45	1.84	0.00	0.00
Neturia	557	3.59	3.23	5.03	3.23	1.97	5.03	8.65	7.39

(continued)

Table 1 (continued)

Name of the block	Number of SHG formed since inception	SHGs formed in 2011–12 (%)	SHGs passed Grade I in 2011–12 (%)	Percentage of SHGs passed Grade II in 2011–12	SHGs for which RF sanctioned in 2011–12 (%)	SHGs for which second installment of RF sanctioned in 2011–12 (%)	SHGs economically assisted in 2011–12 (%)	SHGs formed from 2012 to February 2015 (%)	Pre-NRLM SHGs provided for revolving fund (RF) (2013 to 15 February 2015) (%)
Para	1055	3.22	7.01	4.83	7.01	5.59	4.17	0.00	0.00
Raghunathpur-I	515	2.72	3.50	7.96	3.50	3.11	7.96	5.94	2.16
Raghunathpur-II	768	3.65	4.69	12.50	4.69	5.21	12.50	3.81	3.81
Arsha	1221	6.72	8.52	0.74	8.52	10.48	0.74	6.22	1.23
Barabazar	1180	4.58	13.64	0.85	13.64	8.14	0.59	0.42	0.00
District Total	22314	3.50	6.10	3.04	6.10	5.68	3.15	3.71	2.95

Source Block-level data collected from District Rural Development Cell, Purulia

1.2 The Impact of Microcredit Programs on the Lives of Women: What Does the Existing Literature Say?

For our study, we have undertaken a survey of the literature to know about different sorts of possible impacts of SHGs on women. Since the 2000s, a number of empirical studies have been published on analysis of impacts of SHGs on the lives of the commoners, particularly women (e.g. Barnes et al. 2001; Dunn and Arbuckle 2001; Mosley 2001). These studies have found positive and significant impacts of microcredit through group formation on economic benefits and welfare levels of program participants (Duvendack et al. 2011; Kono and Takahashi 2010; Deininger and Liu 2009). In this respect, the empirical study based on a primary survey in Andhra Pradesh concluded that there is a positive impact on female empowerment, consumption, and nutritional intake in program areas (Deininger and Liu 2009). Focusing on the SHG programs in India, studies by Swain and Varghese (2009, 2011) found positive impacts on asset accumulation, livestock income, and salaries of program participants, although the studies found a negative impact on total income. Another study finds that microfinance has little impact on the poorest because loans are disproportionately obtained by wealthier participants (Coleman 2006). Studies find the possible existence of spillover effects from villages included in the microfinance initiative to control villages (Pitt and Khandker 1998). Khandker (2005) finds a spillover pathway between participants who have access to loans and those who do not discriminate by microlevel data. Regarding the social impact of microfinance, some authors have shed light on its potential to create social capital and facilitate female empowerment through microfinance programs (Garikipati 2008; Rai and Ravi 2011; Swain and Wallentin 2009). Economic theories prove that abundance of microfinance approaches based on SHG programs promotes social interactions among group members within the same community and brings significant monetary and nonmonetary returns in comparison with regular interaction (Kreps et al. 1982; Feigenberg et al. 2010).

As women live in a marginalized conditions and are more vulnerable to different shocks, different research studies have discussed women empowerment through SHGs and explained current position of women empowerment in India. According to some studies, SHGs have benefited women group members in numerous ways; not only through the creation of assets, incomes, and employment opportunities for them, but also by creating bonding and agency development process. This ultimately enhanced the equality of status of women as participants, decision makers, and beneficiaries in the democratic, economic, social, and cultural spheres of life (Thangamani and Muthuselvi 2013; Narang 2012; Reji 2011; Suguna 2006). A study based on the progress of SHGs in Bangladesh has demonstrated how participation in SHGs has increased the mobility of women, their decision-making power, purchasing power, asset possession at the household level, legal and political awareness, and strength to overcome the gender barriers, and led to empowerment of women (Hashemi et al. 1996). Another study suggests that participation of women in SHGs has lowered domestic violence against women at the household level (Hashemi et al. 1996). Thus, we find that SGSY had not only generated economic benefits for women, but it has also initiated the process of empowerment of women in familial and social sphere.

1.3 SGSY and Women Empowerment: Findings from the Survey

As has already been mentioned, at the panchayat level, SGSY/NRLM is the government's attempt to mobilize women and to reduce poverty among rural women through SHGs. The SHGs formed under SGSY comprise 10–15 individuals of homogeneous nature. These groups are formed so that the group members can stand for themselves in need. Formation and upgradation of groups is a continuous process over time. As groups go through different stages, members associated with the groups also go through a subsequent transformation. Over time a habit of saving, loan repayment, and enterprising activities is developed among the group members. These factors naturally lead toward empowerment of the group members. In India, women being less educated and not endowed with assets, are in a vulnerable position. Therefore, government intervention through SHGs focuses on mobilizing women. In this section we discuss on the basis of a microlevel study, the impacts of SHGs on rural women and examine whether these groups are contributing in any way toward women empowerment.

While pursuing with the exercise, we have done a comparative analysis between two categories of SHG members. One category comprises the group members, who are associated with SHGs for many years and have succeeded to receive small loans. On the other hand, the other category consists of the group members, who have associated themselves with groups for fewer years and have not received any loans. Specifically, the comparative analysis is undertaken to know the difference between the impacts on the lives of women members, who have received loans and who have not received loans. Our intention is to know how far group bonding and group loans widen the scope of women empowerment.

The study is a village-level study in Arsha block, which is one of the most backward blocks of Purulia. We have collected data from two villages—Tuma Jhalda and Kanchanpur—under Beldi Gram Panchayat (GP). About 150 women belonging to different SHGs were interviewed. A stratified random sampling was done while collecting data to make a comparative study between the group members who have availed loans and the new group members who have not received any group loans.

We have considered different types of behavioral patterns of the women group members to investigate different facets of empowerment, such as economic, political, and social. Therefore, data were collected on the economic utilization of loans taken by women members, their dependence on self-employment, the impact of group loans on the consumption pattern, their decision-making power, political

Empowerment of Women Through Public Programs ...

involvement, attachment with social network, social bonding, and democratic practice to explore different dimensions of empowerment. We have tried to investigate to what extent involvement with an SHG influences empowerment of women and how far group loan widens the scope of women empowerment.

In Tables 2 and 3, we present social and marital status of the group members who have availed loans vis-à-vis those who have not. It is often seen that familiarity to the village community increases the chance to be included in a group and also to avail the loan. We have investigated the number of years of living of the group members in the village to know whether recognition of an individual matters in availing group membership and a loan. It has been seen from the village-level data (Table 2) that women coming new to the village do not get a membership. In most of the cases, for women, years of marriage is equal to the number of years she is residing in the village. Newly married women are not well known in their community or in many cases they are not aware of different aspects of the village. Women living in the village at least for five years can manage a group membership and group loans. Therefore, it can be said that recognition of a woman individually determines group membership of women in SHGs.

It can also be seen from Table 2 that women belonging to 'other backward castes' (OBC) category are highly interested in SHGs and have managed to get group loans too. People belonging to higher caste do not show much interest in getting involved with SHGs. Involvement of SC people is also very low, which is surprising. Tribals are involved with groups but in a low proportion, and they are

Table 2 Social status of women group members

Caste status			Years of living in the village		
Caste	Percentage of loan-availing women	Percentage of nonloan-availing women	Years	Percentage of loan-availing women	Percentage of nonloan-availing women
SC	4.08	0	Up to 5	0	0
ST	20.41	37.74	5–15	36.73	35.85
OBC	75.51	62.26	15–25	16.33	18.87
GEN	0	0	Above 25	49.94	45–28

Source Primary data collected by the authors in 2015

Table 3 Marital status of the group members

	Percentage of loan-availing women	Percentage of nonloan-availing women
Married	87.76	92.45
Single	0.00	0.00
Widow	8.16	5.66
Separated/divorced	4.08	1.89

Source Primary data collected by the authors in 2015

least interested in the functioning of the group. Another interesting feature is that while allotting loans, they are neglected. In some cases, they have been included recently in newly formed groups. In many instances, their ignorance, unawareness, and absence of saving habit have resulted in the complete breakdown of groups. Therefore, in most of the cases, although tribal people are attached with groups, they do not succeed to receive loans. On the other hand, OBC women are comparatively more attached with groups because they are socially more recognized, aware of different facts, and associated with panchayats and panchayat functionaries. Therefore, they are preferred as group members in the primary phase of the execution of the program. Such groups functioned properly, and group members had succeeded to receive loans.

The widow and separated women, who are in a severely vulnerable position, are neglected in SHGs (refer to Table 3). Over 90% of the group members are married. Separated or divorced women and the widows have remained deprived of group benefits. While forming groups, women living above the poverty line are also included. However, loans are given only to the women below the poverty line. This shows the necessity of the program in helping the marginalized section in its endeavor to come out of the abject poverty. Nevertheless, caste and marital status wise, it can be stated that the poorest section of the village women, who are more vulnerable to shocks, are unable to avail benefits. Therefore, some doubts arise about the detection of below-poverty-line (BPL) status of the women. Some external factors may influence confirmation of the BPL status.

In Table 4, we depict a picture of what the group members achieved regarding the availability of basic amenities. About 28% of the loan-receiving families have managed support from the panchayats for implementing sanitation. This statistics is quite higher than the support available to the families without any loan from the groups. Again, around 76% of the loan-receiving families have availed panchayat support for electrification. On the other hand, the figure for the women's families without loans is 51%. It can be said from the data on panchayat's support for sanitation and electrification that women attached with groups for a longer time and managing to get loans are more aware of the contemporary aspects at the village level. Therefore, they can raise their demand and can ask for institutional help to fulfill their needs. Groups are definitely organizing women toward their rights and claims, and are helping to spread awareness. Here, we have to add that group loans leave a higher impact. Availability of loans from the groups might have helped the families to complement economic support of the panchayats for electrification and

Table 4 Electrification and sanitation status of SHG members' families

	Percentage of loan-availing women	Percentage of nonloan-availing women
Electrification by the panchayat on basis of below the poverty line status	75.51	50.94
Sanitation by the panchayat scheme	28.57	5.66

Source Primary data collected by the authors in 2015

sanitation. However, we do not find any enhancement in expenditure as a result of group association or group loans.

Table 5 shows that women without loans join MGNREGS for work in a higher proportion. This implies that women in comparatively less vulnerable condition have managed to get group loans. In another way round, it can be said that women after receiving loans have uplifted their economic position to some extent and are less interested in unskilled wage work.

We have considered economic status of the women group members by an annual income of the households. It may be said from Table 6 that families with women members availing loans earn a comparatively higher annual income. Group loans perhaps have helped women to increase the annual income of their families. We have also calculated the mean annual income of the households in the two groups. Mean annual income of the families with women availing loans is INR 40,492 and not availing loans is INR 33,935.

However, it is evident from Table 6 that percentage of annual food consumption is greater for the families, where women have not received loans. This supports the economic theory that poorer sections spend more on food. We have also tried to show in this table the impact of group loans for the women on the education of children in their families. Here, we see that a higher proportion of women with group loans can manage for greater education expenditure annually. It can be said that families, where women have managed group loans, can afford higher education for children in upper classes. We have also collected data on the impact of group loans on medical expenditure. No significant difference was noticed in this respect.

We have also traced out the utilization pattern of loans by the group members to explore economic empowerment of group members. Table 7 demonstrates that 57% of the members after receiving loans invested in livestock like milch animals and ducks or hens. About 69% of women members have managed to invest loans for enhancing income. This reflects the positive impact of the program in generating entrepreneurship among the women.

Table 8 shows that 67% of women with loans are self-employed, while 40% of the group members without loans are self-employed. This implies that loans have made women self-dependent in terms of income generation and economic empowerment. We have learnt from the survey that women without loans, depending on self-employment for earnings, are involved with hazardous and low-paid income generating work, such as bidi, bamboo basket, and rope making.

Table 5 Benefit received by the group members by other popular schemes

Government schemes availed by women	Percentage of loan-availing women	Percentage of nonloan-availing women
JSY	2.04	3.77
MGNREGS	42.86	49.06

Source Primary data collected by the authors in 2015

JSY Janani Suraksha Yojana; MGNREGS Mahatma Gandhi National Rural Employment Guarantee Scheme

Table 6 Annual income, food expenditure, and expenditure for children's education of the women group members

Annual income (in INR)	Percentage of loan-availing women	Percentage of nonloan-availing women	Annual food expenditure (in INR)	Percentage of loan-availing women	Percentage of nonloan-availing women	Annual expenditure on children education (in INR)	Percentage of loan-availing women	Percentage of nonloan-availing women
Less than 10,000	24.49	13.21	**Less than 10,000**	6.12	1.89	**Less than 10,000**	42.86	54.72
10,000–20,000	12.24	35.85	**10,000–20,000**	28.58	16.98	**10,000–20,000**	10.2	3.78
20,000 and above	63.27	50.94	**20,000 and above**	65.31	81.13	**20,000 and above**	8.16	7.55

Source Primary data collected by the authors in 2015

Empowerment of Women Through Public Programs …

Table 7 Utilization pattern of loans from SHGs

Purpose of loan taken	Percentage of loan used
Marriage of daughter	14.29
Family crisis	6.12
Medical purpose	2.04
Animal husbandry	57.14
Cultivation	2.04
Tree plantation	10.20
Total of productive activities	69.38 (57.24 + 2.04 + 10.20)
Group savings	8.16

Source Primary data collected by the authors in 2015

Table 8 Self-employment and training of the group members

	Percentage of loan-availing women	Percentage of non-loan-availing women
Self-employed	67.35	39.62
Trained	75.51	0

Source Primary data collected by the authors in 2015

Another encouraging aspect is that 75.5% of the members with loans have received some training from the panchayats, organized by the local nongovernment organizations (NGOs). From this fact, it can be inferred that being a group member and availing loans a woman can be initiated in the process of being empowered.

Through the survey, we have tried to look into the indicators of social and political empowerment. These include mobility, decision-making power, and consciousness about someone's rights and opportunities. The mobility of the women group members is captured by the number of times they can go out from home for different purposes except for work in a week. We have considered several alternative destinations/purposes, such as going out to market, panchayat, relatives' house, doctors' clinic, and theater. Here, it is quite clear that group members, who have availed loans, go out of homes frequently for different purposes (Table 9). Availability of loans has increased their self-employment opportunities, which have opened their path for communication with the outer world, and thus their outer mobility has increased compared to those who have not availed loans.

Loans can be a steady strategy to increase the decisive power of women at the household level. After receiving loans, the economic position of the women members gets uplifted, and they can involve themselves in various major family decisions. Loans enhance the economic position and confidence of the women family members, as loans are used for further income generation or to resolve some of the temporary domestic crises. Table 10 depicts that 98% of the women after receiving loans involve themselves in important family decisions, while 69% of nonloan-availing women group members can participate in family decisions. Membership in groups has made women aware and helped to raise their voices.

Table 9 Mobility pattern of the group members

Number of times going out of home in a week	Percentage of loan-availing women	Percentage of nonloan-availing women
Upto 1 day	20.41	66.04
2–3 days	48.98	32.08
4–5 days	20.41	1.88
6–7 days	10.20	0.00

Source Primary data collected by the authors in 2015

Table 10 Decision-making power of the women group members

	Percentage of loan-availing women involved in the decision	Percentage of nonloan-availing women involved in the decision
Major family decision	98	68
Family planning	97.96	65.81
Planning for children education	67.35	60.38
Protest against family disturbance	57.14	7.55
Helping others in hard times	22	11

Source Primary data collected by the authors in 2015

We have also tried to capture involvement of group members in vital and sensitive decisions, such as family planning and children's education (Table 10). Family planning is a very sensitive issue, and women's influence in this sort of decision can be a strong index of measuring social empowerment of women. We can see that 98% of women with group loans can speak about family planning, which is a surprising result. Again 65% of women in groups without loans can also participate in family planning, which is impressive. SHG members can also largely influence another major decision, the decision regarding children's education. For women group members with loans 67% of women do have a say about their children's education. On the other hand, this proportion is 60% for women group members without loans. Experience, group bonding, social contact, and presence in different gatherings for a longer time have helped to raise their voices in different spheres of domestic affairs.

Therefore, it can be said that social networking and group bonding through SHGs have helped at large in social empowerment of women. While measuring empowerment in respect of raising voices against any domestic violence or disturbance (refer to Table 10), we can see a massive difference between women with loans and without loans. About 57% of the women group members with loans can gather strength and raise their voices against domestic violence or any assault. On the contrary, only 8% of the group members without loans can raise their protest. This implies that being in SHGs for a long time has many positive impacts. SHGs have succeeded to foster an agency among women and helped them to organize a protest against any disorder.

We have examined another dimension to assess social and economic empowerment. We have tried to investigate how many of the group members with and without loans help other women economically and stand beside them in hard times. The result, which is an interesting scenario, is also depicted in Table 10. We see that 10–22% of group women can help other women in the village at times of distress. About 22% of the women with group loans can do this independently, whereas 10% of women without loans have helped others after joining groups. From this, it can be stated that women are mobilized through groups to act independently, and a sense of womenhood has grown.

Next, we tried to investigate about political empowerment through participation in panchayat activities, group meetings, visit to panchayats, attendance at gram sansads, involvement in politics, and contact with elected representatives. The results are depicted in Table 11. We can see that a large proportion of women group members attend group meetings and different panchayat meetings. Again, members with loans join in group and panchayat meetings in a larger proportion than women members of new groups, who have not availed loans. We use participation at gram sansads (ward-level public forums) organized by the panchayats to discuss problems, file complaints, raise demands, and demand accountability as the measures of the level of democratic practice among group members. Participation at sansads is 26% for group members, who have availed loans and only 15% for new group members without any group loan. The most shocking feature is that politics play the most vital role in selecting group members. All the group members are found to be supporters of the ruling party at the village level. However, active participation in politics measured by participation in party meetings and rallies, which can be an indicator of political empowerment, is not so impressive. Only about 13–14% of the women members of the SHGs actively participate in political meetings and rallies.

Table 11 Women's awareness about their political rights and opportunities

	Percentage of loan-availing women	Percentage of nonloan-availing women
Attending group meeting	93.88	86.79
Attending panchayat meeting	95.92	88.68
Visit to village panchayats	100	90.34
Attending gram sansads	26.53	15.09
Attending political meetings/rallies	14.29	13.21
Relationship with elected representatives at the panchayat level	100	67.92

Source Primary data collected by the authors in 2015

On the other hand, as depicted in Table 11, the relationship of the group members with the ward members and panchayat pradhan is quite strong. It implies that women having a good contact with the elected representatives at the panchayat level have a greater chance to be included in groups. Again, women who have received loans from the groups have a longer association with the groups and panchayat activities. Quite naturally, a higher percentage of women receiving loans will have a good contact with the elected representatives. However, in our case, all the group members who have received loans have good contact with the representatives. When a program starts, panchayat members take the initiative to select beneficiaries from the persons well known to them and having regular contact with them. In this case also group formation started with women who are well connected with the panchayat members and among these women some became group leaders. Thus, political association and contact with the elected representatives appeared to be major determinants of loan distribution.

2 Conclusion

In India, one of the attempts of women empowerment took place by provisioning of microcredit for them through SHGs. In this study, we have tried to assess the impact of SGSY, which is a program aiming at providing microcredit through SHGs, on empowerment of women in a completely rural and distressed situation. Our study based on a village-level survey in the backward district of Purulia of West Bengal finds that involvement in the group can do a lot in terms of women empowerment. Not only empowerment, a feeling of sharing and standing beside the fellow members grows among the group members. Loans from the groups can be a great source to provide self-employment for the involved women, which develops self-esteem among women, helps to raise their voices against any corruption, and uplifts their position in their families. We have tried to know which women are particularly involved in groups and who avail or are given loans. On the basis of the comparison drawn between women being only in groups and women who have availed loans from groups under SGSY, we have examined whether group loans can be a major tool for economic empowerment of women.

As far as socioeconomic factors are concerned, we find that the higher caste women have not participated in SHGs. While conducting the survey, it is also observed that ST and SC women are also less interested in groups compared to OBC women. We can also see that poorest households are not involved with groups. We may say that the poorest families do not associate themselves with groups.

Groups and group loans have substantially contributed to economic empowerment. Women associated with groups are comparatively more aware of different facts and, therefore, have managed to get panchayat's assistance for sanitation and electrification facilities. In most cases, group loans have been used productively for animal rearing, cultivation, and tree plantation. Therefore, an increase in income can be expected from association with groups.

Group loans and association with groups have socially empowered women, as women associated with groups can stand beside other women, largely influence the family decisions, participate more in public and political gatherings, and engage themselves with various types of social gatherings. Group association has progressed largely in empowering women as women associated with groups can influence sensitive issues, such as family planning and education of children. However, again, politics play a major role in benefiting the group members. Women well connected with the ruling political parties and panchayat members have a higher chance of getting included in the groups and receiving group loans.

However, groups have to go a long way regarding organizing women and creating a strong bonding among women. Low-caste and illiterate women till now are least interested in groups as the functioning of groups is a bit complicated, or they are not made aware of their features. A proper continuation of group formation lacks at the villages. Group members do not receive any training about group formation, and members remain in total ignorance. Sometimes, training is given to poultry farming and animal husbandry to the loan bearers, but there also, proper continuity is absent. In many instances, after availing loans, women invest in productive activities, but in the long run, they get disinterested. Implementing agencies do not take any proper initiative in maintaining groups in the long run. Panchayats can take strong initiatives in this regard by involving women properly. Particularly, the transformation of schemes impedes the process of proper implementation of groups. As SGSY is transformed into NRLM, groups are facing lots of hindrances. Group are not organized properly to make the members them aware of the new features, and therefore, they are losing interest in groups. Some blocks are chosen for intensive development of SHGs under NRLM, and the District Rural Development Cell is only caring for those blocks. Panchayats can play a crucial role if they are given responsibility. If the panchayats are entrusted with the responsibility of supervising and executing the process of group formation and functioning, many groups can be saved and can function in the desired manner. All the implementing agencies should work in a coordinated manner to develop SHGs and make their members truly economically empowered. Proper and sincere initiatives should be followed to make the groups sustainable in the long run through purposive economic activities instead of only increasing the number of groups and achieving the number target.

References

Bardhan Pranab and Dilip Mookherjee. 2004. 'Poverty alleviation efforts of West Bengal panchayats. *Economic and Political Weekly*, 965–74.

Barnes, C., G. Gaile, and R. Kibombo. 2001. *The Impact of Three Microfinance Programs in Uganda. AIMS Paper.* Washington, DC: Management Systems International.

Coleman, B.E. 2006. Microfinance in Northeast Thailand: who benefits and how much? *World Development* 34 (9): 1612–1638.

Deininger, K., and Y. Liu. 2009. Economic and social impacts of self-help groups in India. World Bank Policy Research Working Paper Series.

Dunn, E., and J.G. Arbuckle. 2001. Microcredit and microenterprise performance: Impact evidence from Peru. *Small Enterprise Development* 12 (4): 22–33.

Duvendack, M., Palmer-Jones, R., Copestake, J.G., Hooper, L., Loke, Y., and N. Rao. 2011. *What is the Evidence of the Impact of Microfinance on the Well-Being of Poor People?* London: EPPI-Centre, Social Science Research Unit, Institute of Education, University of London.

Feigenberg, B., Field, E.M., and R. Pande. 2010. Building social capital through microfinance, NBER Working Paper No. 16018.

Garikipati, S. 2008. The impact of lending to women on household vulnerability and women's empowerment: evidence from India. *World Development* 36 (12): 2620–2642.

Hashemi, Syed, M., S.R. Schuler and A.P. Riley. 1996. Rural credit programs and women's empowerment in Bangladesh. *World Development* 24(4).

Khandker, S.R. 2005. Microfinance and poverty: Evidence using panel data from Bangladesh. *World Bank Economic Review* 19 (2): 263–286.

Kono, H., and K. Takahashi. 2010. Microfinance revolution: Its effects, innovations, and challenges. *The Developing Economies* 48 (1): 15–73.

Kreps, D.M., P. Milgrom, J. Roberts, and R. Wilson. 1982. Rational cooperation in the finitely repeated prisoners' dilemma. *Journal of Economic Theory* 27 (2): 245–252.

Mosley, P. 2001. Microfinance and poverty in Bolivia. *Journal of Development Studies* 37 (4): 101–132.

Narang, U. 2012. Self help group: An effective approach to women empowerment in India. *International Journal of Social Science & Interdisciplinary Research* 1(8).

Pitt, M.M., and S.R. Khandker. 1998. The impact of group-based credit programs on poor households in Bangladesh: Does the gender of participants matter? *Journal of Political Economy* 106 (5): 958–996.

Rai, A., and S. Ravi. 2011. Do spouses make claims? Empowerment and microfinance in India. *World Development* 39 (6): 913–921.

Reji, E.M. 2011. Microfinance and women empowerment: Evidence from field study. *Journal of Rural Development* 30 (1): 25–44.

Suguna, B. 2006. *Empowerment of Rural Women Through Self Help Groups.* New Delhi: Discovery Publishing house.

Swain, R.B., and A. Varghese. 2009. Does self help group participation lead to asset creation? *World Development* 37 (10): 1674–1682.

Swain, R.B., and A. Varghese. 2011. Reassessing the impact of SHG participation with non-experimental approaches. *Economic and Political Weekly* 46 (11): 51.

Swain, R.B., and F.Y. Wallentin. 2009. Does microfinance empower women? Evidence from self-help groups in India. *International Review of Applied Economics* 23 (5): 541–556.

Thangamani, S and S, Muthuselvi. 2013. A study on women empowerment through self-help groups with special reference to Mettupalayam Taluk in Coimbatore district. *IOSR Journal of Business and Management* 8(6).

Non-farm Employment Among Rural Women: Trend and Determinants

Aparajita Dhara and Biswajit Chatterjee

1 Introduction

As the share of agriculture in gross domestic product (GDP) decreases with economic growth, so does its share in employment. Over time this leads to a shift in the rural occupational structure toward different non-agricultural and non-farm activities. A vibrant rural non-farm sector has the potential of reducing disguised unemployment in agriculture, forced migration toward urban centers, rural poverty, and rural income inequality.

The post-1991 reform years in India have witnessed a rapid transition from agriculture to the services sector, leading to livelihood diversification toward the non-agricultural activities and a transformation of the occupational structure in the rural areas. The share of workers engaged in non-agricultural activities as their main occupation has increased from 21.8–23.7% during the 1990s to 32.1% in 2010. Rural non-farm employment (RNFE) helps farm-based households to spread their risks, offers more remunerative activities to supplement or replace agricultural income during lean seasons, and provides means to cope when farming fails, which in turn has the potential of reducing rural poverty levels and distress-led migration to urban areas. However, these positive developments will be taking place when the occupational shift, from agriculture to non-agricultural activities, reflects the maturing of growth-led forces in the economy and not as a result of demographic pressure on cultivable land coupled with adverse trends in the agrarian sector. It is, therefore, important to identify the reasons behind the change in the rural occu-

A. Dhara (✉)
Department of Economics, Rishi Bankim Chandra Evening College, Naihati, India
e-mail: dhara.aparajita@gmail.com

B. Chatterjee
Department of Economics, Jadavpur University, Kolkata, India
e-mail: biswajitchatterjee0@gmail.com

© Springer Nature Singapore Pte Ltd. 2017
C. Neogi et al. (eds.), *Women's Entrepreneurship and Microfinance*,
DOI 10.1007/978-981-10-4268-3_5

pational structure, to determine whether the growth in RNFE is driven by growth- and prosperity-related 'pull' factors or due to distress-driven 'push' factors.

This chapter focuses on the forces behind the growth of non-farm employment among rural women in India during the post-reform decades. There are two major research questions addressed in this study—how the rural female workforce in India has changed during the post-reform decades, on industrial subsectors and employment status? And which factors drive the growth in rural female non-farm employment during this period—'distress-driven' or 'growth-driven'?

The rest of the chapter is organized as follows. We begin with a brief survey of the literature on determinants of RNFE in Sect. 2 and discuss some major hypotheses. Section 3 introduces the data used in our analysis and Sect. 4 gives a macroeconomic overview of the data. In Sect. 5, we undertake a panel data regression analysis on the dataset, to find out the significant determinants. Section 6 concludes the chapter with some policy suggestions.

2 Literature Review

The factors identified in the literature regarding the growth of RNFE can broadly be grouped into two categories—the macrolevel demand-side determinants (which are mainly concerned with the business environment, policies, and other region-level variables affecting the growth of the non-agricultural sector and employment as a whole) and the microlevel supply-side determinants (which enable an individual rural worker or a rural household to take part in the non-farm sector job market). The macrofactors can further be divided into (i) agricultural growth-led diversification (inter-sectoral linkage hypothesis); (ii) distress-led diversification (residual sector hypothesis); (iii) factors external to agriculture, such as rural infrastructure, human capital, and per capita public expenditure on rural development; and (iv) factors external to the rural economy, such as degree of urbanization and urban agglomeration. We discuss here some of the studies carried out in this regard.

In the early 1970s, it was postulated that due to increasing agricultural productivity a virtuous cycle could emerge between agricultural and non-agricultural activities through inter-sectoral consumption and production linkages (Mellor and Lele 1973; Mellor 1976). With increasing levels of agricultural income, the relative share of consumption expenditure of the rural population on non-food items tends to increase and this, in turn, stimulates the growth of RNFE. Moreover, agricultural growth leads to an increased demand by the agriculturalists for inputs, such as fertilizers, tools, machinery equipment, and their repairing services, as well as an increase in the demand for processing of the agricultural products. These backward and forward production linkages also lead to the growth of non-farm sector employment in the rural areas. Several empirical studies have documented the power of these farm–non-farm linkages in Asia, Africa, and Latin American countries. Johnston and Kilby (1975), Rangarajan (1982), Adelman (1984),

Haggblade et al. (1989), Hazell and Haggblade (1991), Shukla (1991, 1992), de Janvry and Sadoulet (1993), and Srivastav and Dubey (2002) based on the evidence from Asia, sub-Saharan Africa, Latin America, and rural India have argued that production and consumption linkages resulting from agricultural growth stimulated demand for rurally supplied non-farm goods and services.

The linkages were found to be larger in the Asian countries than Africa or Latin America, and consumption linkages were found to be much stronger than production linkages in most of the Asian and African countries. However, not all studies (Sankaranarayanan 1980; Vaidyanathan 1986; Jayaraj 1989; Dev 1990; Unni 1991; Singh 1994; Narayanamoorthy et al. 2002) have found a strong association between consumption linkage and RNFE. According to Vyas and Mathai (1978) skewed income gains in agriculture limit consumption linkage, and inadequate rural infrastructure restricts the ability of rural firms to supply the required inputs and consumer goods, hindering the diffusion of production linkages. Moreover, region- and district-level studies showed that the impact of agricultural growth on rural non-agricultural sector depended on the stage of agricultural prosperity and that the relationship was not monotonic.

Studies undertaken in the different states of India by Harris (1987), Chandrasekhar (1993), Eapen (1994, 1995), Verma and Verma (1995), Chand (1996), Basant et al. (1998), and Mecharla (2002) did not find any significant correspondence between agricultural growth and RNFE too, and they argued that the growth of the non-farm sector was driven by factors outside of agriculture, such as degree of urbanization, population density, rural infrastructure, market integration, and allocation of public sector resources.

A different set of literature argues that due to lack of employment opportunities in agriculture, a large section of rural laborers get 'pushed' into low-productivity casual activities in the non-agricultural sector. In the absence of inter-sectoral linkages or due to the nonexistence of a mechanism for conversion of agricultural growth impulses into non-agricultural employment opportunities, the growth in RNFE can thus be seen as distress diversification. Vaidyanathan (1986) observed a strong positive relationship between unemployment rate (as an indicator of excess labor supply problem in agriculture) and RNFE and formulated this spill-off of the excess labor force from agriculture to the non-agricultural sector as the 'residual sector hypothesis'. The hypothesis had received considerable attention from many scholars such as Dev (1990), Unni (1991), Bhalla (1997), Parthasarathy and Reddy (1998), Kaur (2002), and Srivastav and Dubey (2002), especially regarding the choice of 'unemployment rate' as the measurement of 'distress in agriculture.' Dev (1990) had found a positive association between agricultural prosperity and rural unemployment rate, whereas Unni (1991) and Biradar and Bagalkoti (2001) argued that higher unemployment rate should have reduced both agricultural and non-agricultural wage rates as an indication of excess supply of labor, and if the excess labor from agriculture moves to the non-agricultural sector, then non-agricultural wages should have been lower than the agricultural wage rate, which was not the case observed.

However, the distress movement of labor force into non-agricultural activities from agriculture cannot completely be ruled out, and alternative distress causes, such as population density, proportion of marginal landholdings, and casualization of agricultural labor force were suggested, and they were found to have a positive impact on RNFE in the studies by Verma and Verma (1995), Eapen (1995), Kaur (2002), Biradar (2007), Rajasekhar (1995), and Mecharla (2002). The growth of RNFE was also found to be determined by factors external to agriculture but within the rural economy, such as rural infrastructure (particularly road density, telecommunications, banking facilities, and electricity consumption), human capital, government programmes, and so on. Infrastructure facilitates exchange of goods and services between villages and small rural towns and promotes trade, commerce, and business in rural areas as observed in the studies by Oshima (1994), Lane (1996), Islam (1997), Shukla (1991), Singh (1994), Mecharla (2002), Narayanmoorthy et al. (2002), and Kaur (2002). Nevertheless, the ease of transport between rural and urban areas also confronts rural enterprises with increased competition from urban areas and imports. This is especially true for the small-scale and cottage industries that face competition from cheaper products produced by urban-based large-scale industries or imported from outside the state or country. Moreover, it also affects the taste and preferences of rural households and orients themselves toward urban products, especially in the case of richer households (Islam 1997). Taking literacy rate as a proxy for human capital, Chadha in his studies (1997, 2001, 2004) has found that at the all-India level that the proportion of illiterate workers were higher in agriculture than non-agriculture, the participation in non-farm activities tended to increase with increase in the level of education, and there is a shift from casual non-agricultural jobs to regular employment. Jayaraj (1989), Eapen (1994), Mecharla (2002), Biradar (2007), Narayanmoorthy et al. (2002), and Kaur (2002) all found the strong positive association between literacy rate and RNFE, especially for the male workforce. Moreover, the earning level of the workers in the non-farm sector was also found to depend on the level and quality of education. Apart from these determinants researchers have attempted to understand the role of factors external to the rural economy, such as the degree of urbanization, urban agglomeration, the size of nearby villages/cities, macrolevel policy environment, and the like in influencing the growth of rural non-agricultural employment. Jayaraj (1989) found that rural workers in Tamil Nadu are hesitant to stay in urban areas when better transport and communication facilities were available to commute between rural habitation and urban workplace. The study has also found that villages which were located close to urban towns had a larger proportion of workers in the rural non-farm sector. At the National Sample Survey (NSS) regional level, Unni (1991) found a strong positive impact of urbanization (defined as the share of the population in urban areas to total population) on male participation and a weak negative impact on female participation in RNFE. Parthasarathy and Reddy (1998) also found a positive association, but it was not statistically significant.

During the past two decades researchers have also been studying the potential of the rural non-agricultural sector as a pathway out of poverty. However, the extent to which the rural non-farm sector can reduce poverty depends on the rural households' and individuals' access to such employment and income sources, which in turn depends on the households' and individuals' characteristics, especially regarding their asset endowments. The asset of an individual or household can be categorized into three major types—physical and financial capital (wealth-land-savings-credit); human capital (skill-knowledge-education); and social capital (contacts social network)—and these form the most important supply-side microlevel determinants for the rural labor force in gaining access to the non-farm job market. Unequal asset endowments generate inequitable participation patterns, whereby some manage to engage in non-farm activities as part of an accumulation strategy, whereas other remain trapped in low-return activities. Hoffman (1991) argues that individual characteristics play a key role in sorting people across low- and high-productivity employment, and the decision of individuals to participate in the rural non-farm labor market is based on the individual's self-selection rather than random assignment. Individuals with higher initial wealth and human capital are more able to engage in high-return non-farm activities and benefit most from the RNFE (Barrett et al. 2005). As Banerjee and Newman (1993) theorize, in the presence of capital market imperfections, the ex ante poor tend to choose wage labor, while the ex ante rich become entrepreneurs. At the broader country-wide level Ravallion and Datt (1995) show that the effectiveness of non-farm growth in reducing poverty has varied widely across states and argue that this reflects systematic differences in initial conditions.

For our study, we focus on a mix of these 'pull' and 'push' factors to estimate their impact on the growth of non-farm employment among rural women in India during the post-reform period, separately for industry and employment status of the non-farm workers.

3 Data Source

The study is based on official secondary data published by the National Sample Survey Office (NSSO) under the Ministry of Statistics and Programme Implementation, Government of India (MOSPI, GOI), the Central Statistical Office (CSO) (under MOSPI, GOI), and the National Accounts Statistics (NAS), Government of India.

The NSSO has been carrying out detailed sample surveys on the 'Employment and Unemployment Situation in India' every five years since 1972–73 and the employment related data have been collected from the NSS reports as well as extracted from the unit-level data files for the 43rd, 50th, 55th, 61st, and 66th rounds of these surveys. The population figures have been interpolated from the decennial census reports for 1981, 1991, 2001, and 2011. The data on value-added regarding net state domestic product at factor cost (NSDP) have been obtained from the National Accounts Statistics and converted to constant 2004–2005 base-year prices to arrive at comparable figures. Any other data used or mentioned in the analysis have also been taken from different official government sources.

The analysis covers the 16 major states of India which account for 89.27% of India's rural area and 97.66% of India's rural population. These states are—Andhra Pradesh (AP), Assam (ASM), Bihar (BHR), Gujarat (GUJ), Haryana (HRY), Himachal Pradesh (HP), Karnataka (KNT), Kerala (KER), Madhya Pradesh (MP), Maharashtra (MHA), Odisha (ODS), Punjab (PUN), Rajasthan (RAJ), Tamil Nadu (TN), Uttar Pradesh (UP), and West Bengal (WB).[1]

The NSSO defines the activity status of a person during the reference period of 365 days preceding the date of survey, on which the person spent relatively long time as usual principal status (UPS) of a person, and we have taken the UPS workforce for our analysis and segregated them by one-digit Industrial Classification Code. The study covers all the workers residing in rural areas, irrespective of their place of work, which may be from the village, outside the village but within rural areas, in urban areas, or without any fixed location.

The authors would like to mention here the following notations which are used subsequently—RNFE for rural non-farm employment, AGRI for agriculture and allied activities, NONAGRI for non-agricultural activities, MFG for manufacturing activities, CON for construction, TRD for trade, hotel, and restaurant activities, TRA for transport, storage, and communication, SVS for all other service sector activities (banking, finance, public administration, community services, and so on), OTH for mining-quarrying-electricity, and so on (which have been deliberately left out from detailed study as they employ only around 1% of the total workforce). As for the employment status of the workers, SELFEMP will be denoting all own-account workers, proprietors, and employers, HELPER will mean unpaid family workers involved in the household enterprise, REGULAR imply salaried employment, and CASUAL will be consisting of all other casual workers.

4 Macroeconomic Overview

As presented in Table 1, in Indian economy the share of non-agriculture in total value-added has increased from 69.5% to 84.8% during 1988–2010, while its share in employment increased from 33.8% to 48.8%. At the same time, India's population has been growing at an average annual rate of 2.3%, resulting in about 6.9% average annual rate of growth in per capita national output.

At a rural–urban disaggregated level, one finds that the ratio of percent change in employment and percent change in output (which can be termed employment

---

[1]The newly formed states, namely Jharkhand, Chhattisgarh, and Uttarakhand, have been merged with their parent states Bihar, Madhya Pradesh, and Uttar Pradesh, respectively, to maintain data comparability over the period.

Non-farm Employment Among Rural Women …

Table 1 Share of subsectors in output and employment in India during 1988–2010

	Share in total output 1987–88	Share in total output 2009–10	Share in total employment 1987–88	Share in total employment 2009–10
Agriculture	30.50	15.18	60.11	51.19
Non-agriculture	69.50	84.82	33.89	48.81
Manufacturing	14.66	13.83	11.07	11.57
Construction	6.99	8.32	3.54	9.62
Trade	13.03	18.09	6.17	11.35
Transport	5.30	10.07	1.99	4.51
Storage and communication	24.80	31.49	9.09	10.88

Source Author's calculations based on NSSO, CSO, and population census data

elasticity of output) was greater for the urban non-agricultural workforce than their rural counterpart. However, during the second decade, we find that the elasticity of rural non-agricultural workforce became greater than the urban workforce, indicating a higher growth of the rural non-farm sector employment in the later years.

Probing into the growth of RNFE, one finds that rural–urban ratios for the rates of growth of rural population and rural workforce have been less than that of the urban population and urban workforce. This is due to the process of urbanization of the country—the percentage of population living in urban areas have been rising continuously with the development process, and much of rural areas are getting redesignated as urban areas. Nevertheless, at the same time, we find that for the non-agricultural workforce, the ratio is greater than 1, and that has been through the CON, TRD, and TRA sectors during 2000–10. This indicates that a high proportion of the rural workforce is getting absorbed in these three sectors. Further calculations reveal that while the rural agricultural workforce has been growing at an average rate of 1.4%, the rural non-agricultural workforce has been increasing at 4.2%, with the figures for CON, TRA, and TRD being 12.8, 11.4, and 5.9%, respectively. This reflects the occupational transformation in the rural areas of India during the post-reform decades, especially for the later period, when 1.12% of the net addition to the rural workforce has diversified toward non-agricultural employment.

Disaggregation of the rural workforce in India by gender shows that for the male workforce (which accounts for 72% of rural workers), the share of agriculture has fallen from 75% to 63% and most have gone toward CON, TRA, and TRD. On the other hand, for the female workforce, the share of agriculture has fallen from 85% to 79% during the same period, with CON, MFG, and SVS being the major attractors.

Table 2 shows the trend in the share of non-farm employment among the rural female workforce, and here we can see that it is the younger section of the population who are going more toward non-farm activities, and in 2009–10, more than one-third of the rural female workers in the age-group of 15–29 years have taken up non-farm jobs. Table 3 presents the changing share of the different subsectors over

Table 2 Share of non-farm employment among rural women—total workforce and 'young' workforce

Year	% share of total	% share of youth
1987–1988	15.9	15.9
1993–1994	15.3	16.1
1999–2000	17.6	18.5
2004–2005	23.1	25.8
2009–2010	30.8	33.5

Source Author's calculations based on NSSO, CSO, and population census data

Table 3 Composition of rural female workforce in India—segregated by industrial subsectors

	% of rural female workforce 1987–88	% of rural female workforce 2009–10
Agriculture	85	79
Non-agriculture	7	9
Manufacturing	3	5
Construction	2	3
Trade	3	0
Transport	0	5
Storage and communication	0	0

Source Author's calculations based on NSSO, CSO, and population census data

Table 4 Composition of rural female non-farm workforce—by employment status

	Manufacturing	Construction	Trade	Transport	Storage and communication
SELFEMP	55.85	0.59	33.42	0.75	9.06
HELPER	39.20	1.08	49.06	0.28	9.80
REGULAR	6.58	1.00	3.16	1.37	86.93
CASUAL	19.06	65.81	1.05	1.20	9.53

Source Author's calculations based on NSSO, CSO, and population census data

our chosen time period, while Table 4 shows the data segregated by employment status. Here one can see that while the women are engaged in manufacturing and trading activities as self-employed, construction work is mostly casual in nature and other services are providing more regular employment opportunities to rural women. With this brief macroeconomic overview of the situation, we begin our empirical analysis in the following section, where we would like to analyze the determinants of this livelihood diversification among rural women.

5 Empirical Analysis

5.1 Econometric Modeling

The analysis of the growth of the rural non-farm sector employment was done in terms of the changing share of the non-farm workforce in the total rural workforce during the period. Most of the studies discussed in the literature focus on the non-farm sector as a whole, but we would like to take a look at the growth of the sector at a disaggregated level also, in the hope that this will help in understanding the dynamics better. Our basic econometric model consists of the variables presented in Table 5.

We have taken up AGRI-PC as our growth-related 'pull' factor as per the inter-sectoral linkage hypothesis. It is proposed that with agricultural prosperity in the economy, there will be consumption and production linkages with the non-agricultural sector. More purchasing power in the hands of (rural) agricultural workforce will lead to increased demand for non-agricultural goods and services. Moreover, increase in agro-processing activities and increase in demand for agricultural inputs (fertilizer, equipment, and their maintenance) will lead to growth in related non-farm goods and services, resulting in forward and backward production linkages.

Data revealed that the growth in India's per capita value-added has been led by growth in the non-agricultural sector, and our decomposition analysis has shown a non-agricultural 'pull' on the employment of the workforce. Moreover, the study found that quite a large proportion of this addition to the non-farm workforce has gone to the rural sector. Thus, with non-agricultural prosperity also there are consumption and production linkages with the rural non-farm workforce. Hence, we also include a variable NONAGRI-PC as another explanatory variable.

Table 5 Introducing the variables for regression analysis

Variable	Definition	Unit	Expected sign
Dependent variable			
RNFE Share	Rural non-farm workers/total rural workers	%	Positive
Explanatory variables			
UNEMP	(Rural labor force-rural workforce)/rural labor force	%	Positive
Ln (DENSITY)	Rural population/rural area	%	Positive
Ln (AGRI-PC)	Agricultural value-added/total population	%	Positive
Ln (NONAGRI-PC)	Non-agricultural value-added/total population	%	Positive
URBAN	Urban population/total population	%	Positive
Literacy	Rural literates/rural population	%	Positive

On the other hand, distress in agriculture will be reflected in the increase in unemployment among the rural workforce, due to lack of opportunities in the agricultural sector. In such a situation, the unemployed labor force will be forced to take up non-farm activities out of duress, even at a lower wage rate. Therefore, as per the residual sector hypothesis, we have taken up UNEMP as the 'push' factor.

As for the factors external to agriculture but within rural economy, the important determinants are population pressure on land, development of human capital base, and infrastructural development (electricity, road density, telecommunication, banking system, and so on), and from here we have taken DENSITY and LITERACY as our determinants. The degree of urbanization, presence of urban agglomeration, and governmental policies are other important determining factors external to the rural economy, and we have taken URBAN from this set.

Thus, in our model, UNEMP and DENSITY represent the distress-driven factors, AGRI-PC and NONAGRI-PC represent the growth-related factors; LITERACY is the proxy for human capital, and URBAN is the extra-rural influence.

The pair-wise correlation matrix and the variance inflation factors show the presence of a high degree of multicollinearity if we use all the explanatory variables together in our multiple regression equations, and so we estimate the determinants by two separate models:

Model—1 (with distress factors and growth factors)
RNFE-SHARE = f (UNEMP, Ln(DENSITY), Ln(AGRI-PC), Ln(NONAGRI-PC))
Model—2 (with distress factors and other factors)
RNFE-SHARE = f (UNEMP, Ln(DENSITY), URBAN, LITERACY)
(The models have been checked for multicollinearity and endogeneity problems.)

6 Methodology

The data that we are working with covers 16 states of India over five NSSO rounds. This makes the dataset possess some characteristics of both the cross-sectional studies and time-series studies. We can pool the data to arrive at a bigger dataset and run simple ordinary least squares (OLS) linear regression. However, since we are dealing with the same set of entities over the time points, we can attempt to utilize the panel regression methods also, which examine individual-specific effects, time effects, or both, to deal with observed or unobserved heterogeneity, which are not captured by the explanatory variables of our model. These effects are either fixed or random effects.

A *fixed-effect model* examines if intercepts vary across group or time period, whereas a *random-effect model* explores differences in error variance components across individual or time period. Following Greene (2008), the estimation of panel data model is presented as follows.

If individual effect u_i (cross-sectional or time-specific effect) does not exist (i.e., $u_i = 0$), OLS produces efficient and consistent parameter estimates.

OLS model:

$$y_{it} = \alpha + \beta X_{it} + \varepsilon_{it}, (u_i = 0)$$

If individual effect u_i is not zero in longitudinal data, heterogeneity may influence some of the core assumptions of OLS estimation. Then, panel data models provide a way to deal with these problems.

The functional forms of one-way fixed and random-effect models are as follows:
Fixed-effect (FE) model:

$$y_{it} = (\alpha + u_i) + \beta X_{it} + v_{it}$$

Random-effect (RE) model:

$$y_{it} = \alpha + \beta X_{it} + (u_i + v_{it})$$

where u_i is a fixed or random effect specific to individual (group) or time period that is not included in the regression, and errors are *independent identically distributed*, $v_{it} \sim IID (0, \sigma v^2)$.

Fixed effects are tested by the F test, while random effects are examined by the Lagrange multiplier (LM) test (Breusch and Pagan 1980). If the null hypothesis is not rejected in either test, the pooled OLS regression is favored. The Hausman specification test (Hausman 1978) compares an RE model to its fixed counterpart. If the null hypothesis that the individual effects are uncorrelated with the other regressors is not rejected, an RE model is favored over its fixed counterpart.

7 Results

Table 6 presents the summary statistics of the variables used in the models, and the results of the panel data regression analysis are presented in Tables 7 and 8. We find that on average 22.3% of the rural female workers are engaged in non-farm activities, with a standard deviation of about 15%, while manufacturing sector employment is at 8.9%. It can also be noted that the majority (34.7%) are engaged as helpers in family business.

The Breusch–Pagan Lagrange Multiplier test indicates the presence of state-specific unobserved heterogeneity for all the subsectors of RNFE in both of the models. The Hausman specification test (which checks whether that unobserved heterogeneity is correlated with our explanatory variables or not) shows that the omitted variables are sometimes correlated and sometimes non-correlated for the different industrial subsectors and also for the different sections of the workforce, and we have taken the robust fixed-effect and random-effect results accordingly.

The regression results show that the MFG and TRD, as well as SVS sector jobs are often aided by a high-population density, while TRA and SVS are driven by a higher overall unemployment rate. Agricultural prosperity seems to lower female

Table 6 Summary statistics of the dependent and independent variables of the models

	Mean	SD	Min	Max
Dependent variables				
RNFE	22.29	15.35	4.00	70.00
MFG	8.90	7.92	1.20	35.80
CON	2.43	2.97	0.00	20.30
TRD	2.70	1.59	0.20	7.20
TRA	0.23	0.40	0.00	2.40
SVS	7.75	8.61	0.90	49.30
SELFEMP	22.82	14.41	5.10	80.20
HELPER	34.72	17.31	4.50	72.00
REGULAR	9.74	10.46	1.10	46.40
CAUSAL	32.72	14.58	1.30	57.10
Independent variables				
UNEMP	2.02	2.14	0.23	11.46
Ln (DENSITY)	5.53	0.59	4.38	6.60
Ln (AGRI-PC)	3.93	0.38	3.12	4.77
Ln (NONAGRI-PC)	4.96	0.56	4.02	6.21
URBAN	26.38	10.26	8.37	47.89
LITERACY	53.22	13.98	24.99	86.60

Number of observations = 80

SD Standard Deviation

Source Author's calculations from NSSO, CSO, and NAS data, and values are in percent

CON-sector participation, whereas non-agricultural growth seems to emerge as the major 'pull' factor, especially for CON workforce. At the same time, non-agricultural prosperity seems to lower the participation in MFG sector. Rising urbanization increases the scope of TRD activities among rural females.

Analysis on employment status shows that a higher degree of unemployment pushes a rural female worker to take up self-employment activities, and a high-population density and agricultural prosperity induce them toward unpaid family labor in household non-farm enterprises, which are mostly carried out by the male members. On the other hand, regular salaried employment is aided by the non-agricultural prosperity of the area, and urbanization has increased the demand for casual work.

The NSS reports reveal a high degree of self-employment among the rural manufacturing sector, and it might be that the distress-driven diversification is toward the self-employment in home-based job works in the manufacturing sector. Some distress diversification is also toward the transport and low-paying service activities, in which we found a positive and significant impact on the unemployment rate. However, it is not that the rural non-farm sector is always acting as a 'sponge' or 'sink' for the low-skilled labor displaced from agriculture, as is evident from a non-agricultural 'pull' in the SVS sector. It might be that better wages are encouraging the workers to shift toward non-farm activities if they possess the

Non-farm Employment Among Rural Women …

Table 7 Regression results for rural female workforce—by industrial subsectors

Dependent variables		RNFE	MFG	CON	TRD	TRA	SVS
Model 1							
UNEMP	Coeff.	0.31**	0.05	-0.02	0.03	0.07***	0.25***
	Robust SE	0.12	0.09	0.05	0.02	0.02	0.07
Ln (DENSITY)	Coeff.	11.35	10.23***	1.64	1.50***	0.81*	-0.18
	Robust SE	9.36	2.15	3.61	0.29	0.40	5.86
Ln (AGRI-PC)	Coeff.	-11.68	-0.49	-11.35	0.66	0.03	-0.45
	Robust SE	7.72	1.60	5.44	0.55	0.16	2.30
Ln (NONAGRI-PC)	Coeff.	5.42*	-1.82*	2.86**	0.34	-0.01	3.76
	Robust SE	3.00	1.05	1.13	0.30	0.10	2.24
Constant	Coeff.	-22.80	-36.87***	23.84	-9.95***	-4.66**	-9.30
	Robust SE	45.86	11.13	24.04	2.01	1.75	25.33
Breusch–Pagan Test	Chibar2	29.75	113.48	1.89	16.67	0.04	15.51
	Prob > chiba	0.00	0.00	0.05	0.00	0.04	0.00
Hausman Test	Chibar2	14.46	2.10	12.42	4.79	21.56	13.55
	Prob > chiba	0.01	0.72	0.02	0.31	0.00	0.01
Model		FE	RE	FE	RE	FE	FE
Model 2							
UNEMP	Coeff.	0.31**	0.06	-0.03	-0.01	0.07***	0.37***
	Robust SE	0.12	0.09	-0.04	0.02	0.02	0.06
Ln (DENSITY)	Coeff.	7.42	3.95***	-0.77	0.74	1.06	3.96***
	Robust SE	23.08	2.54	0.90	1.75	0.62	1.50
Urban	Coeff.	0.47	-0.04	0.02	0.12***	0.01	0.21
	Robust SE	0.49	0.10	0.04	0.03	0.01	0.17
Literacy	Coeff.	0.08	-0.06	0.03	-0.01	-0.01	0.06
	Robust SE	0.29	0.05	0.03	0.03	0.01	0.04

(continued)

Table 7 (continued)

Dependent variables		RNFE	MFG	CON	TRD	TRA	SVS
Constant	Coeff.	−36.12	−42.90***	5.04	−4.46	−6.06*	−23.93***
	Robust SE	125.49	11.99	5.58	4.74	3.20	9.33
Breusch–Pagan Test	Chibar2	37.01	107.96	2.47	17.87	2.07	55.81
	Prob > chiba	0.00	0.00	0.05	0.00	0.04	0.00
Hausman Test	Chibar2	10.30	4.70	17.29	10.69	25.88	7.75
	Prob > chiba	0.04	0.32	0.00	0.03	0.00	0.10
Model		FE	RE	FE	FE	FE	RE

*, **, *** denote significance levels of 10%, 5%, and 1% respectively

FE Fixed effect; *RE* Random effect

Source Panel data regression on data from NSSO, CSO, and NAS

Non-farm Employment Among Rural Women ...

Table 8 Regression results for rural female non-farm workforce—by employment status

Dependent variables		Share in different employment status			
		SELFEMP	HELPER	REGULAR	CAUSAL
Model 1					
UNEMP	Coeff.	2.03**	−0.93	0.17	−0.98
	Robust SE	1.00	1.09	0.77	1.00
Ln (DENSITY)	Coeff.	−7.39	63.86***	−6.26	−8.49
	Robust SE	6.65	16.26	5.68	19.24
Ln (AGRI-PC)	Coeff.	−4.18	23.50*	−1.98	4.40
	Robust SE	11.61	13.04	1.43	8.38
Ln (NONAGRI-PC)	Coeff.	−4.76	−8.55	6.18***	−6.41
	Robust SE	3.00	6.73	2.02	4.52
Constant	Coeff.	99.62	−366.33***	21.10	96.11
	Robust SE	65.80	90.81	27.89	85.29
Breusch–Pagan Test	Chibar2	21.56	5.70	63.98	77.78
	Prob > chiba	0.00	0.01	0.00	0.00
Hausman Test	Chibar2	0.01	38.61	10.86	38.28
	Prob > chiba	0.89	0.00	0.03	0.00
Model		RE	FE	FE	FE
Model 2					
UNEMP	Coeff.	2.72	−1.65	0.36	−1.44
	Robust SE	1.63	1.48	0.75	0.8
Ln (DENSITY)	Coeff.	−54.87	82.13	−4.84	−23.11
	Robust SE	39.16	35.56	10.60	19.21
Urban	Coeff.	0.09	0.32	0.47	0.88**
	Robust SE	0.54	0.47	0.28	0.32
Literacy	Coeff.	0.20	−0.47	0.13	0.14
	Robust SE	0.52	0.48	0.16	0.24
Constant	Coeff.	307.48	−399.11**	16.28	178.78*
	Robust SE	196.00	173.98	53.00	97.49
Breusch–Pagan Test	Chibar2	36.57	12.57	73.30	61.21
	Prob > chiba	0.00	0.00	0.00	0.00
Hausman Test	Chibar2	13.75	18.92	10.16	13.90
	Prob > chiba	0.01	0.00	0.04	0.01
Model		*FE*	*FE*	*FE*	*FE*

*, **, *** denote significance levels of 10%, 5%, and 1% respectively
FE Fixed effect; *RE* Random effect
Source Panel data regression on data from NSSO, CSO, and NAS

required skills. However, it is found that for the rural female workers, the non-farm sector shows some sign of being a 'residual sector' in some of the states where the average wage rate in the non-farm activities undertaken by the female workers is lower than the prevailing agricultural wage rate, and the ratio has been found to have decreased between 1993–94 and 2004–2005. Hence, the 'residual sector hypothesis' cannot be completely ruled out, especially for the female non-farm workforce.

The other 'distress' factor—low land–man ratio or high-population density—has emerged as an important determinant of RNFE, especially for the trade-related workforce, but apart from being just a 'push factor' high-population density seems to facilitate trading activities by lowering the transaction cost.

A rising trend in the share of non-food expenditure in a household's average monthly consumption expenditure in the rural areas indicates a rise in the demand for non-agricultural goods and services by a rural household. There will be a corresponding rise in the demand for non-agricultural labor also, which will be met by the rural and urban workforces. The inter-sectoral linkages through agricultural prosperity lead to such increase in the demand for non-farm activities through consumption linkages. However, our regression results do not show the much positive impact of agricultural growth on the growth of non-farm employment in the rural areas, and it seems that the urban sector mostly supplies the rural demand for non-farm goods. Thus, the 'inter-sectoral linkage hypothesis' led by agricultural prosperity in the economy is not much supported by our dataset, as the linkages are not found to be that much significant. However, the linkages are growing within the non-agricultural sector itself due to the growth in non-agricultural output, and these are spreading among the rural workforce also to a large extent.

8 Conclusion

As the share of agriculture in GDP decreases with economic growth, so does its share in employment. Over time this leads to a shift in the rural occupational structure toward different non-agricultural and non-farm activities. A vibrant rural non-farm sector has the potential of reducing disguised unemployment in agriculture, forced migration toward urban centers, rural poverty, and rural income inequality. Yet, the extent of success depends on whether such livelihood diversification is driven by growth-related 'pull' factors or distress-driven 'push' factors. Based on data from the quinquennial surveys on 'Employment and Unemployment Situation in India' carried out by the NSSO and other official sources, this chapter analyzes the determinants of non-farm employment among the female workforce in rural India, segregated by industrial subsectors and employment status, during the two post-reform decades 1990–2010. From the study, it is observed that during the post-reform decades, the rural non-farm sector seems to have emerged as a dynamic employment generator and the regression analyses point toward the existence of both 'push' and 'pull' factors in the dynamics behind the growth of RNFE in India. It seems that the female workforce is taking up low-paid home-based manufacturing employment in the face of the general unemployment situation, and because of limited mobility possibility and lower education levels they cannot take up better-paid opportunities created by non-agricultural growth. Policy makers should attempt to take these aspects of rural occupational transformation into account for a better utilization of the economy's labor force and for making the growth process more inclusive in nature. Suitable schemes may be undertaken to tap rural female labor more effectively and increase their entrepreneurial capacity by proper training, credit availability, and marketing channels.

References

Adelman, I. 1984. Beyond exported growth. *World Development* 12(9).

Banerjee, A., and A. Newman. 1993. Occupational choice and the process of development. *Journal of Political Economy* 101: 274–298.

Barrett, C.B., M. Bezuneh, D. Clay, and T. Reardon. 2005. Heterogeneous constraints, incentives and income diversification strategies in Rural Africa. *Quarterly Journal of International Agriculture* 44 (1): 37–60.

Basant, R., B.L. Kumar, and R. Parthasarathy. 1998. *Non-agricultural Employment in Rural India*. Jaipur, India: Rawat Publications.

Bhalla, Sheila. 1997. The rise and fall of workforce diversification process in rural India. In *Growth, Employment and Poverty: Change and Continuity in Rural India*, eds. Chadha, G.K., and Alak. N. Sharma, 145–183. New Delhi: Vikas Publishing House.

Biradar, R.R. 2007. Growth of rural non-farm activities in Karnataka: Emerging issues and prospects. In *Rural Karnataka,* ed. Jayasheela. New Delhi: Serial Publications.

Biradar, R.R., and S.T. Bagalkoti. 2001. Changing facets of employment in rural India: Emerging issues and challenges. *Indian Journal of Agricultural Economics* 56 (3): 538–552.

Breusch, T.S., and A.R. Pagan. 1980. The lagrange multiplier test and its applications to model specification in econometrics. *Review of Economic Studies* 47 (1): 239–253.

Chadha, G.K. 1997. Access of rural households to non-farm employment: Trends, constraints and possibilities. In *Growth, Employment and Poverty: Change and Continuity in Rural India*, eds. Chadha, G.K., and Alakh N. Sharma. New Delhi: Vikas Publishing House.

Chadha, G.K. 2001. Impact of economic reforms on rural employment: No smooth-sailing is anticipated. *Indian Journal of Agricultural Economics* 56 (3): 491–525.

Chadha, G.K. 2004. Human capital base of the Indian labour market: Identifying worry spots. *The Indian Journal of Labour Economics* 47 (1): 3–38.

Chand, Ramesh. 1996. Agricultural diversification and farm and Nn-farm employment in Himachal Pradesh. *The Indian Journal of Labour Economics* 39 (4): 841–851.

Chandrasekhar, C.P. 1993. Agrarian change and occupational diversification: Non-agricultural employment and rural development in West Bengal. *The Journal of Peasant Studies* 20 (2): 205–270.

de Janvry A., E. Sadoulet. 1993. Rural development in Latin America: Re-linking poverty to growth. In *Including the Poor*, eds. Lipton, M., and J. van dir Gaag. Washington D.C.: World Bank.

Dev, Mahendra S. 1990. Non-agricultural employment in rural India: Evidence at a disaggregated level. *Economic and Political Weekly* 26 (28): 1526–1536.

Eapen, Mridul. 1994. Rural non-agricultural employment in Kerala: Some emerging tendencies. *Economic and Political Weekly* 29 (21): 1285–1296.

Eapen, Mridul. 1995. Rural non-agricultural employment in Kerala: Inter-district variations. *Economic and Political Weekly* 30 (12): 634–638.

Greene, William H. 2008. *Econometric Analysis*, 6th ed. NJ: Prentice Hall.

Haggblade, S., P. Hazell, and J. Brown. 1989. Farm-non farm Linkages in Sub-Saharan Africa. *World Development* 17 (8): 1173–1201.

Harris, Barbara. 1987. Regional growth linkages from agriculture and resource flows in the non-farm economy. *Economic and Political Weekly* 22 (1–2): 31–46.

Hausman, J.A. 1978. Specification tests in econometrics. *Econometrica* 46 (6): 1251–1271.

Hazell, Peter B.R., and S. Haggblade. 1991. Rural-urban growth linkages in India. *Indian Journal of Agricultural Economics* 46(4): 515–529.

Hoffman, W.E. 1991. Multiple jobholding among farm families. In *Agricultural Households Survey and Critique, (Chapter 5)*, ed. J.L. Findeis, M.C. Hallberg, and D.L. Lass. USA: Iowa State University Press.

Islam, Nurul. 1997. The Non-farm Sector and Rural Development: Review of Issues and Evidence. Food Agriculture and Environment Discussion Paper 22. Washington: International Food Policy Research Institute.

Jayaraj, D. 1989. Determinants of Rural Non-agricultural Employment. Working paper No. 90. Madras: Madras Institute of Development Studies.

Johnston, B.F., and P. Kilby. 1975. *Agriculture and Structural Transformation: Economic Strategies for Late Developing Countries*. London: Oxford University Press.

Kaur, Kuldip. 2002. Determinants of rural non-agricultural employment: An inter-state analysis. *The Indian Journal of Labour Economics* 45(4).

Lane, D.W. 1996. Political base and rural industrialisation: Korea and Taiwan. In *Towards the rural-based development of Commerce and Industry: Selected experience from East Asia*. Washington D.C.: World Bank.

Mecharla, Prasad Rao. 2002. Determinants of inter-district variations in rural non-farm employment in Andhra Pradesh. *The Indian Journal of Labour Economics* 45 (4): 807–820.

Mellor, John. 1976. *The New Economics of Growth: A strategy for India and the Developing World*. Ithaca, New York: Cornell University Press.

Mellor, J.W., and U.J. Lele. 1973. Growth Linkages of the New Food Grain Technologies. *The Indian Journal of Agricultural Economics* 18(1).

Narayanamoorthy, A., Queenie Rodrigues, and Ashwini Phadnis. 2002. Determinants of rural non-farm employment: An analysis of 256 districts. *The Indian Journal of Labour Economics* 45 (4): 759–769.

Oshima, H.T. 1994. *The significance of off-farm employment and incomes in post-war East-Asian growth*. Manila: Asian Development Bank.

Parthasarathy, G., Shameem and B. Sambi Reddy. 1998. Determinants of rural non-agricultural employment: The Indian case. *Indian Journal of Agricultural Economics* 53(2): 139–54.

Rajasekhar, D. 1995. Rural non-farm employment in Karnataka: a dis-aggregated analysis at the district level. *Agricultural Situation in India*, August.

Rangarajan, C. 1982. Agricultural Growth and Industrial Performance in India. Research Report No. 33. Washington D.C.: IFPRI.

Ravallion, M. and G. Datt. 1995. Growth and Poverty in Rural India, Working Paper Series 1405. Washington, D.C.: World Bank.

Shankaranarayanan, V. 1980. Inter-state Variation in Rural Non-agricultural Employment: Some Tentative Results. Working Paper No. 104. Trivandrum: Centre for Development Studies.

Shukla, Vibhooti. 1991. Rural non-farm activity: A regional model and its empirical application to Maharashtra. *Economic and Political Weekly* 26 (45): 2587–2595.

Shukla, Vibhooti. 1992. Rural non-farm employment in India: Issues and policy. *Economic and Political Weekly* 27 (28): 1477–1488.

Singh, A.K. 1994. Changes in the structure of rural workforce in Uttar Pradesh: A temporal and regional study. In *Non-agricultural Employment in India: Trends and Prospects*, ed. P. Visaria, and R. Basant. New Delhi: Sage Publications.

Srivastav, N., and Amaresh Dubey. 2002. Rural non-farm employment in India: Spatial variations and temporal change. *The Indian Journal of Labour Economics* 45 (4): 745–758.

Unni, Jeemol. 1991. Regional variations in rural non-agricultural employment: An exploratory analysis. *Economic and Political Weekly* 26 (3): 109–122.

Vaidyanathan, A. 1986. Labour use in rural India: A study of spatial and temporal variations. *Economic and Political Weekly* 21 (52): 130–146.

Verma, B.N., and N. Verma. 1995. Distress diversification from farm to non-farm employment in rural sector in the Eastern Region. *Indian Journal of Agricultural Economics* 50 (3): 422–429.

Vyas, V.S., and George Mathai. 1978. Farm and non-farm employment in rural areas: A perspective for planning. *Economic and Political Weekly* 21(52).

Part II
Microfinance in India

Efficiency and Mission Drift—Debate Revisited in Indian Context

Chandralekha Ghosh and Samapti Guha

1 Introduction

Microfinance institutions (MFIs) have two-folded objectives—serving the poor and marginalized section of the clients, especially women, known as outreach, and at the same time achieving efficiency and financial self-sufficiency. Many observers are concerned about the likely trade-off between these two aims, called mission drift (Kar 2012). Does excessive profit motive really outweigh original social mission of microfinance (MF)? Will it lead MFIs to focus more on better-off clients with bigger loans? Will all types of MFIs under different legal framework namely nongovernment organization (NGO)-MFI, cooperative credit societies, non-banking financial companies (NBFCs) perform in the same way in meeting these goals? There is a huge debate. Researchers such as Hermes et al. (2011), Brett (2006), and Woller et al. (1999) state that higher profit motive worsens outreach objective of the MFIs, as MFIs with higher profit objective generally target better-off clients. While there is another group of researchers according to whom profit-oriented MFIs are better capable of reaching the poorest because they are more efficient in their performance. The proponents of this view are Schreiner (2002), Christen and Drake (2002), and Rhyne (1998). Kar (2012) has explored the impact of profitability on the depth of outreach in MFIs, a trade-off between outreach and efficiency which is commonly known as 'mission drift.'

There are two approaches of MF sector—welfarist and institutionalist. The 'welfarists' believe that MF is primarily meant for poverty reduction with improving capabilities which lead to the empowerment of poor women, as opposed to the 'institutionalists' who believe in the sustainability of the MFIs along with

---

C. Ghosh (✉)
West Bengal State University, North 24 Parganas, Kolkata, West Bengal, India
e-mail: ghoshchandralekha@yahoo.com

S. Guha
School of Management and Labour Studies, Tata Institute of Social Sciences,
Centre for Social Entrepreneurship, Mumbai, Maharashtra, India

© Springer Nature Singapore Pte Ltd. 2017
C. Neogi et al. (eds.), *Women's Entrepreneurship and Microfinance*,
DOI 10.1007/978-981-10-4268-3_6

minimal services. Ghosh (2013) concludes that MF cannot be seen as a silver bullet for development and that profit-oriented MFIs are problematic. To fulfill even some of its progressive goals, it must be regulated and subsidized, and other strategies for viable financial inclusion of the poor and of small producers must be more actively pursued (Saad and Khan 2014).

In the case of India, microfinance (MF) sector passed through a crisis after 2010 as due to double dipping, the people who had lesser capacity to repay the loans were given two to three loans. In the process, many borrowers, especially from Andhra Pradesh, committed suicide due to indebtedness, and the state government had to intervene to formulate new regulation for the MF sector. In this context, our objective is to examine whether in case of India there is any trade-off between efficiency of performance and outreach to poor clients.

In this chapter, we have examined the technical efficiencies and cost efficiencies of MFIs in Indian context using stochastic frontier analysis, and then we have also tried to identify the determinants of both technical and cost efficiency. Subsequently, we have attempted to examine the factors affecting the efficiency of the MFIs. Further, we have analyzed whether there is any incidence of mission drift in terms of increase in average loan size and increase in efficiencies.

The rest of the chapter is organized as follows. Section 2 provides a brief account of literature survey. Section 3 discusses data and methodology adopted in the analysis. Section 4 provides empirical results, and finally Sect. 5 concludes the study.

2 Related Studies

In several countries, competition among MFIs has increased rapidly over two decades (Rhyne and Otero 2006). The consequences of this increased competition for MFIs can be manifold.[1] One of the outcomes of this competition is mission drift. Movement of MF in India was initiated by nonprofit institutes such as NGOs. The problem of these organizations arose of limited financial activities. Legally they were not allowed to raise equities, channelize public savings, and so on. Their problems increased manifold when for-profit banks joined the movement. In the context of India, the success of the pilot project on self-help group (SHG)-bank linkage of National Bank for Agriculture and Rural Development (NABARD) during the 1990s attracted other banks and NBFCs to take up microfinancial activities. The main reason for this attraction was high profitability and low non-performing assets of this project. This forced the NGO-MFIs to face the competition. As a result, transformation of NGO-MFIs to for-profit MFIs in India has

---

[1]For example, lower interest rates, lower costs, more efficiency, and the introduction of new financial services, such as savings accounts, pension, and insurance services.

Efficiency and Mission Drift—Debate Revisited in Indian Context

happened. This kind of transition was found in other developing nations too. In this context, Bolivia is an example of a country that has experienced increasing competition in the MF industry since the late 1990s (Rhyne and Otero 2006). The studies by Navajas et al. (2003) have contributed to outreach versus sustainability debate. They have discussed the Bolivian MF market developments since the mid-1990. They have shown that due to increased competition, MFIs changed their lending technologies and the target clients.

In some countries, commercial banks are getting involved in lending to the poor. K-REP in Kenya and the Commercial Bank of Zimbabwe are two examples of commercial banks that have become involved in lending to the poor[2] recently (Hermes et al. 2011). Moreover, in some countries the government has actively stimulated commercial banks to become involved in MF. Again, this may have put pressure on MFIs to reduce interest rates and costs and raise efficiency. This has happened in the case of India where Reserve Bank of India under directives of government has directed commercial banks to lend to MFIs under priority sector lending. Moreover, the profitability of MF sector influenced commercial banks and investors, especially those from developed countries, to increasingly finance MFIs. Along with the profitability of MF sector, it is important that regulatory pressure of this sector is also increasing which demand efficiency and self-sufficiency but not outreach (Cull et al. 2007). In this context, the debate of efficiency versus outreach has caught the attention of the development professionals.

Manos and Yaron (2009) stated in their work that there may be trade-off between outreach and sustainability in the short run, but in the long run both can be improved through various innovations. Many researchers such as Navajas et al. (2003), Schreiner (2002), Rhyne (1998), and Von Pischke (1996) have shown that due to greater transaction costs in dealing with large number of small loans outreach in terms of small loan size leads to cost inefficiency. Similar views have been elucidated by Lariviere and Martin (1999), Paxton (2007), and Cull (2007). According to them, MFIs dealing with individual loans are more profitable than others as they can target wealthier clients. This event is known as 'mission drift.'

Cull et al. (2011) have provided further evidence of existence of trade-off between outreach and commercialization. Based on large, global surveys of different types of MFIs,[3] the authors have observed a conflict between meeting social goals and maximizing financial performance. Olivares-Polanco (2005) identified the determinants of outreach in terms of the loan size of MFIs, using data for 28 MFIs in Latin America during the period 1999–2001. He has depicted in his study the prevalence of a trade-off between sustainability and outreach. Makame and Murinde (2006) while examining balanced panel data set for 33 MFIs in five East African countries for the period 2000–2005 further confirmed existence of a trade-off between outreach and sustainability and efficiency.

---

[2]Referred to as 'downscaling.'

[3]MFIs are registered either as an NGO or an NBFIs or a bank or credit cooperative society. Bank and NBFIs are regulated by the Central Bank of the Country.

Some studies have tried to measure the efficiency of the MFIs using either data envelopment analysis (DEA) or stochastic frontier analysis (SFA) technique (Qayyum and Ahmad 2006; Gutiérrez-Nieto et al. 2007; Pal 2010). These studies have made an attempt to capture different dimensions of the efficiency of MFIs in South Asian and Latin American nations. It is observed that efficiency of MFIs varies from country to country and within the country from location to location. It also depends on the institutional types of MFIs. Pal (2010) has found that technical efficiency is positively related with borrower per staff, age, value of asset, return on asset, return on equity level, and yield on gross portfolio. It is also shown that southern states in India have fared better in terms of technical efficiency.

Paxton (2007) showed that the differences in efficiency of 190 Mexican popular savings and credit institutions are associated with differences in technology, average loan size, rural outreach, and the age of the institution. Caudill et al. (2009) using a mixed modeling approach estimated cost functions, allowing for heterogeneity of cost functions of MFIs. Based on their analysis, they have shown that MFIs become more efficient over time, yet this is dependent on their size and whether they offer deposits, as well as on the extent to which they receive subsidies. Hermes et al. (2011) examined whether there is a trade-off between outreach of the poor and efficiency of MFIs. The study of Tariq and Izhar (2010) on Indian MFIs for the period 2005–2008 showed that the MFIs become technically efficient with age and with an increase of asset. In this context, our main objective is to examine whether the technical efficiency and cost efficiency increase with an outreach of the poor clients.

3 Context of the Study

In India, MF is a flourishing sector, and in many cases, it is the sole provider of finance for the poor. The loan assets are likely to increase by INR 35,000 crore by March 2015 (Crisil 2014). There was 43% of the growth of MFI's loan assets during 2013–2014. According to Crisil (2014), the profitability will decline due to lowering of the margin, but in the course of time, the profitability will increase due to increase in efficiency. This analysis has shown that MFI's efficiency has increased by increasing the branch efficiency. It has been observed that larger MFIs have fared well than the smaller ones.

The MF movement in India can be divided into two phases. From 1970s to 1990s, microfinancial services were delivered by NGOs and community-based organizations (CBOs). Most of the operations of these MFIs were grant based. They played the role of facilitators. The mission of these MFIs was economic empowerment of the low-income groups. In the second phase after 1990s, while banking sector joined the movement, these MFIs faced hard competition, and they started to transform into NBFCs, banks, and cooperative societies to scale up their operations. This transition has demanded operational efficiency and self-sufficiency of the MFIs to sustain their services, which have impacted outreach.

Efficiency and Mission Drift—Debate Revisited in Indian Context

In recent years, MFIs such as SKS Microfinance going for public offerings to raise more funds for further commercialization indicates the importance of efficiency of MFI. For high commercialization of operation, an MFI needs to meet the demand of the investors rather than the clients. In this premise, this study first attempts to calculate both technical and cost efficiency using stochastic frontier production and stochastic frontier cost function, respectively, for the period 2010–14. In India, after financial crisis in 2010, MFI industry has also been hit by financial crises, as many of the borrowers could not pay back their loans, leading to many borrowers committing suicide.

One of the causes of this crisis is that very high rates of interest have been charged by the MFIs. This prompted RBI, the central bank of India, to bring MFIs under its supervision in December 2011. RBI stipulated that there would be only three components in the pricing of loans—an interest rate cap of 26% (on reducing balance); processing charge (1% of loan amount); and insurance premium (Arun and Kamath 2015). The phase after the crisis has been taken into consideration to examine whether the efficiency in performance and the mission of reaching to the poor actually got hampered after the period of crisis or not.

4 Methodology

In this chapter, we have tried to examine the efficiency of operation and cost efficiency of MFIs in India after the period of crisis in 2010. Then, we have tried to find out whether there is any trade-off between efficiency and outreach of MFIs. In order to examine efficiency, we have used SFA. It is a suitable approach for efficiency measurement of MFIs since (1) it allows the observed production of a particular institution to deviate from the efficient frontier due to either random events and/or possible inefficiencies; and (2) this technique incorporates an error term that captures inefficiencies in the MFI sector, a convenient property when examining information from developing countries (Servin et al 2012).

In empirical studies, selection of input and output for financial institutions is mainly based upon two different concepts, namely the production approach and the intermediation approach (Berger and Humphrey 1997). Under the production approach, banks or financial institutions, in general, are viewed as institutions making use of various labor and capital resources to provide different products and services to customers. Thus, the resources being consumed, such as labor and operating cost, are deemed as inputs, while the products and the services, such as loans and deposits, are considered as outputs (Gebremichael and Gessesse 2016). Under the intermediation approach, financial institutions are viewed as financial intermediaries who collect deposits and other loanable funds from depositors and lend them as loans or other assets to others for profit. MFIs are also financial institutions, but their approach and motive differ from other financial institutions. They are special banks that target mainly the poor often without any collateral requirements (Gutiérrez-Nieto et al. 2007; Tariq et al. 2010).

Specifically, outputs in this study are defined to include gross loan portfolio. To produce these outputs, the study assumes MFIs use two main inputs: labor and operating expenses.

The stochastic frontier production function is

$$y_{it} = \alpha + x'_{it}\beta + \varepsilon_{it}, \quad i = 1, 2, \ldots N, \quad t = 1, 2, \ldots T \tag{1}$$

$$\varepsilon_{it} = v_{it} - u_{it} \tag{2}$$

Then, the technical efficiencies m are regressed on a set of factors denoted by z. Next,

$$m_{it} = \delta_o + \sum_n \delta_{nit} z_{nit} \tag{3}$$

$$u_{it} \sim N^+ \left(m_{it}, \sigma_u^2 \right) \tag{4}$$

$$v_{it} \sim iidN(0, \sigma_v^2) \tag{5}$$

ε_i represents a random disturbance term.

v_{it} is the random 'noise' component of the error term which represents random, uncontrollable factors that affect total production, such as weather, probabilistic factors, labor strikes, or machine performance. These factors (and their impact on production) are assumed to be independent of each other. They are identically distributed as normal variables, and the value of the error term in the production relationship is, on average, equal to zero.

u_{it} is a nonnegative technical inefficiency component that represents firm's specific production deviations or errors which are due to factors that are under the control of the management of the MFI. Such factors include the quantity of labor, capital, or other inputs hired or employed in the production of the firm's products and services and the amount chosen to be produced.

The inefficiency term u_i is drawn from a nonnegative half-normal distribution, truncated at u, and independent and identically distributed (*i.i.d.*) with $u_i \sim N(\mu, \sigma_u^2)$. It carries a negative sign because all inefficient firms will operate below the efficient production frontier. Then, technical efficiency for MFI i is defined as:

$$TE_i = E[\exp(-u_i)|\varepsilon_i] \tag{6}$$

This measure ranges between zero and one, where one indicates a fully efficient MFI. The frontier functions are estimated by maximum likelihood methods. In the

Efficiency and Mission Drift—Debate Revisited in Indian Context

estimation, the terms σ_u^2 and σ_v^2 are re-parameterized by $\sigma^2 = \sigma_v^2 + \sigma_u^2$, $\gamma = \frac{\sigma_u^2}{\sigma^2}$, and $\lambda = \sigma_u/\sigma_v$. If λ is close to zero, little structural inefficiency exists and standard ordinary least squares (OLS) estimation may be appropriate. The parameter λ represents the share of inefficiency in the overall residual variance and ranges between zero and one. A value of one for λ suggests the existence of a deterministic frontier, whereas a value of zero represents evidence in favor of a standard OLS estimation (see Coelli et al. 1988 for further discussion). After the estimation of cost efficiency, the determinants of the efficiency are obtained by running a Tobit regression on some explanatory variable.

Next,

$$m_{it} = \delta_o + \sum_n \delta_{nit} z_{nit} \tag{7}$$

In this model, m stands for technical efficiencies and 'z' is the vector of factors explaining the technical efficiency.

In the case of the stochastic frontier production function, the output variable we have taken is the log of the gross loan portfolio (measured in INR). Number of personnel (PRSNL) and cost per borrower (CPB) (measured in INR) are taken as input variables. Then the inefficiency terms have been regressed on MFI-related variables to identify which variables lead to the efficiency of the MFIs in India after 2010 crisis.

Outreach variables have been taken as determinants of efficiency. In the MF literature, average loan size is taken to be an indicator of outreach (Bhatt and Tang 2001; Cull et al. 2011; Schreiner 2002). The reason for considering average size of the loan is that poor people have lesser capacity to borrow higher size loans, as they have a low level of income, assets, and savings than the people belong to the richer class. Although MFIs lend collateral-free loans, they also check the repayment capacity of the clients before disbursing the loans. It also establishes the fact that the average loan size is low if the MFIs target the poorest of the poor or economically active poor. Apart from this, there is a maximum cap on loan size provided by MFIs. Even if some poor clients are members of an MFI for a long time, every time their repayment capacity is checked before loan disbursement. To reach the maximum size of the loans, they need to show that they are capable of repaying that higher size loans. The low size of an average loan of an MFI is an indicator of outreach.

The percentage of woman borrowers is another indicator of outreach (Dowla and Barua 2006). Here, women are considered as a vulnerable group of the society. More women customers mean that the MFI is meeting the social mission of MF sector. Group lending is another pointer of outreach (Aghion Armendariz de and Morduch 2005; Ghatak and Guinnane 1999). Here group-lending technique helps

MFIs to reach more clients easily. The explanatory variables taken accordingly for the inefficiency model are type of lending of the MFIs, namely individual, group, or both, regulatory framework of the MFI, namely NGO-MFI, NBFC-MFI, or other types, asset of the MFIs, number of active borrowers, percentage of woman borrowers, average loan size of the borrowers, and the age of the MFIs.

After this analysis, we have carried out estimation of the stochastic frontier cost function.

The general Battese and Coelli (1995) model specifies a stochastic cost frontier with the following properties:

$$\ln C_{it} = \beta_i + \beta_y \ln y_{it} + \sum_n \beta_n \ln w_{nit} + v_{it} + u_{it} \tag{8}$$

where C_{it} is the total cost MFI i faces at time t, and $(C_{it}, w_{it}; \beta)$ is the cost frontier. In this cost frontier y_{it} represents the logarithm of output of MFI i at time t, w_{it}, is a vector of the logarithm of input prices of MFI i at time t, and β is a vector of all parameters to be estimated. The term u_{it} captures cost inefficiency and is independent and identically distributed with a truncated normal distribution. v_{it} captures measurement errors and random effects; for example, favorable and unfavorable probabilistic factors and is distributed as a standard normal variable. Both u_{it} and v_{it} are time and MFI specific and can be represented as standard normal:

$$u_{it} \sim N^+ (m_{it}, \sigma_u^2) \tag{9}$$

$$v_{it} \sim iidN(0, \sigma_v^2) \tag{10}$$

The variance parameters are expressed in terms of $\gamma = \frac{\sigma_u^2}{\sigma_u^2 + \sigma_v^2}$.

A value of γ of zero indicates that the deviations from the frontier are due entirely to noise, while the value of 1 would indicate that all the deviations are due to cost inefficiency.

Following Coelli (1996), the equation $CE_i = \frac{E(C_i/u_i, P_i)}{E(C_i/u_i=0, P_i)}$ is used to calculate the cost inefficiency for each of the states from the estimated stochastic frontier. P_i is the vector of input prices, and $E(.)$ refers to the expected value. In the cost function, the CE_i takes the value between 1 and ∞. The value of inefficiency can be interpreted as follows: an efficiency score of 1.329 means that the MFI's cost is 32.92% higher than the cost of an equivalent MFI that is efficient. The reciprocal of cost inefficiency is taken as the measure of cost efficiency (Kumbhakar and Knox Lovell 2003).[4]

---

[4]After estimating stochastic frontier cost function, we have estimated the cost efficiency $CE = \exp\{-E(u|e)\}$, where $E(u|e)$ is the (post-)estimate of cost inefficiency obtained through the Jondrow et al. (1982) estimator. In the case of a cross-sectional normal-half-normal cost frontier, this estimator corresponds to Eq. 4.2.12 of Kumbhakar and Knox Lovell (2003). Equivalently, another estimator (the estimator implemented in the post-estimation command of both -frontier- and

Next

$$m_{it} = \delta_o + \sum_n \delta_{nit} z_{nit} \tag{11}$$

In Eq. (11), z represents the vector of n variables that determine the efficiency (m) of MFI i at time t. The δs represent the coefficients. Equations are solved in one step by using maximum likelihood.

Here, we have assumed a Cobb–Douglas form of the model. There are two inputs, labor and capital, and the input prices are salary and interest paid on the capital. For the specification of the cost function, we use the model developed by Sealey and Lindley (1977), who state that a bank acts as an intermediate between funders and borrowers.

Operating expense by asset has been taken as the input price of labor, and financial expense by asset has been taken as the input price for capital. Gross loan portfolio by assets has been taken as a proxy for output. Total cost here means that total cost has been normalised by total asset. Then, Eq. (11) is estimated taking same variables as that of technical efficiency variables of Eq. (7). The outreach variables, as well as some of features of MFIs, have been taken as the determinants of MFIs efficiency.

We use data from the Microfinance Information Exchange Network,[5] a global web-based MF platform that provides individual data on MFIs. The platform is among one of the most renowned and extensive databases on worldwide MF and provides high-quality information. We have extracted data for 86 MFIs operating in India over the period 2010–14. We construct a panel set of financial and outreach indicators.

5 Description of Indian MFIs

The publicly available MIX database now provides data on more than 200 Indian MFIs. We have selected 86 MFIs for whom all the concerned variables for analysis are available for the time period 2010–14. For the rest of the MFIs, the recent year data are not available.

(Footnote 4 continued)

-xtfrontier-) can be obtained using the Battese and Coelli (1995) approach $CE = E(\exp\{-u\}|e)$, which it is still bounded in the unit interval (in the case of a cross-sectional normal-half-normal cost frontier this estimator is reported in Eq. 4.2.14 of Kumbhakar and Knox Lovell 2003). Hence, a strategy to avoid the problem is to take the reciprocal of what the -frontier- (or -xtfrontier-) command is giving you to get approximated Battese and Coelli (1995) point estimates of cost efficiency predict ce, te replace $ce = 1/ce$.

[5] www.mixmarket.org.

There are 86 MFIs in the study. Of them, 41 provide individual loans, 34 provide joint lending, and 10 provide both individual and joint lending. There are 51 NBFIs, 4 credit unions, 38 NGOs, one rural bank, and two other types of MFIs. Among 86 MFIs, 51 are regulated. Here, according to the registration of the institutions only NBFIs are registered under The Reserve Bank of India Act, 1934, 45 1(B) and banks are regulated by the Reserve Bank of India. Other MFIs that are registered as NGO-MFI, cooperative credit union, or NBFIs that are registered under Section 8 of The Companies Act, 2013 and so on, are not regulated. In this dataset, 52 are for-profit organizations,[6] 4 are not-for-profit organizations, and 40 are nonprofit organizations.

We have presented the descriptive statistics of the features of the MFIs in Appendix Table 5. The mean age of the MFI is 11 years. The average number of persons working in an MFI is 973, and the lowest value is 11 (see Appendix Table 5). We have obtained descriptive statistics of some of the important financial variables. The average financial revenue by assets and yield on the gross portfolio are 21.43 and 30.00, respectively. The details on the asset, equity, capital/asset ratio, and number of outstanding loans are given in Table 6. The descriptive statistics of different types of expenses are represented in Appendix Table 7. The outreach variables, such as average loan per borrower and percentage of female borrowers are depicted in Annexure Table 8. It is observed that average percentage of female borrowers is 97%, hence it can be inferred that MFIs considered for analysis are mostly targeting the woman borrowers.

We have clubbed all NBFI-MFI together to understand the asset position of the MFIs. The reason for the same is that NBFI-MFIs are allowed to raise the equities and shares, and these institutions are earn private profits, whereas in the case of credit unions, although they earn a profit, it is distributed among the member–borrowers. NGO-MFIs do not earn a profit at all by design. Hence, apart from NBFI-MFIs, other MFIs are grouped in the same category. RBI regulates NBFI-MFIs. We have compared asset, capital by asset ratio, and gross portfolio for NBFI-MFIs versus other types of MFIs. It has been observed that all these variables are significantly higher for the NBFI-MFIs compared to others. We have compared other financial variables, such as equity, debt to equity ratio, return to asset, return on equity, and yield to the gross portfolio for the NBFI-MFIs versus others. The mean value of all these variables is greater for NBFI than others but only in case of equity; this value is statistically significant than others (see Appendix Tables 9 and 10).

---

[6]Here 'for profit organizations' are non-banking financial companies or intermediaries. Some of them are registered under Section 8 of The Companies Act, 2013, and The RBI Act, 1934 45(B). Both types of organizations are allowed to make profit. The NBFIs registered under Section 8 of The Companies Act, 2013 cannot enjoy the private profit as they have to invest it in their business. NBFIs registered under The RBI Act, 2013 can enjoy share of total profit as dividend.

5.1 Cost Structure

We have tried to compare the different types of costs. In Appendix Table 11, we have provided the details of the cost structure. It has been observed that mean level of operating expense by asset and personnel expense by the asset are significantly higher for the NBFI-MFIs than other types of MFIs. The average total expense is significantly higher for the NBFI-MFIs compared to others (Appendix Table 11). The performance variables have been compared between two types of MFIs, which is discussed in the previous section. Loans per loan officer and loans per staff members are significantly higher for the NBFI-MFIs than other types of MFIs (Appendix Table 12). The outreach variables are also compared between two types of MFIs, and it is found that NBFI-MFIs are having a significantly higher percentage of female borrowers than others. The average loan size is significantly lower for the borrowers taking a loan from NBFI-MFI than other types of MFIs (see Appendix Table 13).

6 Econometric Analysis

We have applied stochastic frontier and then applied Jondrow et al. (1982) formula to determine technical efficiency. The value of efficiency ranges between zero and one. Higher the value of technical efficiency, the more efficient will be the firm.

From Table 1 it is observed that a number of personnel are positively influencing the dependent variable and gross loan portfolio. The value of γ is 0.65, hence there

Table 1 Estimates of stochastic frontier production function

Dependent variable is log of gross loan portfolio		
Explanatory variables	Coefficients	Level of significance
Ln personnel	0.897*	0.0
Ln cost per borrower	−0.145**	0.042
Constant	12.74	0.0
μ	1.2	
$\sigma 2$	0.559	
γ	0.651	
σu_2	0.36	
σv_2	0.192	
Log likelihood	−288.264	
Wald chi2(2)	486.47	
Prob > Chi2	0.0	
Number of observations	344	

*Significant at 1% level, **significant at 5% level, and ***significant at 10% level

Table 2 Tobit results

Dependent variable is technical efficiency (value ranges between 0 and 1)			
Explanatory variables	Coefficient	Standard error	Significance
Average loan balance	0.0005217*	0.0000888	0.0
Age	0.0074562*	0.00146	0.0
Regulate_Dummy	0.1236*	0.0154	0.0
Percentage Female_Borrowers	−0.0283	0.072	0.626
Assets	4.86(e−10)*	8.16(e−11)	0.0
Loan_Type_2	−0.0145	0.0156	0.32
Loan_Type_3	−0.0892*	0.020	0.0
Constant	0.113	0.074	0.132
σ	0.134	0.0061	
Log pseudo-likelihood = 188.31, pseudo-R2 = −1.71			

*Significant at 1% level, **significant at 5% level, and ***significant at 10% level

is a high level of variance of technical inefficiency. Moreover, statistical tests have confirmed stochastic frontier model over deterministic model. Then, the technical efficiencies have been regressed on other variables. As the technical efficiency ranges between zero and one, we have performed Tobit regression. The results have been represented in Table 2.

From Table 2, it has been observed that with age of the MFIs, the technical efficiency increases. Regulated MFIs, that is NBFI-MFIs, perform better than unregulated MFIs. The MFIs providing individual and joint lending are inefficient than those who are providing individual loans. Lariviere and Martin (1999) also have shown this fact in their study. As the loan size increases, the technical efficiency increases. Therefore, there is a mission drift because higher loan size indicates that poor people are deprived of the loan. As previously mentioned, loan size is generally taken as one of the outreach variables. Smaller loan size indicates that a larger number of borrowers can be reached; on the other hand larger loan size indicates reaching only few large borrowers. There is a significant positive association between loan size and technical efficiency in our study. After estimating stochastic frontier production function, we have estimated stochastic frontier cost function.

6.1 Estimation of Stochastic Frontier Cost Function

From Table 3, it is found that in this model, the value of γ is quite high indicating presence of variation in the cost efficiency term. Statistical tests have been carried out that have confirmed the acceptance of the stochastic model over the

Efficiency and Mission Drift—Debate Revisited in Indian Context

Table 3 Estimates of stochastic frontier cost function

Explanatory variables	Coefficient	Standard error	Significance
Ln_Operating Expenses	0.47*	0.036	0.0
Ln_Financial_Expenses	0.045	0.030	0.135
Ln_Outstanding_Balance	−0.0147	0.033	0.657
Ln_Active_Borrowers	0.019	0.014	0.177
Constant	−0.483	22.13	0.983
Mu	2.03	22.13	
Sigma2	0.111	0.015	
Gamma	0.760	0.039	
Sigma u_2	0.0185	0.015	
Sigma v_2	0.026	0.00243	
Log likelihood	22.09		
Wald chi2(2)	148.02		
Prob > Chi2	0.0		
Number of observations	344		

*Significant at 1% level

deterministic model. Operating expenses positively and significantly influence the cost function.

In the next step, we have carried out a Tobit analysis of the cost efficiency on outreach variables. MFIs providing both group and individual loans are less efficient than MFIs providing individual loans. Table 4 represents results of the Tobit regression. It is found that MFIs, which have provided individual loans have provided the same to the richer customers. It is easy for them to achieve efficiency as the loan size is bigger. For group lending, MFIs need to bear monitoring cost and higher transaction cost. It is difficult for them to achieve efficiency. The regulated MFIs are found to be less cost efficient than the unregulated ones. Regulated MFIs, need to bear the cost of regulation in terms of administrative and operational cost (Cull and Demirguc-Kunt 2011). The cost efficiency increases with the age of the MFIs. As time goes, the MFIs learn how to run institutions efficiently, which includes the cost efficiency. There is a positive association between loan size and cost efficiency. The study indicates that there is a chance of mission drift in the context of Indian MFIs operating during the period from 2010 to 2014. In terms of the technical and cost efficiency analysis the gender of the borrower as woman borrower is insignificant in influencing the efficiencies. However, in India, MFIs are mostly woman-centric, and thus, women are the targeted clients. During the past four years, there is a low variation in the percentage of woman borrowers in the case of MFIs concerned, and the mean level of woman borrowers is about 97%, hence, it is not possible to show the mission drift in terms of percentage of women borrowers in the case of India during this period of study.

Table 4 Determinants of cost efficiency: estimates of Tobit regression

Explanatory variables	Coefficient	Robust standard error	Significance
Avg_Loan_per_Borrower	0.0012**	0.00050504	0.011
Age	0.0006171**	0.002916	0.035
Regulate_Dummy	−0.004626***	0.0035	0.072
Percentage_Female borrowers	0.0095	0.020	0.643
Loan_Type2	−0.0038	0.0034	0.280
Loan_Type_3	−0.007***	0.0038	0.080
Sigma	0.026	0.00172	
Number of observations	344		
Log likelihood	−786.0147		
Pseudo Rsq	−0.041		

**Significant at 5% level, and ***significant at 10% level

7 Conclusions

In this study, important stylized facts have been analyzed. It is found that the technical and cost efficiency of Indian MFIs are increasing along with the increase of loan size. In the literature on mission drift of MFIs, it is ascertained that an increase in loan size could be an indicator of mission drift. According to this explanation of mission drift, this study has also observed that mission drift is present in Indian MFIs. Further, it is seen that technical efficiency is positively related to the regulation dummy. It indicates that MFIs who are registered as NBFIs and banks have a higher chance of achieving technical efficiency than other types of MFIs. Both the efficiencies are positively related to age as well as the assets of the MFIs. It implies that experienced MFIs and MFIs who own the assets achieve both the efficiencies. This finding along with the increase in loan size establishes the fact that MFIs are diverting their objective of serving poor clients. In conclusion, we can say that efficiency and mission drift are positively correlated in Indian MF sector.

Appendix

See Tables 5, 6, 7, 8, 9, 10, 11, 12, 13, 14 and 15.

Efficiency and Mission Drift—Debate Revisited in Indian Context

Table 5 Descriptive statistics of MFI characteristics

	Minimum	Maximum	Mean	Std. deviation
AGE	1.00	49.00	11.3169	8.34854
Personnel	9.00	22733.00	9.7348E2	2266.88773

Table 6 Descriptive statistics between financial indicators of MFIs

	Minimum	Maximum	Mean	Std. deviation
Equity	52835	1.E9	5.69E7	1.361E8
Asset	52300	1.E9	5.53E7	1.358E8
Gross loan portfolio				
Capital/asset ratio	−103.69	3020.00	33.9797	171.60577
Yield gross portfolio	22	2230	30.34	119.84
Equity	678	4.E8	1.17E	3.34E7
Number of loans outstanding	291	4.81E7	6.6694E5	3.73535E6
Financial revenue/assets	3.05	38.55	21.45	5.3

Table 7 Descriptive statistics of some important expenses of MFIs

	Minimum	Maximum	Mean	Std. deviation
Financial expense/assets	0.12	19.31	8.5833	2.61099
Operating expense/assets	2.88	34.98	10.3360	4.97
Cost per borrower	2	1300.00	23.3864	70.96
Administrative expense/assets	0.65	20	4.2	2.3
Personnel expense/assets	0.79	20.83	6.46	3.17
Average salary per GNI per capita	0.10	231	2.4022	12.5
Total expense/assets	0.00	73.56	21.0227	8.91341

Table 8 Descriptive statistics of some outreach variables

	Minimum	Maximum	Mean	Std. deviation
Average loan balance per borrower	22	835	159.06	74.15
Percent of female borrowers	48.26	100.00	97.0597	7.84946
Borrowers per loan officer	1.00	967	391.31	213.99

Table 9 Independent *t*-test of some financial indicators based on legal framework of MFIs

	LEGAL DUMMY	Mean	Std. deviation	Std. error mean	Independent *t*-test	Significance
ASSETS	NBFI	8.27E7	1.647E8	1.171E7	4.25	0.0
	Others	2.10E7	6.650E7	5580860.722		
GROSS_PORT_FOLIO	NBFI	8.14E7	1.642E8	1.155E7	4.35	0.0
	Others	1.82E7	6.406E7	5375879.807		
Capital/asset ratio	NBFI	44.9326	223.10965	15.69794	1.68	0.094
	Others	18.3989	16.15149	1.35540		

Efficiency and Mission Drift—Debate Revisited in Indian Context

Table 10 Independent *t*-test of some important indicators of MFIs based on legal framework

	LEGAL_DUMMY	Mean	Std. deviation	Std. error mean	Independent *t*-test	Significance
Non-earning liquid assets as % of total assets	NBFI	18.009	12.070	0.849		
	Others	14.454	13.079	1.097	2.56	0.011
Gross loan portfolio to total assets	NBFI	90.65	33.801	2.378	−1.488	0.139
	Others	168.61	747.415	62.722		
Portfolio at risk > 90 days	NBFI	9.638	31.890	2.243		
	Others	6.298	43.968	3.689	0.733	0.40
Profit margin	NBFI	−55.938	436.571	30.717		
	Others	1.991	53.827	4.517	−1.572	0.117
Yield on gross portfolio (real)	NBFI	20.073	92.130	6.48227	0.543	0.587
	Others	15.956	46.722	3.92089		

Table 11 Independent *t*-test of some important types of expenses of MFIs based on legal framework

	LEGAL_DUMMY	Mean	Std. deviation	Std. error mean	Independent *t*-test	Significance
Financial expense/assets	NBFI	8.589	2.796	0.197	0.045	0.964
	Others	8.576	2.333	0.196		
Operating expense/assets	NBFI	10.839	5.178	0.364	302.000	0.033
	Others	9.620	5.217	0.438		
Operating expense/loan portfolio	NBFI	13.112	6.866	0.483	204.000	0.918
	Others	13.228	12.087	1.014		
Cost per borrower	NBFI	25.534	91.604	6.510		0.441
	Others	20.392	16.708	1.402	215.000	
Administrative expense/assets	NBFI	4.261	2.365	0.166		
	Others	4.011	2.781	0.233	0.871	0.385
Cost per loan	NBFI	18.173	10.319	0.739		
	Others	18.959	16.504	1.437	−0.487	0.627
Personnel expense/assets	NBFI	6.622	3.297	0.232		
	Others	5.646	3.149	0.264	2.776	0.001
Personnel expense/loan portfolio	NBFI	8.966	5.529	0.389	0.500	0.617
	Others	8.631	6.496	0.545		
Average salary of the staff per GNI	NBFI	3.070	16.420	1.170	1.348	0.179
	Others					
Total expense per asset	NBFI	1.410	0.771	0.060		
	Others					

Table 12 Independent *t*-test of some performance indicators of MFIs based on legal framework

	LEGAL_DUMMY	Mean	Std. deviation	Std. error mean	Independent *t*-test	Significance
Loan per officers	NBFI	2.0367E2	232.36332	16.51334	5.122	0.0
	Others	88.3083	141.42287	12.26292		
Loans per loan officer	NBFI	4.2812E2	235.02597	16.78757	3.5	
	Others	3.3854E2	212.48247	18.49423		0.0
Loans per staff member	NBFI	3.0649E2	137.05508	9.76477	4.6	0.0
	Others	2.2941E2	160.99568	13.96010		
Personnel	NBFI	9.7110E2	2564.45686	195.53800	−0.22	0.983
	Others	9.7673E2	1792.52734	159.69103		

Table 13 Independent *t*-test of outreach variables of MFIs based on legal framework

	LEGAL_DUMMY	Mean	Std. deviation	Std. error mean	Independent *t*-test	Significance
Percent of female borrowers	NBFI	97.8329	5.60162	0.39413	2.91	0.029
	Others	95.9596	10.15274	0.85200		
Average loan balance per borrower	NBFI	1.5275E2	47.49186	3.34152	−2.71	0.014
	Others	1.7518E2	115.98502	9.73325		
Average loan balance per borrower/GNI per capita	NBFI	0.10	0.032	0.002	−2.481	0.014
	Others	0.12	0.078	0.007		
Number of active borrowers	NBFI	3.2033E5	8.71990E5	66682.73000	0.078	0.9
	Others	3.1316E5	6.24954E5	55897.59052		
Number of loans outstanding	NBFI	5.6194E5	1.11417E6	78392.56600	−0.584	0.560
	Others	7.9860E5	5.60857E6	4.70661E5		

Table 14 Correlation among the continuous variables

	AGE	ASSETS	Return on asset	Average loan balance per borrower/GNI per capita	Average loan balance per borrower	Percent of female borrowers
AGE	1	0.111*	−0.064	0.150**	0.153**	−0.170**
		0.040	0.236	0.005	0.004	0.002
ASSETS	0.111*	1	−0.087	0.063	0.063	−0.105
	0.040		0.110	0.244	0.243	0.053
RETURN_ASSET	−0.064	−0.087	1	0.024	0.024	0.144**
	0.236	0.110		0.664	0.660	0.008
Average loan balance per borrower/GNI per capita	0.150**	0.063	0.024	1	0.995**	−0.121*
	0.005	0.244	0.664		0.000	0.025
Average loan balance per borrower	0.153**	0.063	0.024	0.995**	1	−0.115*
	0.004	0.243	0.660	0.000		0.033
Percent_female_Borrowers	−0.170**	−0.105	0.144**	−0.121*	−0.115*	1
	0.002	0.053	0.008	0.025	0.033	
	0.937	0.002	0.210	0.812	0.817	0.851
	0.530	0.165	0.452	0.611	0.617	0.170

*Significant at 1% level
**Significant at 5% level

Table 15 Association between type of lending and legal framework of MFIs

Joint lending and group lending			LEGAL_DUMMY		Total
			Others	NBFI	
Individual	Count		46	118	164
	% within joint lending and group lending		28.0%	72.0%	100.0%
	% within LEGAL DUMMY		33.3%	58.4%	48.2%
Joint_Lending	Count		72	64	136
	% within joint lending and group lending		52.9%	47.1%	100.0%
	% within LEGAL DUMMY		52.2%	31.7%	40.0%
Individual and joint lending	Count		20	20	40
	% within joint lending and group lending		50.0%	50.0%	100.0%
	% within LEGAL DUMMY		14.5%	9.9%	11.8%
Total	Count		138	202	340
	% within joint lending and group lending		40.6%	59.4%	100.0%
	% within LEGAL DUMMY		100.0%	100.0%	100.0%

Chi-square tests

	Value	df	Asymp. Sig. (2-sided)
Pearson chi-square	20.769[a]	2	0.000
Likelihood ratio	21.064	2	0.000
Linear-by-linear association	15.414	1	0.000
No of valid cases	340		

[a] 0 cells (0.0%) have expected count less than 5. The minimum expected count is 16.24

References

Aghion Armendariz de, B., and J. Morduch. 2005. *The Economics of Microfinance*. MIT Press.

Arun, T., and R. Kamath. 2015. Financial inclusion: Policies and practices. *IIMB Management Review* 27 (4): 267–287.

Battese GE, Coelli TJ. 1988. Prediction of Grm-level technical efficiencies: With a generalized frontier production function and panel data. *Journal of Econometrics* 38: 387–399.

Battese, G.E., and T.J. Coelli. 1995. A model for technical inefficiency effects in a stochastic frontier production function for panel data. *Empirical Economics* 20: 325–332.

Berger, A.N., and D.B. Humphrey. 1997. Efficiency of financial institutions: International survey and directions for future research. *European Journal of Operational Research* 98 (2): 175–212.

Bhatt, N., and S.-Y. Tang. 2001. Delivering microfinance in developing countries: Controversies and policy perspective. *Policy Studies Journal* 29 (2): 319–333.

Brett, J.A. 2006. We sacrifice and eat less: The structural complexities of microfinance participation. *Human Organization* 65 (1): 8–19.

Caudill, S.B., D.M. Gropper, and V. Hartarska. 2009. Which microfinance institutions are becoming more cost effective with time? Evidence from a mixture model. *Journal of Money, Credit, and Banking* 41: 651–672.

Christen, R., and D. Drake. 2002. Commercialization. The new reality of microfinance. In *The commercialization of microfinance: Balancing business and development*, ed. D. Drake, and E. Rhyne, 2–22. Bloomfield: Kumarian Press.

Crisil Report India's Leading 25 MFIs, Report. 2014. http://www.crisil.com/pdf/ratings/indias-25-leading-mfis.pdf. Accesses on March 2, 2015.

Cull, R., A. Demirguc-Kunt, and J. Morduch. 2007. Financial performance and outreach: A global analysis of lending microbanks. *Economic Journal* 117: F107–F133.

Cull, R., and A. Demirguc-Kunt. 2011. Does regulatory supervision curtail microfinance profitability and outreach? *World Development* 39 (6): 949–965.

Dowla, Asif, and Dipal Barua. 2006. *The Poor Always Pay Back: The Grameen 2 Story*. Bloomfield: Kumarian Press Inc.

Gebremichael, Bereket Zerai, and Hailemichael Tesfay Gessesse. 2016. Technical efficiency of Microfinance Institutions (MFIs): Does ownership matter? Evidence from African MFIs. *International Journal of Development Issues* 15 (3): 224–239.

Ghatak, Maitreesh, and Timothy Guinnane. 1999. The economics of lending with joint liability: Theory and practice. *Journal of Development Economics* 60 (1): 195–228.

Ghosh, Jayati. 2013. Microfinance and the challenge of financial inclusion for development. *Cambridge Journal of Economics* 37 (6): 1203–1219.

Gutiérrez-Nieto, B., C. Serrano-Cinca, and C. Mar Molinero. 2007. Microfinance institutions and efficiency. *Omega* 35 (2): 131–142.

Hermes, N., R. Lensink, and A. Meesters. 2011. Outreach and efficiency of microfinance institutions. *World Development* 39 (69): 938–948.

Jondrow, James, C.A. Knox Lovell, Ivan S. Materov, and Peter Schmidt. 1982. On the estimation of technical inefficiency in the stochastic frontier production function model. *Journal of Econometrics* 19 (2–3): 233–238

Kar, Ashim Kumar. 2012. Mission drift in microfinance: are the concerns really worrying? Recent Crosscountry results. *International Review of Applied Economics* 27 (1): 44–60.

Kumbhakar, Subal C., and C.A. Knox Lovell. 2003. *Stochastic Frontier Analysis*. Cambridge University Press.

Lariviere, S., and F. Martin. 1999. Innovations in rural microfinance: the challenge of sustainability and outreach. In *Innovations in Microfinance for the Rural Poor: Exchange of Knowledge and Implications of Policy*, ed. M. Zeller, and M. Sharma, 85–110. Washington, DC: International Food Policy Research Institute.

Makame, A.H., and V. Murinde. 2006. Empirical findings on cognitive dissonance around microfinance outreach and sustainability. Unpublished paper. Birmingham: University of Birmingham.

Manos, R., and J. Yaron. 2009. Key issues in assessing the performance of microfinance institutions. *Canadian Journal of Development Studies* 29: 101–122.

Navajas, S., J. Conning, and C. Gonzalez-Vega. 2003. Lending technologies, competition and consolidation in the market for microfinance in Bolivia. *Journal of International Development* 15: 747–770.

Olivares-Polanco, F. 2005. Commercializing microfinance and deepening outreach: Empirical evidence from Latin America. *Journal of Microfinance* 7 (1): 47–69.

Pal, Debdatta. 2010. Measuring technical efficiency of microfinance institutions in India. *Indian Journal of Agriculture Economics* 65 (4): 639–657.

Paxton, J. 2007. Technical efficiency in a semi-formal financial sector: The case of Mexico. *Oxford Bulletin of Economics and Statistics* 69 (1): 57–74.

Qayyum, A., and M. Ahmad. 2006. Efficiency and sustainability of microfinance institutions in South Asia. Islamabad: Pakistan. Institute of Development Economics (PIDE). Retrieved on March 3, 2015. http://saneinetwork.net/Files/06_07.pdf.

Rhyne, E. 1998. The yin and yang of microfinance. Reaching the poor and sustainability. *MicroBanking Bulleti* 2: 6–9.

Rhyne, E., and E. Otero. 2006. Microfinance through the next decade: Visioning the who, what where, when and how. Paper commissioned by the Global Microcredit Summit 2006. Boston MA: ACCION International.

Saad, S.A., and A. Khan Sr. 2014. Microfinance and client protection under existing Indian framework. *Intercontinental Journal of Finance Research Review* 2 (9).

Schreiner, M. 2002. Aspects of outreach: A framework for the discussion of the social benefits of microfinance. *Journal of International Development* 14 (5): 591–603.

Sealey Jr., C.W., and J.T. Lindley. 1977. Inputs, outputs, and a theory of production and cost at depository financial institutions. *Journal of Finance* 32: 1251–1266.

Servin, R., Robert Lensink, and Marrit van den Berg. 2012. Ownership and technical efficiency of microfinance institutions: Empirical evidence from Latin America. *Journal of Banking & Finance* 36 (7): 2136–2144.

Tariq, M., and A.M. Izhar. 2010. Technical efficiency of microfinance institutions in India—A stochastic frontier approach. Munich Personal RePEc Archive (MPRA) Paper No. 25454.

Von Pischke, J. 1996. Measuring the trade-off between outreach and sustainability of microenterprise lenders. *Journal of International Development* 8 (2): 225–239.

Woller, Gary M., Christopher Dunford, and Warner Woodworth. 1999. Where to Microfinance? *International Journal of Economic Development* 1 (1): 29–64.

Microfinance and Human Development: A Cross-Generation Study

Arijita Dutta and Sharmistha Banerjee

1 Introduction

In recent years microfinance (MF) initiatives have been highlighted as a key strategy to alleviate poverty in the poorest countries in the world. Initially developed as a model for offering soft loans without collateral to vulnerable women in the developing countries, it is expected to support the immediate consumption needs, as well as long-term investment requirements in the human capital formation of these households. It has been widely discussed that accumulation of human capital is an effective and indispensable part of the long-term goal of alleviation of poverty (Schultz 1961; Bils and Klenov 2000). Additionally, MF is believed to contribute to this objective by ameliorating the welfare and the quality of life of the next generation in developing countries through the human capital formation in education and health. Service providers of MF with long-term, routine, and trusting relationships with clients are well positioned to improve access for the poor to a range of important health-related services (Leatherman et al. 2011). This chapter seeks to diagnose the premise that besides offering more purchasing power and empowerment among the women, MF goes beyond creating prosperity of the present borrowers up to the next generation of daughters and daughters-in-law. This chapter also examines the impact of MF loans on the educational attainment, general and maternal health, and decision-making indicators of daughters, and labor force participation of daughters-in-law of first-generation MF borrowers in Bangladesh, the haven of MF activities.

A. Dutta (✉)
Department of Economics, University of Calcutta, Kolkata, India
e-mail: dutta.arijita@gmail.com

S. Banerjee
Department of Business Management, University of Calcutta, Kolkata, India

© Springer Nature Singapore Pte Ltd. 2017
C. Neogi et al. (eds.), *Women's Entrepreneurship and Microfinance*,
DOI 10.1007/978-981-10-4268-3_7

There is a large body of literature on the effect of MF on educational attainment of the children of MF users. Findings related to children's education and cognitive development were overall mixed and depended on the category of impact measured. As a systematic review of the topic and a few studies included hypothesize, households may spend loan money directly on education-related expenses, improving short-term outcomes, but fail to improve the household's overall financial standing (USAID 2015). MF users practice the proposition that continued education is based on the underlying hypothesis that women as MF borrowers have relatively stronger preferences for education than men (Pitt and Khandker 1998; Thomas 1990). However, this premise is expected to work only when the formal loan entitlement brings about an effective shift of power toward women within the family to the extent they can influence the family decision of sending the child (especially the girl child) to school. However, children may be more likely to attend school if a MF loan enables smooth consumption pattern by alleviating financial pressures. Automatically, this would decrease the propensity of the parents to keep their children out of school as MF would generate extra income for the household. Littlefield et al. (2003) find that children of MF clients are more likely to go to school and stay in school longer, resulting in lower student dropout rates among MF client households. In a joint study by BIDS and World Bank in Bangladesh findings supported the claim that MF programs promote the poor household's investment in human capital through schooling and the contraceptive behavior of fámilies (Khandker 1988; Pitt and Khandker 1998). However, the results of some studies challenge usual assumptions in MF programs. Holvoet (2004) states that direct individual bank-borrower lending in South India does not induce any effect at all on children's educational inputs and outputs. Using the panel data collected by the Townsend Thai Project between 1997 and 2007 in eight provinces of Thailand, no statistically significant correlation between the number of loans and enrollment in school was found (Hytopoulos 2011). In another study on Ghana by Joseph et al. (2009), it emerged that participation in the program has enabled established clients to own savings deposits and subscribe to a client welfare scheme to pay off debts in times of illness or death. They were in a better position to contribute toward the education of their children, payment of health care for members of their households, and the purchase of household durables. The authors further noted that clients who remained in MF programs for longer periods of time suffered from diminishing marginal returns. It was suggested that there should be some form of upscaling to accommodate these clients or they should be able to join other financial service providers in the formal sector in order to sustain the benefit generated at the initial stages of MF transactions.

Maldonado et al. (2005) suggests that access to loans has differential effects on school enrollment across different strata of society. On the one hand, loans increase the demand for education as a result of increased income, risk management, and gender and information effects. On the other hand, credit-constrained households that run labor-intensive microenterprises or cultivate own land need more labor hours (even from children), either for working or taking care of siblings, while the mothers operate the business. In another study, by Blume and Breyer (2011), it was evident that access to MF—as one tool—can be used to prevent, mitigate, and reduce child labor, but when applied incorrectly, MF can also contribute to the creation of child labor.

It is believed that although the primary objective of the microfinance institutions (MFIs) was to reduce poverty, it also accrued with its positive impacts on the social sphere, including women's power or agency control (Hulme and Moore 2008). One of those indicators of women control over the household assets and spousal communication regarding family planning and childbearing is the age of marriage of women. Child marriage below the age of 18 years is particularly low in South Asian countries, including Bangladesh (UNICEF 2014). However, the average age of marriage does not seem to have increased in Bangladesh, in spite of large-scale involvement of a generation of women in MF. There is no notable difference between so-called *empowered* versus *un-empowered* women and their families in the ways decisions about the timing of marriage and childbearing were made. In general, daughters of empowered women with MF experiences were much the same as daughters of less empowered non-borrowers regarding the timing of marriage, as was expected of them (Schuler and Rottach 2011).

Given this vast body of existing literature, this chapter attempts to locate the impact of MF on human capital formation and health indicators of next-generation women in Bangladesh. Section 2 briefly discusses the methodology. The discussion of results is presented in Sect. 3, while Sect. 4 contains the conclusions and suggestions for a way forward.

2 Data and Methodology

The chapter uses primary survey of 1200 households in 17 districts of Bangladesh, with partner organizations (PO) of *Palli Karma-Sahayak Foundation* (PKSF) offering MF. Six hundred households receiving MF loans from these POs since 1995 or before have been considered to be part of treatment group, while another 600 households from the same or neighboring village without MF services have been selected under control group. From a list of 57 POs enrolled before 1995, 15 POs (five each from large, medium, and small categories) have been selected using stratified random sampling technique.

The sample size of the study has been determined to estimate the result of the study within 5% of the true value with 95% confidence level. In order to select respondent households, at the first stage, two branches from each of the selected POs and two sub-POs or *samities* established before 2000 from each branch were selected. At the second stage, 10 households who have been receiving microcredit since 15 years were selected from each of the selected *samities* using simple random sampling technique. Thus, the total number of respondent households under treatment group for each PO stands at 40. Similarly, a total of 40 control households from each PO and 10 from each of the treatment or neighboring villages were selected using the same technique. The survey was conducted during May to September 2015.

This chapter uses simple statistical data explorations and propensity score matching (PSM) analysis to capture the impact of long-term microcredit on the human capital formation of the second generation of the borrowers. PSM technique is effective in simulating an experiment and measuring treatment impacts in non-experimental studies, especially only for studies observing the post-treatment effects (Khandekar et al. 2010). In this method, each treated person is compared with a non-treated person using the nearest neighbor matching (NNM) technique and the average difference of the outcome variable is taken as average treatment effect on the treated (ATT). The technique is expected to remove the selection bias by balancing the sample on the characteristics that potentially determine the possibility of selection of cases into the treatment group. Balancing for selection bias is done using a probit model, whose estimates were used to obtain the propensity scores for selection into the program (Dehejia and Wahba 2002). Propensity scores are the predicted probabilities to receive the treatment. Once the scores had been generated, we checked whether the selection bias had been removed by performing bivariate tests against the treatment variable on all the variables used to remove selection. If the differences for treatment indicator emerge as insignificant after balancing, it can be concluded that the selection bias has been successfully removed and our subsequent models would be balanced. The model is expected to capture the average treatment effect on the treated (ATT) in terms of the outcome variable, several measurements of entrepreneurship of individuals.

3 Results and Discussion

While surveying 1200 households with women aged between 45 and 60 years, information on 1418 daughters and daughters-in-law (aged 14 and above) was collected, of which 788 were daughters-in-law, and the rest 630 were daughters. Some married daughters could not be interviewed directly, and hence their information were recorded from their mothers. Among those women from next generation, 706 belonged to households where the mother or mother-in-law had taken loans from MF about 15 years back, while the rest 712 belonged to control group of households without such long-term involvement in MF. Information was primarily collected on the human development aspects, their involvement in income-generating activities (IGA), and financial inclusion.

Table 1 depicts the information of these women across both the generations in terms of crucial attributes. It is clear that education reached the next generation of women in Bangladesh far better than the earlier one. Also, there was a jump in the share of women completing primary education for those women whose first generations were MF borrowers. This may suggest that the borrowers continued their daughter's schooling, while also preferred brides with better education to be married to their sons. Interestingly, a different picture emerged in the case of years of education for these women. The primary borrowers had a higher mean of years of education than the non-borrowers. The difference got reversed in the second generation, while the mean of years of education for borrowing households was a bit higher, though the difference remained insignificant across generations. There was no such difference in median years of education also. No mention-worthy leap was observed over a generation in case of financial inclusion. Less than 10% of women from both treatment and control groups had access to bank accounts in the study area. Although women from the second generation in the treatment group had better involvement in IGAs, there was a significant drop observed across generations. This has been partly reflected in encouragement offered by women of first generations to their daughters and daughters-in-law. Less than half of those treated groups provided 'enough' encouragement as per their records, while 15% reported offering no encouragement at all. Although a quarter of primary respondents received some vocational training, there was a significant drop in that activity among the second-generation women. Only a minuscule share of the latter had access to some vocational training.

Looking at the age of marriage and age of first delivery, there was a marginal improvement across generations. Although in second generation the mean age of marriage and age of first delivery were higher among treatment groups with long-term access to MF, the median values do not differ much. In fact, the median age of first delivery was higher among the control groups. Interestingly, primary women borrowers appear to offer active advice and control on crucial issues related to childbirth and family planning of daughters and daughters-in-law more than the control households, hinting toward the fact that the primary respondents exercised their control and empowerment on issues, which ideally should be decided within the dyad of husband and wife.

However, it must be accepted that this type of comparison of means might not reflect the actual picture as there might be a strong sample bias among households to get *treated* or in this case to receive MF a decade and a half back. Often it is found that women from the poorest and most vulnerable households opt for MF loans to escape the immediate poverty trap. Based on this possibility of presence of sample bias, considering the case of Grameen Bank's beneficiaries in Bangladesh, it is found that the per capita consumption among program participants is lower than that of non-participants prior to program intervention because Grameen Bank targeted low-income families as they had lower per capita food consumption to begin with (Khandekar et al. 2010). Thus, judging the program's impact by comparing the food consumption of program participants with that of non-participants might involve strong participation bias. What is needed is to compare what would have happened to the food consumption of the participating women *had the program not existed*. Again, one might compare ex-post outcomes for beneficiaries with data on their outcomes before the intervention. However, such a simple difference method would again yield incorrect assessment because many other factors (outside of the program) might have changed over the period. Essentially, these two issues call for a proper comparison group; that is, a close *counterfactual* of program beneficiaries is needed. Since observation of same individuals cannot belong to both treatment

124 A. Dutta and S. Banerjee

Table 1 Attributes of human development across generations

Attributes	Generation 1		Generation 2	
	MF borrowers	Non-borrowers	MF borrowers	Non-borrowers
Completed primary education	26.67	24.37	90.45	83.85
Mean years of education	2.28 (0)	2.57 (0)	7.06 (7)	6.33 (7)
Access to bank accounts	14.50	5.68	7.72	6.66
Involvement in IGA	78.67	60.43	39.47	30.45
Access to any vocational training	26.42	1.51	1.40	0.15
Average age of marriage	14.61 (14)	14.45 (14)	16.86 (17)	16.44 (17)
Average age of first delivery	17.65 (17)	17.66 (17)	18.49 (18)	18.86 (19)
Encouragement for IGA to second generation	NA			
Enough encouragement			44.74	35.88
Little encouragement			40.25	41.67
No encouragement			15.01	22.46
Advice for birth of children to second generation	NA			
Enough encouragement			40.92	31.21
Little encouragement			36.89	42.55
No encouragement			22.19	26.24
Advice for birth of children to second generation	NA			
Enough encouragement			38.53	31.63
Little encouragement			37.09	39.15
No encouragement			29.22	29.22

Figures in parenthesis represent median values. *IGA* Income-generating activities
NA Not applicable
Source Analysis of primary data

and control group of counterfactuals, the next best alternative is to compare outcomes of treated individuals with those of a comparison group that is very similar to the treated group such that those who received treatment would have had outcome similar to those in the comparison group in the absence of treatment.

In this chapter, we first attempt to locate the factors that drive the mothers or mothers-in-law to choose MF or not, or in other words, to get treated or not. This is done with the help of probit regression, and hence we calculate the propensity score of each woman to participate or not. Results posit that woman from Hindu households and residing away from pucca roads opted for MF more. Also, women who were married late preferred these loans. Societal encouragement, as perceived

Microfinance and Human Development: A Cross-Generation Study

Table 2 Results of probit regression analysis of accepting MFI loans (0 = not accepting loans or control group, 1 = accepting loans or treatment group)

Variables	Coefficient	$P > |z|$
Religion Hindu (ref. Muslim)	0.28**	0.01
Distance from pucca road (in minute)	−0.01*	0.07
Age at joining (in years)	0.06**	0.05
Square of age at joining	−0.01***	0.00
Personal education above primary (ref. primary)	−0.05	0.99
Age at first delivery	−0.01	0.63
Perception about society's acceptance: does not like (ref. likes)	−0.29**	0.00
Constant	−0.44	0.44
LR chi-square	238.56***	
Pseudo R^2	0.12	
Number of observations	1417	

Source Analysis of primary data
*Significant at 10% level
**Significant at 5% level
***Significant at 1% level

by the respondents, makes a big difference in choice of MF. Interestingly, women's educational status does not make a significant impact (Table 2).

Once the regression is run, we attempt to match each second-generation woman from a treated household to one second-generation woman from a non-treated or control group household by the method of NNM. This way, we calculate ATT as the mean of these differences. We measure the impact of the policy choice on several outcome measures of entrepreneurship, as reported in Table 3.

Results in Table 3 posit that there is no significant difference in educational status between the women of the first and of the second generations of the two groups. Additionally, the results are insignificant when we analyze the daughters and daughters-in-law separately, although, on average, the control group members appear to complete their daughters' education more. Similar insignificant differences emerge with regard to possession of bank account and the age of first delivery. However, the involvement in IGAs is almost 40% higher in the treated group, with 1% significance. The long-term MF borrowers also prefer their daughters and daughters-in-law to be married at a 2% older age, though significant at only 10% level, the result is significant for daughters only. In all cases, the overwhelming majority of observations (more than 98%) were lying within the common support area.

Table 4 depicts that in the case of most of the variables, the sample was unbalanced before matching (as shown by significant t statistic at unmatched cases). However, after balancing, that is, matching one treated and one control household, the difference in all variables become insignificant, meaning that the two fragmented samples of treatment and control groups become similar in all major and observable aspects and possible sample bias is removed. The final mean bias after

Table 3 Impact of MF on several measures of human development for the second generation

Impact on several measures of attributes of second-generation women	Mean of treatment group	Mean of control group	Difference %	t-stats
Education more than primary level	0.90	0.88	2.72	0.73
Age of marriage* (years)	16.87	16.51	2.18	1.61
Age of first delivery (years)	18.50	18.43	0.40	0.23
Involvement in IGA***	0.39	0.28	39.28	2.86
Possession of bank account	0.08	0.07	14.28	0.06
Education more than primary level for daughters	0.94	0.95	−1.06	−0.22
Education more than primary level for daughters-in-law	0.87	0.88	−1.36	−0.19
Age of marriage for daughters	16.95***	15.92	6.47	2.64
Age of marriage for daughters-in-law	16.83	16.56	1.63	1.07

Source Analysis of primary data
*Significant at 10% level
***Significant at 1% level

matching is 12.9, below the thumb rule of 15.0. Also, a good matching needs the use of as many controls as possible and low repetition of same control household. In the present matching, 85% matching involved using one control household less than four times and 95% matching involved using same control less than six times.

This study attempts to locate the impact of long-run involvement of poorest Bangladeshi women in the human development process of the next-generation women, namely daughters and daughters-in-law. While literature does identify income effect and risk-smoothing effects of MF borrowers to improve education and health indicators of their next generation, the continued engagement of mothers in IGA often indirectly pulls children out of school, which may affect access to education adversely. However, MF is found to have an improving impact on age of marriage of daughters and daughters-in-law, though the similar impact on age of childbearing seems to be insignificant.

While looking at the results of probit model, it is found that overall more vulnerable, relatively older women from religious minority group (Hindus in Bangladesh) and residing far off from motorable *pucca* road had self-selected themselves more into MF activities, hinting toward the fact that women from more vulnerable strata and location prefer to join MF more, as also identified in the literature. The significance of the squared age term points out a nonlinear relationship between age and acceptance of MF. It is also clear that the women valued the society's preference, as perceived by them, in making their choice to opt for the loans themselves.

Microfinance and Human Development: A Cross-Generation Study

Table 4 Balancing of the sample before and after matching

Variables	Mean value in treatment group	Mean value in control group	t-statistic for the mean difference	$P > \lvert t \rvert$
Religion Hindu (ref. Muslim)				
Unmatched	1.15	1.09	3.05	0.002
Matched	1.15	1.13	1.00	0.319
Distance from pucca road (in minutes)				
Unmatched	6.93	8.12	−2.92	0.004
Matched	6.93	6.55	1.08	0.280
Age at joining (in years)				
Unmatched	32.82	35.99	−7.08	0.000
Matched	32.82	32.53	0.72	0.96
Square of age at joining				
Unmatched	1134.5	1381.0	−7.38	0.000
Matched	1134.5	1117.9	0.59	0.556
Personal education above primary (ref. primary)				
Unmatched	0.25	0.22	1.35	0.17
Matched	0.25	0.26	−0.42	0.57
Age at first delivery				
Unmatched	17.67	17.66	0.00	0.997
Matched	17.67	17.86	−1.37	0.172
Perception about society's acceptance: does not like (ref. likes)				
Unmatched	0.02	0.17	−9.40	0.000
Matched	0.02	0.03	−0.17	0.868
Sample				
Unmatched	Mean bias 26.14		Bias 83.0	
Matched	Mean bias 3.4		Bias 12.9	

Source Analysis of primary data

The results presented in this chapter are crucial in understanding the entire pathway of development in this poor Asian country. With a primary survey of 1200 households spread across the districts of Bangladesh, the study identifies no significant impact of MF on educational access of Bangladeshi women. Although there is a clear jump in the share of women completing primary education across both borrowers and non-borrowers, this might have occurred due to other features of development policies in Bangladesh, especially those related to the overall movement toward the education of girl students. PSM technique removing all sample bias identified both the treatment households (with women having MF loans for more than 15 years) and control households (with no such long-run involvement) to be reacting in similar ways in imputing human capital among their women in next generation.

The involvement in the labor market, however, shows a different trend. MF is found to improve labor market participation of daughters and daughters-in-law in the economy, though overall there is a drop compared to an earlier generation. This result is surprising in the backdrop of higher participation of women in labor market across the world. Probably, this is correlated to the fact that the next-generation women have hardly accepted loans from the MFIs, and there is a clear shrinkage of the net of loanees.

However, there appears to be a marginal impact of MF on the age of marriage of daughters and daughters-in-law. This impact is not highly significant, though. As identified in a systematic literature review by U.S. Agency for International Development (USAID 2015), health-related indicators for next-generation women appear to improve, albeit very little. The difference is highly significant for daughters separately. This might hint toward the fact that the women with long-term exposure to MF prefer to keep their daughters unmarried for a longer time, though they do not continue education in most of the cases. This can have two separate trends. First, the daughters are engaged more in labor market and also in household chores to support the business of their mothers. Secondly, they inherit higher chances to be involved in IGA even after marriage. However, no such effect is observed for the age of the first childbearing. Thus, the impact of MF seems to fizzle out without sustainability, representing a sure sign of mission drift.

4 Conclusion

The overall perception presented in this chapter submits that in spite of a decade-long experience with MF, Bangladesh could not free her women from the shackles of low human capital and improper childbearing age. MF did impact a higher female participation in labor market among the households with a long history of MF, although that seemed to be dwindling over the generations. Contextualizing the results in the macroframe of Bangladeshi development model, it must be accepted that the economic situation in Bangladesh a decade and a half back was conducive to the initial success of MF initiatives. The aim at that point of time was alleviation of abject poverty. This has surely and successfully been achieved, albeit with various fallouts. The small sum of collateral-free money that reached the vulnerable and poorest women in rural Bangladesh was more like a windfall. It not only provided for immediate consumption needs including basic hygiene but also encouraged traditional IGA to continue for generating just enough for loan repayments. With time the country has evolved, and the role of MF initiatives are now being scrutinized through a complex sieve.

Understanding the limited success of human capital formation among women in Bangladesh, it is probably the right time that MF activities take up different shapes and forms in different markets. Instead of questioning the validity of collateral-free small loans, which serve the bottom-most layers of society in underdeveloped countries, it may be worthwhile to look at a reengineered form of MF for countries such as Bangladesh where the initial challenges of basic living have been overcome. It is probably time for a much-needed makeover of the MFI, which may, in more ways than one, contribute to the human capital formation, in varying degrees and forms in developing countries, in its homeland. The users of collateral-free small loans may be guided through trained usage of such loans in economically sustainable and socially meaningful ways. The newer MF offers may aim at proactive modes of empowering women in the second generation by using their names not only to obtain loans but also to engage them in responsible and participative IGA.

References

Bils, Mark, and Peter J. Klenow. 2000. Does schooling cause growth? *American Economic Review* 1160–1183.
Blume, Jonas, and Julika Breyer. 2011. *Microfinance and Child Labour, ILO.*
Dehejia, R., and S. Wahba. 2002. Propensity score matching methods for non-experimental causal studies. *The Review of Economics and Statistics* 84: 151–161.
Hulme, D., and K. Moore. 2008. Assisting the poorest in bangladesh: Learning from BRAC's 'targeting the ultra-poor' programme. In *Social Protection for the Poor and Poorest*, 194–210. UK: Palgrave Macmillan.
Joseph A. Kimos, Thankom Arun, and Farhad Hossain. 2009. *The Role of Microfinance in Asset-Building and Poverty Reduction: The Case of sinapi aba Trust of Ghana*, University of Manchester.
Holvoet, N. 2004. Impact of microfinance programs on children's education: Do the gender of the borrower and the delivery model matter? *Journal of Microfinance* 6 (2): 27.
Hytopoulos, Evelyn. 2011. The Impact of Microfinance Loans on Children Educational Attainment in Rural Thailand. Undergraduate Honors Thesis Fall 2011. Economics Department Berkeley, University of California
Khandker, Shahidur. 1988. *Fighting Poverty with Microcredit: Experience in Bangladesh*, Oxford University Press for the World Bank.
Khandekar, Shahidur, Gayatri Koolwal, Hussain Samad. 2010. *Handbook on Impact Evaluation: Quantitative Methods and Practices*, The World Bank.
Leatherman Sheila, Christopher Dunford, Marcia Metcalfe, Myka Reinsch, Megan Gash, and Bobbi Gray. 2011. Integrating microfinance and health: Benefits, challenges and reflections for moving forward. In *Global Microcredit Summit Commissioned Workshop Paper*, November 14–17, 2011. Valladolid, Spain.
Littlefield, E., J. Murduch, and S. Hashemi. 2003. *"Is Microfinance an Effective Strategy to Reach the Millennium Development Goals?" CGAP Focus Note 24.* Washington, D.C.: Consultative Group to Assist the Poor.
Maldonado, Jorge Higinio, Claudio González-Vega, and Vivianne Romero. 2005. *The Influence of Microfinance on the Education Decisions of Rural Households: Evidence from Bolivia*, Universidad de los Andes.
Pitt, M., and S. Khandker. 1998. The impact of group-based credit programs on poor households in bangladesh: Does the gender of participants matter? *Journal of Political Economy* 106 (October): 958–996.
Schuler, Sidney Ruth, Elisabeth Rottach. 2011. Why does women's empowerment in one generation not lead to later marriage and childbearing in the next? Qualitative findings from Bangladesh. *Journal of Comparative Family Studies*, 253–265.

Schultz, T.W. 1961. Investment in human capital. *American Economic Review*, 51 (1): 1–17 ((March) No. 468. Washington, D.C.: Inter American Development Bank).

Thomas, D. 1990. Intra-household resource allocation: an inferential approach. *Journal of Human Resources* 25 (1990): 635–664.

UNICEF. 2014. *Ending Child Marriage*: *Progress and Prospects*, New York

USAID. 2015. *The Impact of Microcredit Loans on Child Outcomes: A Review of the Literature. Supporting Transformation by Reducing Insecurity and Vulnerability with Economic Strengthening (STRIVE)*.

Microfinance for Women-Owned Small Business in India: Challenges and Opportunities

Avijit Brahmachary

1 Introduction

The formal financial sector assumes that providing small loans and deposit services to the poor people would be unprofitable because the cost of delivering small-scale financial services at the local level is too high for non-subsidized institutions. They assume that informal financial service providing institutes, such as nongovernmental organizations (NGOs), may offer some solution to meet such demand. However, with very few exceptions, these institutions (i.e., NGOs) can operate only on a very limited scale. Poor people who require small loans and deposit services are usually unable to inform informal market (due to their low or zero bargaining power) about their creditworthiness or about their demand for saving services and loans. Accordingly, these services are not provided to them. 'Those who had the power do not understand the demand; those who understand the demand do not hold power' (Robinson 2001).

The implementation of any formal lending program (subsidized as well as non-subsidized) directed toward the poor is often beset by some important difficulties (Hulme and Mosley 1996). The major issue is the problem of exact targeting and the failure of supply-led financial programs to reach the targeted poor. Besides, the screening problem of distinguishing the good (creditworthy) from the bad (not so creditworthy) borrowers, high transaction costs associated with small loans, and so on, prompted the formal lending agencies to leave the poor unbanked (Hulme and Mosley 1996; Yunus 1999). The failure of formal lending program insists that the policy makers find an alternative lending mechanism to minimize the said gap on the one hand and to provide a smart loan to the poor protecting themselves from the usurious informal money lending activities on the other. Against this backdrop, the group-based

---

A. Brahmachary (✉)
Department of Economics, Kandi Raj College, Kandi, 742137 Murshidabad,
West Bengal, India
e-mail: avijiteco@rediffmail.com

© Springer Nature Singapore Pte Ltd. 2017
C. Neogi et al. (eds.), *Women's Entrepreneurship and Microfinance*,
DOI 10.1007/978-981-10-4268-3_8

microfinance program has evolved as an alternative formal lending program throughout the world specifically in the developing nations to provide different financial services among the collateral-less unbanked poor, specifically women.

However, microfinance during the 1990s was marked by a major debate between the two leading views: the financial system approach and the poverty lending approach. The objective of poverty lending approach is to reduce poverty through credit and other services provided by institutions that are funded by donor and government subsidies and other concessional funds. The primary goal is to reach the poor, especially the poorest of the poor, with credit. As indicated by the term poverty lending, the emphasis is on microcredit, not microfinance. Many institutions, such as Bangladesh's Grameen Bank and some of its replicators in other countries, provide microcredit using poverty lending approach at low cost. In contrast, the financial approach focuses on commercial financial intermediation among poor borrowers and savers. The main emphasis of this system is on institutional self-sufficiency or sustainability. Advocates of financial approach think that government and donor funds alone cannot finance microcredit on a global scale. Financially sustainable institutions, however, can meet such demand without any difficulty. Commercial microfinance institutions (MFIs, who adopt financial system approach) provide loans and voluntary savings services to the economically active poor, and they offer easy access to funds at reasonable cost. At present in India, the microfinance program led by the National Bank for Agriculture and Rural Development (NABARD) to empower rural poor follows the financial approach of microfinance and provides significant credit to the economically active people, especially women for their small or tiny businesses.

Thus, microfinance plays a pivotal role in providing individuals a platform from where they can start a journey to a life in which their potential is realized (Mitra 2002). Encouraging women to participate in business activities not only generates employment opportunities within the economy but also helps to establish their self-worth within the family and also in the society. Voice representation and economic self-sufficiency are the two crucial indicators by which we can crudely measure the actual status of the women in the family and society. Women participation in business to some extent helps to improve these two indicators ensuring a better freedom in the society (ILO 2004).

Unfortunately, at the early age, most people believed that men alone could set up enterprises. The infrastructure and social scenario throughout the world were designed mainly for men. Women joined in this network only due to compulsion. They were compelled to run an enterprise as a sole or partnership owner to generate some income for sustaining themselves and families (Kollan and Parikh 2005). Nowadays, all over the world women are increasingly finding self-employment through small and tiny business activities irrespective of its size. Most of these business activities suffer from the shortage of finance and the women are usually unable to manage the adequate finance from formal institutions. Here, the microfinance program through self-help groups (SHGs) may act as a good alternative to formal financial institutions to provide financial support to the micro- and small businesses.

Microfinance for Women-Owned Small Business in India ...

This chapter presents study of the financing of women-owned businesses in India and the major challenges faced by them. Also, specifically, the role of microfinance to provide an alternative source of finance to the women-led unorganized informal businesses is examined. However, the broad objectives of the present study are:

(i) to evaluate the role of microfinance program as an alternative source of finance for women-owned enterprises;
(ii) to understand the present status of microfinance program in India;
(iii) to evaluate the major factors responsible for encouraging women to set up or to participate in business;
(iv) to review the current scenario of women-owned small businesses in India;
(v) to study the problems and challenges faced by women-owned small enterprises in India and the role of microfinance to provide small finance;
(vi) to analyze the initiatives taken by the government to accelerate women's businesses in India;
(vii) to study the policies, programs, institutional networks, and the involvement of support agencies in promoting women's businesses in India to ensure a better economic and social empowerment.

To fulfill all these objectives successfully, I have planned to divide the analysis into eight sections. Section 1 explains the major objectives of the study. In Sect. 2, I discuss the logical foundation of microfinance as an alternative to formal financial institutions to provide small finance to the women-owned enterprises. In Sect. 3, the global experience of microfinance program is explained briefly. In Sect. 4, the major events of microfinance program in India are elaborated to understand the outreach of such finance program in the country. I have analyzed the major problems faced by women-owned small businesses in India in Sect. 5. Along with gender bias, some specific social and economic factors have been identified, which put major obstacles for women-owned businesses. Since finance is the oxygen of any business activity, in this chapter I have analyzed the issue specifically in Sect. 6. In this section, the demand and supply of finance and the actual finance gap for women businesses, which usually belong to the informal sector, are explained briefly. Besides, this chapter identifies some demand- and supply-side constraints to access finance by women in India. The role of microfinance to minimize such gap and to increase the outreach of the program has been explained briefly. Apart from microfinance program, the other projects and schemes offered by government and private agencies to address the finance gap for women-owned businesses are also explained. Although such programs are not sufficient to meet the total demand for finance, such initiatives are very encouraging for the start-ups of women, specifically for India where women face multiple problems as explained in Sect. 5. The concluding remarks and some probable policy suggestions regarding the microfinance for women-owned small businesses in India are discussed extensively in Sect. 7.

2 Microfinance: An Alternative Source of Finance and Global Experience

The implementation of any formal lending program (subsidized and non-subsidized) directed toward the poor is often beset by some important difficulties (Hulme and Mosley 1996). The first is the problem of exact targeting and the failure of supply-led financial programs to reach the targeted poor. It has often been found that (i) large-scale subsidized programs generally do not reach low-income households; (ii) subsidized credit programs, especially in state-owned institutions, have high default rates; (iii) subsidized credit programs are often controlled by political leaders and local elites and, once offered, is difficult to withdraw—lists of 'poor' borrowers who receive credit subsidies usually include local political leaders, their relatives, and supporters; (iv) in subsidized credit programs, the borrower bears high transaction costs—receiving credit is a time-consuming and cumbersome process including high transportation costs for borrowers together with corruption, requirement of bribes for staffs, and so on increasing the transaction costs unexpectedly; (v) loan products are often inappropriate for borrower's needs; and (vi) subsidized credit retards the development of sustainable financial institutions (Yaron et al. 1997). Secondly, it faces the screening problem of distinguishing the good (creditworthy) from the bad (not so creditworthy) borrowers, which in turn generates an adverse selection and moral hazard in the rural credit market. Thirdly, these agencies may not be able to monitor and ensure productive usage of the loans. Further, if the loan repayment runs into a problem, they may not be able to take legal action against the borrowers, often on account of the absence of any collateral. Besides, due to high transaction costs that have to be incurred in lending to the poor, formal lending agencies often leave the poor unbanked (Hulme and Mosley 1996; Yunus 1999).

These are the logical foundations for the emergence of the concept of 'microfinance' for reaching the target population (Nair 2001). Microfinance was promoted in the 1980s as a response to doubts and research findings of the state of delivery of subsidized credit to poor farmers. Beginning in the mid-1980s, the subsidized targeted credit programs supported by many donor agencies were the object of steady criticism because most programs accumulated larger loan losses and required frequent recapitalization to continue operating (Von Pischke 1992; Gonzalez-Vega 1993). Failure of state-led subsidized credit program associated with increasing demand for small credit by microenterprises (due to increasing demand for low-cost goods and services produced by informal microenterprises) persuaded policy makers in some countries to reexamine their approach to the informal sector. This led to a new approach that considered microfinance as an integral part of the overall financial system and treated it as a market-based solution to the problem. Thus, emphasis shifted from the disbursement of subsidized loans to target populations toward the building up of local, sustainable institutions to serve the poor (Ledgerwood 1999; Robinson 2001).

3 Global Experience with Microfinance

Many countries across the world have established microfinance programs with the objective of reducing poverty by providing small amounts of credit to the poor to generate self-employment in income-earning activities. The group-based lending approach with small-scale microfinance programs provides microcredit rather than traditional financial institutions in rural areas (World Bank 1996).

Bangladesh is a leader among low-income countries offering microfinance among the poor households. Grameen Bank, founded in 1976 as a project and transformed into a specialized bank in 1983, is the best-known microfinance program in the world. By 1994, it had mobilized more than 2 million members, 94% of them being women, and had achieved a loan recovery rate of more than 95%. Grameen Bank's group-based lending approach is the guiding principle for more than 750 NGOs operating small-scale microfinance programs in Bangladesh. Two other large microfinance programs in Bangladesh are the Bangladesh Rural Advancement Committee (BRAC), with more than 1 million members, and the Rural Development Project-12 (RD-12) of the Bangladesh Rural Development Board (BRDB), with about 0.5 million members. BRAC is an NGO; RD-12 is a government program.

The success of Grameen Bank in recovering loans and lending to the poor without collateral has attracted worldwide attention. The group-based approach to lending is replicated in more than 45 countries, including the USA. Action International and Women's World Banking is working to expand microfinance programs in many countries. Different donor agencies, such as US Agency for International Development (USAID), International Fund for Agricultural Development (IFAD), Canadian International Development Agency (CIDA), and Swedish International Development Authority (SIDA), play major roles in the development of MFIs in many countries.

In 1995, the World Bank provided grant funding of $30 million to establish Consultative Group to Assist the Poorest (CGAP) fund of $100 million to directly support and spread microfinance programs in developing countries. The main task of CGAP is to strengthen microfinance programs by providing grants to support and extend banking to the poor. It also identifies best practices, develops guidelines for microfinance programs, and channels funds to poor, especially women, through microfinance activities. The World Bank is also financing microfinance programs directly, as well as indirectly, through various social fund projects (CGAP 1997; Khandker 1999).

By end 2013, about 280 million clients across the world were being serviced by about 7900 MFIs. India's share in the global microcredit market in 2013 was 17% of all clients and 19% of the poorest clients. India, thus, is home to one of the largest microfinance/microcredit programs in the world (World Bank Report).

4 Microfinance in India—Attempts and Major Events

The official involvement in informal group lending in India commenced during 1986–87 on the initiative of the NABARD. During 1986–87, the Mysore Resettlement and Development Agency (MYRADA) sponsored an action research project 'Savings and Credit Management of SHGs,' which was partially funded by NABARD. During 1988–89, in collaboration with some of the member institutions of the Asia-Pacific Rural and Agricultural Credit Association (APRACA), NABARD undertook a survey of 43 NGOs in 11 states in India with respect to the functioning of SHGs in microfinance activities and the collaboration possibilities with the formal financial institutions. Both the research projects revealed an encouraging experience about the linkage of SHGs with banks as a part of microfinance program, and NABARD responded by initiating a pilot project called the SHG-bank linkage project in 1992 (NABARD 1992; Satish 2005).

To initiate the pilot project, NABARD also held extensive consultation with Reserve Bank of India (RBI). In 1991, RBI issued a policy circular to all commercial banks to participate and extend finance to SHGs (RBI 1996). NABARD also issued a set of guidelines in February 1992, to the formal rural banking system for financing SHGs under the pilot project that aimed at financing 500 SHGs across the country through the banking system.

However, microfinancing by non-formal financial organizations had started in India much earlier than NABARD's involvement in this regard. The earliest step in microfinance in India was taken by Self-Employed Women's Association (SEWA) in 1975. SEWA, an association of women belonging to petty trade groups, was established on cooperative principle in 1974 in Gujarat. The main objective of SEWA was to provide banking services to the poor women employed in the unorganized sector of Ahmedabad. Shri Mahila SEWA Sahakari Bank was set up by registering it as an urban cooperative bank. Since then, the bank has been providing banking services to the poor and self-employed, working as hawkers, vendors, domestic servants, and so on. Similarly, in Tamil Nadu, Working Women's Forum (WWF), a cooperative society, started microfinancing among their members from 1980. A similar organization, Shreyas, in Kerala has been actively involved in microfinance operations since 1988. At the national level, some renowned NGOs also involved themselves in experimenting with the microfinance program, introducing the SHG approach. MYRADA mobilized multipurpose SHGs around group savings and introduced credit. PRADAN in its Madurai project formed women's SHGs with the objective of mobilizing saving and rotating this as a credit to group members, with the goal of eventually forming a community banking system. During the pilot project period, the Association of Sarva Seva Farms (ASSEFA) of Chennai promoted 214 groups; People's Rural Education Movement (PREM) of Odisha promoted 829 groups; PRADAN (Madurai) promoted 313 groups; and Community Development Society (CDS) of Kerala promoted 350 groups (RBI 1996).

Although all these microfinance activities were started during the 1980s and early 1990s, such initiative was extremely scattered over the country, and except few institutions (few NGOs and cooperatives), all suffered from considerable uncertainties and had projected, at best, an unclear picture about their microfinance activities. It is to the credit of NABARD for the first initiative to promote such a program with a clear objective. To implement the program successfully all over India, NABARD has provided extensive guidelines and policy support, both to MFIs and to the formal banking sector.

The policy interest in the whole concept of SHG-bank linkage was institutionalized with the RBI establishing in 1994 a working group of NGOs and SHGs comprising representatives from NABARD, bankers, and development practitioners. Encouraged by the success of SHG-bank linkage program launched by NABARD, the working group advocated some policy support and RBI, in 1996, issued the following policy: (i) lending to SHGs should be considered as a normal lending activity and the banks may consider lending to SHGs as part of their 'mainstream credit operations' both at policy and implementation levels; (ii) financing SHGs should be accepted as a separate segment under priority sector lending; (iii) lending to SHGs will be a part of the service area plan of a branch; (iv) SHGs may be allowed to open savings bank account with the bank branches; and (v) SHG lending, although unsecured, must remain outside the purview of non-performing asset (NPA) norms (RBI 1996).

The Government of India has also recognized the importance of the SHG-bank linkage program as an important instrument for delivery of financial services to the poor. In the Union Budget for 1999–2000, Finance Ministery announced the linkage of 50,000 SHGs by NABARD and SIDBI during the year. Further, as announced in the Union Budget for 2000–2001, NABARD has created a fund called 'Microfinance Development Fund' with an initial corpus of INR 100 crore with contributions from RBI, NABARD, banks, and other institutions. Besides these initiatives, Government of India has also launched a parallel microfinance scheme, namely Swarnajayanti Gram Swarozgar Yojana (SGSY) in 1999 (NABARD 2001; Sriram 2005).

Along with these policy supports, NABARD regularly takes different kinds of initiatives for up-scaling the SHG-bank linkage program. To increase the number of partner banks, NABARD has been conducting extensive awareness-generating programs for the bank officers. More and more NGOs are being encouraged to participate in the program, and NGOs having good past records are also being provided with grant assistance for the promotion and linkage of new SHGs (NABARD 2002; Brahmachary 2014).

As per the NABARD record, during 2015–2016 about 79.03 lakh SHGs had savings linked with banks and mobilized INR 13,691.39 crore throughout the country. Among these, 86% were women SHGs who mobilized about INR 12,035.78 crore with banks and other financial institutions. In the case of credit linkage, about 16.29 lakh women SHGs received loan of INR 34,411.42 crore from different formal financial institutions mainly from banks. Although all these credit or loans that have been given to the women SHGs do not flow for financing any formal business activity, always a significant amount of such loan has been used to finance various informal, unorganized petty businesses concentrated mainly in rural India. Thus, microfinance has opened an avenue to the rural unbanked poor to finance their small businesses for their livelihood from formal sources through alternative ways (Annual Report: NABARD 2016).

4.1 Women-Owned Small Businesses in India

Participation and Status

The Government of India has defined women businesses as an enterprise owned and controlled by women having a minimum financial interest of 51% of the capital and giving at least 51% of the employment generated in the enterprise to women (Goyal and Prakash 2011). According to Khanka (2012), 'Women Entrepreneurs are those women who think of a business enterprise, initiate it, organize and combine the factors of production, operate the enterprise and undertake risks and handle economic uncertainty involved in running a business enterprise.' According to Micro, Small, and Medium Enterprise Development (MSMED) Act, 2006, the MSMEs are divided into two classes, namely manufacturing enterprises and service enterprises. The limits of investment for manufacturing and service enterprises as specified by the Government of India are as follows:

Enterprise	Manufacturing sector (investment in plant and machinery)	Service sector (investment in equipment)
Micro-enterprise	Does not exceed INR 25 lakh	Does not exceed INR 10 lakh
Small enterprise	More than INR 25 lakh but less than INR 5 crore	More than INR 10 lakh but less than INR 2 crore
Medium enterprise	More than INR 5 crore but less than INR 10 crore	More than INR 2 crore but less than INR 5 crore

Source www.dcmsme.gov.in

However, women in India have to play multiple roles within the household (mother, wife, daughter, and so on), as well as in the community settings. As a result, sometimes they suffer from a dilemma whether entry to a business is merely a window to earn money for the family or it is a challenge to establish the self-worth and value within the society where males are dominating. Women with high education accept business activity as a challenge, whereas people with low or no education think of business as merely an earning potential for their family. Even women with the strong financial background do not always come forward to establish a business venture due to family obstacles, lack of ideas, inner strength and so on, whereas women with very little or no financial background are very keen to commence a business venture because they want to earn some money and gain self-worth. Here, some 'pull' and 'push' factors play a very crucial role (Kollan and Parikh 2005).

Although many social and economic factors are responsible for women participating in business activities, I have depicted only the major ones behind such decision through Fig. 1.

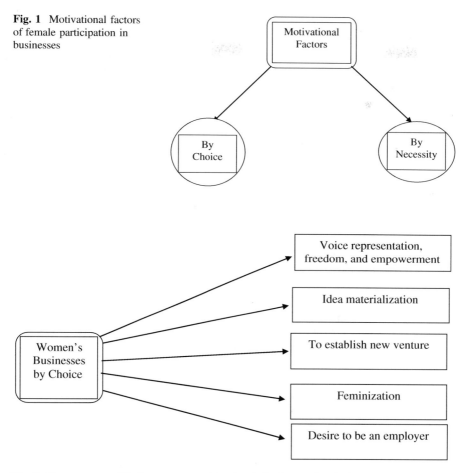

Fig. 1 Motivational factors of female participation in businesses

Fig. 2 Factors responsible for women participation in businesses by choice

In the twenty-first century, the educated woman are not willing to bind themselves within the household activities only. Researchers found different factors that encourage woman to set up new business venture or to participate in the existing family business. The major motivational factors that are responsible to influence woman to join in the businesses are of two types—business by choice and business by necessity (Schumpeter 1950). Both the factors have explained briefly in Fig. 2.

Most of the women are willing to join in business by choice due to the five major factors mentioned earlier (Fig. 2). Educated woman have own voice and, therefore, always try to transform their ideas into capital formation. They find themselves more suitable as an employer rather than a mere employee. Their objective is to establish a valued self-worth within the family and society and to carry forward this moral value over generations. Researchers well found that successful entrepreneurship very much depends on the series of succession over generations. That is, the ownership shifts from father or mother to son or daughter to grandson or granddaughter, and so on. If anybody is absent in a generation (i.e., no inheritance at all) in the series, then the harmony may break. This is true for small or medium enterprises. In the case of large firms, rivals come forward to take over the zero-inheritance firm and try to run the business under own ideas and capacity.

However, the majority of the women who fall in this category are usually from affluent section of the society. Most of them have strong financial background or have channels and ideas to accumulate capital for the new project and are capable of transforming ideas into capital formation or output production through high education and management skills to mobilize inputs properly. The successes of businesses guided by these types of women are comparatively higher than others due to such positive factors.

The determining factors that make women to become a business woman due to necessity are shown in Fig. 3. There are many socioeconomic factors by which woman are motivated to participate in businesses due to necessity. Due to poor economic conditions of the family, sometimes woman are motivated to set up a small business. They also cooperate with their husband or family members to establish a new business setup to overcome the financial crisis. In India, such initiatives have been well observed in SHG-based microfinance programs. Here, women form a group and set up a small business form different small setup (such as animal husbandry, fishery, weaving industry, and so on) to earn some money usually spent on the well-being of the family instead of self-consumption. Although all these activities are very small and the capital generation from such activities is negligible, they a great value for employment generation.

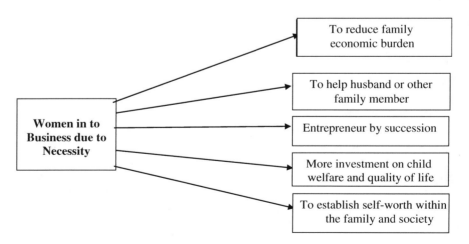

Fig. 3 Determinating factors of women participation in businesses due to necessity

Unfortunately, the poor always suffer from diverse financial crunch, low or no education, and various family and social bottlenecks. Since quality employment requires high education and technical or managerial skills, most of these women fail to get good employment and, therefore, find way to participate in small business activities as a good alternative to earn some money. Microfinance program mainly focuses on these types of women to provide small finance and other services.

However, there is a big question about the long-term sustainability of such ventures. Most of these businesses are set up under the umbrella of government or some other financial agencies and motivated only by the self-interest. Some researchers believe that it is a waste of social capital and, therefore, the governments should stop the supply-based pro-poor microfinance lending program for such businesses immediately. However, various studies are under way to track all such unpalatable issues related to the microfinance programs which requires specific, focused attention, and research.

5 Major Problems of Women-Owned Small Businesses in India

Running a business is not easy. Researchers opine that the path which a business follows from incubation to the maturity stage is not a step-by-step journey. It is a complex journey where problems may overlap and experience tells that most of the start-ups have to pass this road with high managerial efficiency. Although in practice, the same process is followed by both men and women, there are many problems which are being faced specifically by business woman in India. The major problems are discussed in the following paragraphs (Dangi and Ritika 2014; Goyal and Prakash 2011; Mahajan 2013):

(A) *Gender Bias and Male Dominancy in the Society*

Gender bias is a serious problem throughout the world and is also prevailing significantly in India where the mind-set of most people is backward and risk averse. They think business is not suitable for women since it requires large mobility outside the home or village/town and the woman has to work with men who come from diverse strata. They think women are best suited to only the household activities and, therefore, compel them to stay within that limit (Vossenberg 2013).

(B) *Conflict between Dual Liabilities (Household and Workplace)*

Working women always have to balance their duties between workplace and households. On the one hand, they have to perform their mandatory duties in the workplace, and on the other hand, they look after the welfare of the household simultaneously. Even in the twenty-first-century globalization era, the educated families still believe that women are more suited to the household activities and, therefore, they try to find out only those types of employments where they can balance both the domestic and work liabilities simultaneously.

Unfortunately, a businessperson cannot bind his or her working hours within a time limit like a government or other organized-sector employee. As a result, women are increasingly discouraged from participating in a business activity on the assumption that it may hamper their household duties. They are strongly restricted to stay within the household or compelled to join only in those activities where they can perform their domestic activities very well.

(C) *Inadequate Financial Resources and Working Capital*

Developing countries like India usually suffer from the capital crisis and, therefore, experience a slow growth of business. The crisis is more serious for business woman. It is believed that due to complex inheritance laws and social psychology, most of the financiers are not willing to give a loan to women-owned businesses and therefore, suffer these businesses from working capital crunch. Moreover, the problem exaggerates among the low-educated zero-collateral-based business woman who usually have no access to formal financial resources, such as banks, and are totally dependent on informal sources for their financial needs. Few women having strong recommendations (political or administrative) may avail some financial support from the formal sources for their business.

(D) *Lack of Proper Education and Managerial Skills*

Proper education is very important for a successful business. Unfortunately, except few cases, most of the poor women undertake business due to necessity and usually have very low level of education. Even if they have some education, it may not be suitable for their business. Thus, the improper or low level of education and lack of managerial skills emerge as a major problem for women-owned businesses in India.

Apart from these problems, lower mobility of women outside home, lack of family support, particularly the male support, obsolete social customs, inability to take risks in businesses, improper knowledge about marketing of the products, inability to face market competition, and so on, are the other notable problems faced by business woman in India.

All these problems are of very serious concern to the policy makers, since the nature and magnitude of such problems are quite different and overlapping across various women-owned businesses. Some of the issues as stated earlier, such as financial problem, lack of managerial skills, and improper knowledge about marketing may be addressed with adequate policy support (if possible), but prejudice, psychological factors, social restrictions, male dominance within the society,

Microfinance for Women-Owned Small Business in India … 143

improper education, and so on, cannot be addressed promptly at will. A long-term all-round effort along with enough capacity-building programs is needed to address all these issues successfully. In India, government and some other private agencies are trying to address some of these issues, in particular, the financial issues very seriously to accelerate the growth of women-owned businesses in the country and for this purpose offer different supportive measures in different strata of the society at local, regional, and national levels.

6 Financing Women-Owned Businesses in India

Funding is the oxygen of a business. Researchers found that gender bias is a big issue in accessing capital. Women entrepreneurs are less funded than their male counterparts. Financiers believe that women-led lead businesses are often controlled by one person and, therefore, do not have the high growth potential resulting in less or no funding to the women enterprises. In India, a large number of women fail to access the formal finance due to the asymmetric information about their credit worthiness. Usually, banks and non-banking financial institutions initially judge the credit worthiness of the borrower before deciding the approval of any loans. Unfortunately, due to zero collateral and lack of family support, these institutions are less interested in women-owned businesses. Even if they have some good quality collateral, banks often investigate about the management of the business, and if it is found that no family or male support is present, they forthwith reject their loan application. In addition, if they find that male family members are present in the management of the business, they inquire about the creditworthiness of those male members also assuming that the male members are actually operating the business behind female face and that for the easy and prompt loan approval under the women-centric policies, female members have been made to apply for that loan. If any information is unfavorable in this process, the women applicant fails to receive the loan. Thus, due to zero collateral, asymmetric information about the creditworthiness of the female applicants, and lack of male presence in the business management, the formal financial institutions, such as banks, often refuse to supply finance to business woman (Vossenberg 2013; Siddiqui 2012). At this juncture, microfinance, however, has made an attempt to bridge such gap in Indian context and tried to provide formal financial support to the women-owned small enterprises in the country.

In India, nearly 78% of women enterprises belong to the service sector that contributed 3.09% of total output and 8 million employments in 2012 (IFC 2014). Most of these enterprises are categorically small or micro in nature. The financial requirement for all these enterprises together was about INR 8.68 trillion in 2012, and unfortunately, 90% of these financial requirements were met through informal sources (Tables 1 and 2).

The study conducted by International Finance Corporation (IFC) on women-owned MSMEs in India found that there is a significant gap between

Table 1 Demand for financing from women-owned MSMEs, 2012

Type	Financing demand from formal sector (INR in trillion)	Financing demand from informal sector (INR in trillion)
Micro	0.19	1.86
Small	3.91	2.50
Medium	0.21	0.00
Total	4.31	4.37

Source IFC Report, 2014

Table 2 Sources of finance of women-owned enterprises (MSMEs), 2012

Financial sources	Percentage share
Formal financial institutions	3.1
Semi-formal financial institutions	4.8
Informal institutions	92.1

Source IFC Report, 2014, State Level Bankers Committee Report, 2012

demand and supply of financing for women enterprises and, therefore, women relied heavily on informal sources, such as family, friends, and professional moneylenders to meet the seed money and working capital requirements.

The study identified some demand- and supply-side constraints to access finance for women entrepreneurs:

(A) **Demand-Side Constraints**

(1) *Lack of Adequate Collateral against Loan*

The lack of collateral, specifically for women MSMEs, arises mainly from social and legal restrictions on inheritance and landownership rights. Even though the loan is sanctioned to a woman, often it requires the signature of husband or father to approve the loan application. Sometimes, they fail to manage such signature to approve the loan due to the non-cooperation of these family members.

(2) *Lack of Financial Awareness*

Low level of financial literacy and lack of awareness about available financial options puts a further constraint to access finance by women from formal channels. Poor financial literacy contributes low financial management and less confidence of the women to cope with formal financial institutions. At present, with the rapid introduction of information and communication technology (ICT) in the financial sector in India, the nature of services of banks and other financial institutions have changed drastically. To avail such ICT-based products and services, some ICT knowledge and good financial awareness among the beneficiaries are required which are absent among low-educated unbanked women.

Microfinance for Women-Owned Small Business in India …

(3) *Lack of understanding of financial Products/Services*

Due to lack of proper financial awareness and knowledge, women fail to understand properly about the available financial resources, the cost and benefit of such financial options, the proper channel to avail such services, and so on. Besides, they fail to understand which financial products are suitable for their business and what are the major conditions associated with such loan products. Thus, poor financial literacy and lack of confidence to approach formal financial institutions put some restrictions on women to access the formal financial products/services.

(4) *Lack of family support particularly from male members*

As stated earlier, banks and financial institutions often inquire whether male or family support for a woman-led business is present. They assume that male participation in any business contributes better success and hence better loan repayment. For this reason, most of the banks require the signature of husband or father/brother (for unmarried women) to ensure that there is a male support in the business. Failing such requirements, the loan application of women entrepreneur may be rejected.

(B) **Supply-Side Constraints**

(1) *High-risk investment to the finance due to absence of collateral*

On the supply side, most of the finance suppliers believe that investment on women-owned ventures is very risky due to the lack of adequate and transparent collateral. Some institutions think lending to unmarried women is very risky as they could change the locality and profession after marriage and thereby entailing a very high probability of loan defaults. For married woman, though such problem does not arise since they get both the assets of their father and husband simultaneously due to the inheritance law in India, still the finance suppliers do not think these as a good collateral and, therefore, put a large margin against such loans resulting in a very low or inadequate financing of the business. Besides, they believe that women enterprises are operating mostly in the informal sector and usually are of micro nature and therefore less creditworthy than male-operated MSMEs.

(2) *High-risk group due to lack of any guarantee or support by male family members*

Banks think that women solely cannot run a successful business without the male support and, therefore, leave the business unbanked if any male or family support is not there. Usually, throughout the world, finance to single women entrepreneurs is considered as a risky investment due to lack of any guarantee or support by male members and, therefore, often require male support/guarantees to offset the risk of any future loan default.

(3) *High transaction cost for women-owned enterprises*

The high transaction cost of women-owned enterprises is also a serious problem to the formal financial institutions. It is estimated by IFC (2014) that the average finance needs of male-owned enterprises are 2.4 times higher than those of women-owned enterprises, which indicate that the finance needs of women enterprises are below average due to its small volume of business as compared to male-owned businesses. As the administrative and serving cost, processing fees, and another cost of sanctioning a loan is more or less similar irrespective of the size of the loan, banks frequently tend to focus on large loan demands leaving most of the women applicants out, since their loan demand is very small.

(4) *Women enterprises are less attractive due to lack of reliable information about their financial management and strength*

Asymmetric information about women's creditworthiness is a very serious concern to the supplier of finance. Due to lack of reliable information about the financial management and strength of the women-led businesses, most formal financial institutions often refuse to provide financial services to these business activities. Besides, banks have very limited knowledge about the financial management of women enterprises, since they do not maintain the necessary financial documents in proper format, and usually, the women loan applicants interact with banks through the third party (say, local political leaders, local club members, and so on). In these circumstances, the bank fails to assess the actual creditworthiness of the enterprise and therefore, is reluctant to finance these ventures.

(5) *Bank loans are not often suited for the needs of women enterprise*

Besides, although different agencies offer specific finance schemes for women-owned MSMEs, most of them are inadequate in respect of total demand, and supply only in some specific geographical locations. In other areas, such products/services are not available, and if available, are not always suitable for women's business needs. In such circumstances, they often meet their demand from informal sources such as professional moneylenders, friends, and relatives at a very high rate of interest.

The supply–demand gap of finance in India for women MSMEs (as on 2012) as estimated by IFC is depicted in Table 3. The table shows that in 2012 there was 73.40% of total finance gap (INR 6.37 trillion) for women-owned enterprises in India. The gap is more prominent for small enterprises (78.30%) followed by micro (20.40%) and medium enterprises (1.30%). The picture indicates that women-owned MSMEs may open a wide business opportunity to Indian formal and semi-formal financial institutions.

The source of the supply of formal finance for women enterprises as estimated by IFC in their report (2014) is depicted in Table 4. The total supply of finance from formal sources for women-owned MSMEs was about INR 2.31 trillion in India on 2012, and Table 4 indicates that public sector banks supplied about 68% of total finance of formal institutions.

Microfinance for Women-Owned Small Business in India ... 147

Table 3 Supply–demand gap of finance of women MSMEs as on 2012

	Total finance demand (INR in trillion)	Total finance supply (INR in trillion)	Gap (INR in trillion)	Percentage share of total gap
Micro	2.05	0.76	1.30	20.40
Small	6.42	1.43	4.99	78.30
Medium	0.21	0.13	0.08	1.30
Total	8.68	2.32	6.37	100.00

Source IFC report, 2014

Table 4 Formal source of the supply of finance of women-owned MSMEs (2012)

Sources	Share of total formal finance supplied (%)
Public sector banks through microfinance, SHGs	30
Public sector banks directly to MSMEs	38
Prime Minister's Rozgar Yojana	2
Swarnajayanti Shahari Rozgar Yojana	1
Swarnajayanti Gram Swarozgar Yojana	4
Private sector banks	19
Other institutions, say foreign banks, and so on	5

Source IFC report, 2014

6.1 Major Financing Program for Women MSMEs

To encourage women-owned businesses in India and greater participation of financial sector for women-owned MSMEs to address the finance gap as stated earlier, the Government of India has announced different schemes through multiple agencies. Apart from the usual microfinance program, some other finance programs led by different agencies are explained in the following paragraphs.

(A) TREAD Scheme

Trade Related Entrepreneurship Assistance and Development (TREAD) Scheme for women is a popular subsidized scheme in India provided by the Ministry of Micro, Small, and Medium Enterprises, Government of India, to provide better financial access by women. NGOs are the implementing agencies to lend fund to women entrepreneurs. The government provides a subsidy of up to 30% of the total project cost as grant and the remaining 70% by the appraising institutions. Women who have no easy access to credit from banks due to their cumbersome procedures and are unable to fulfill the collateral demand by the bank against their loan application are eligible to get such subsidized loan from the government. Further, the request for subsidy under this scheme must be made by an NGO.

(B) *Bharatiya Mahila Bank*

The Government of India planned to open a full-fledged women's public sector bank for the greater financial inclusion of women and formed the Bharatiya Mahila Bank in 2013. The bank had a target to have 25 branches by March 2014, and currently, the bank has 45 branches across India. The bank focuses mainly on women entrepreneurship with special attention to empowering economically and socially deprived aspirant women who remain unbanked due to multidimensional social problems. Some of the popular loans provided by Bharatiya Mahila Bank for business women are as follows: BMB Shringaar (collateral-free loan of up to INR 1 crore for beauty parlor/saloon/spa or related businesses for a term up to 7 years); BMB Annapurna (loan for food business, collateral free, up to INR 1 crore for a term of up to 3 years); BMB Parvarish (loan for day care centre—collateral free, up to INR 1 crore for a term of up to 5 years); and so on.

(C) *Mahila Coir Yojana*

It is a subsidized scheme aimed to provide self-employment for women artisans in regions where coir fiber is produced. Conversion of coir fiber into yarn on motorized ratts in the household generates significant employment and income in the regions. The scheme is designed to distribute motorized ratts among women artisans at a subsidized rate through NGOs or other organizations.

(D) *Entrepreneurship Development Program (EDP)*

Time to time government announces entrepreneurship development programs, especially for the first generation of women who are willing to be an entrepreneur. Mainly, there are four important institutes that were designed to offer training and skill development, namely National Institute of MSME, Hyderabad; National Institute of Entrepreneurship and Small Business Development, Noida; Indian Institute of Entrepreneurship, Guwahati; and National Small Industries Corporation, New Delhi.

(E) *Schemes Offered by Banks*

Along with the government scheme as stated earlier, almost all the public sector banks in India have designed different loan products especially for women businesses at a discounted rates. Some of the popular schemes under such category are (IFC 2014; Official Website of Banks) as follows:

   i. Mutual Credit Guarantee Scheme—Andhra Bank
   ii. Akshaya Mahila Arthik Sahay Yojana—Bank of Baroda
   iii. Cent Kalyani—Central Bank
   iv. Dena Shakti Scheme for Women Entrepreneurs—Dena Bank
   v. Schemes for Professional & Self-Employed Women—Oriental Bank of Commerce
   vi. Orient Mahila Vikas Yojana—Oriental Bank of Commerce

vii. Priyadarshini Yojana—Bank of India
viii. Udyogini Scheme—Punjab and Sindh Bank
ix. Stree Shakti Package for Women Entrepreneur—State Bank of India
x. Marketing Fund for Women—Small Industries Development Bank of India
xi. Annapurna Scheme for Financing Women—State Bank of Mysore
xii. Mahila Vikas Scheme—State Bank of Travancore
xiii. Special Benefits for Women Entrepreneurs in MSMEs—Canara Bank

(F) *Other General Finance Scheme for Women Businesses and Empowerment*

Time to time different government schemes were operated by different ministries and departments to empower the women in India. Although all these schemes are not designed especially for financing women entrepreneurs, the main focus of these programs is to empower Indian women through their socioeconomic upliftment. Some of the flagship programs under different ministries designed for women empowerment are (Goyal and Praksh 2011; various department websites)

i. Integrated Rural Development Program (IRDP)
ii. Khadi and Village Industries Commission (KVIC)
iii. Training of Rural Youth for Self-Employment (TRYSEM)
iv. Prime Minister's Rozgar Yojana (PMRY)
v. Management Development Program (MDP)
vi. Women's Development Corporations (WDCs)
vii. Marketing of Non-Farm Products of Rural Women (MAHIMA)
viii. Assistance to Rural Women in Non-Farm Development (ARWIND) schemes
ix. Working Women's Forum
x. Indira Mahila Yojana
xi. Mahila Samiti Yojana
xii. Rashtriya Mahila Kosh (RMK)
xiii. SIDBI's Mahila Udyam Nidhi
xiv. Micro and Small Enterprises Cluster Development Program (MSE-CDP).
xv. National Banks for Agriculture and Rural Development's (NABARD) Schemes
xvi. Rajiv Gandhi Mahila Vikas Pariyojana (RGMVP)
xvii. Self-Employed Women Association (SEWA) Bank project

(G) *Microfinance and MSMEs*

As stated in Sect. 4, microfinance program in India has evolved as a good alternative of formal finance for unbanked poor, especially women. Currently, the microfinance programs by various agencies provide a significant formal finance to women-owned businesses as seed capital. As per IFC Report (2014), about 85 million women primarily availed loans for income-generating activities in India in 2012. The Government of India microfinance scheme, namely Swarnajayanti Gram/Shahari Rozgar Yojana, has been recognized as one of the flagship pro-poor finance schemes in the country/world to provide small loans to women for their businesses.

All such microfinance programs can effectively serve the finance need of tiny enterprises only, which have not much potential for employment generation and gross domestic product (GDP) growth of the country as compared to MSMEs, but they go a long way in empowering poor women. The usual microfinance program in India provides seed and working capital only to the tiny home-based business activities and usually leaves the MSMEs out due to their high credit requirements. As stated earlier, the microfinance using SHG mechanism innovatively addresses the problem to access to formal finance by the poor minimizing the information and collateral gap. The SHG-bank linkage program helps the financer to provide a formal loan to the collateral-less business women minimizing the transaction cost associated with loan disbursement and good repayment history due to peer pressure within the group members.

Since it has a great potential to provide formal loan among the zero-collateral unbanked poor people minimizing various problems of formal finance supply, the present restricted view of microfinance to provide loan only for tiny home-based women-owned businesses should be extended by providing adequate loan to women-owned MSMEs. In fact, various MFIs have already started to serve such loans for women-run MSMEs, but due to capital shortage, such initiatives have not been accelerated in India under the umbrella of microfinance.

7 Conclusions

The announcement of liberalization policy in 1991 and 1995 and its effects on the different sectors have started to be felt in India from the first decade of the twenty-first century. From this time on, with the rapid globalization effect all over the world, Indian women started to think about small start-ups as employment opportunities. However, such thinking had mainly remained concentrated among the affluent sections of the society, who started a new business by choice, not by necessity. By the same time, a large number of poor low-educated women were compelled to enter into different, mostly informal, business activities due to shear necessity and faced multiple problems. Although all the problems that are usually faced by women-owned small businesses in India are of serious concerns to every policy maker, in this chapter, I have concentrated mainly on the financial issues related to the women businesses since finance is the oxygen of any business venture, irrespective of its volume and nature.

Policy design should account for this financing problem as a major issue. Although formal financial institutions may offer some good solutions to overcome the finance problem of women-owned businesses, they frequently leave these people unbanked due to the asymmetric information about their creditworthiness, absence of collateral, and lack of family support. Microfinance through SHGs provide some solution in this regard to provide small formal finance to these unbanked business enterprises. Using the 'peer pressure' within the SHG lending mechanism, the microfinance program gives a 'market signal' to the formal lender to offer loan and other financial services to the small borrowers. Unfortunately, the supply of finance under such mechanism of microfinance program is still very low as compared to total demand and, therefore, requires direct intervention of the formal agencies with a bundle of services in adequate volume.

Better quality credit, comprehensive banking relationship, information supply about available financial products and opportunities, and so on, are the predominant factors for a successful business. Furthermore, the financial institutions have to realize the specific problems faced by women in India and should design flexible finance products for them only. From numerous studies, it is revealed that the loan repayment performances of women are far better than men. Therefore, banks should not leave unbanked these potential customers just due to various ill-founded apprehensions (such as property rights, inheritances, and so on) or non-cooperation from male family members as stated earlier.

Also, the government should offer an environment where women can voice their needs and concerns prominently without facing any discrimination. Proper implementation of laws of equal rights on the property, simplification and flexibility of collateral needs, understanding women's status, personality development, friendly work environment, infrastructure development, proper marketing of the products, and so on, should be the prime focus of the government to accelerate successful women business activities. Besides, the present microfinance programs in India mainly focus on tiny home-based earning activities leaving the MSMEs out of their ambit due to their high demand for credit. The government should look into this area specifically, and should provide an adequate fund to the MFIs so that they can adequately finance MSMEs, which have a significant potential to contribute to employment generation and GDP of the country. Initiative to build up a risk capital fund for women and specific support from financial institutions may further enhance the environment to become more healthy and friendly toward women enterprises in the country.

References

Brahmachary, A. 2014. For a better world: Livelihood security measurement of the SHG members. Paper published in the edited book entitled 'Microfinance, Risk-taking Behaviour and Rural Livelihood', ed. Amit K. Bhandari and Kundu, Ashok. Springer. ISBN: 978-81-322-1283-6.

CGAP. 1997. Consultative group to assist the poorest. A Review of the World Bank's Microfinance Portfolio FY 91–FY 96. Washington, D.C.: World Bank.

Dangi, N. 2014. Women entrepreneurship and growth and performance of MSMEs in India. *International Journal of Advanced Research in Computer Science and Management Studies* 2 (4). ISSN: 2321-7782 (Online).

Gonzalez-Vega, C. 1993. From policies to technologies, to organisations: The evolution of the Ohio State University vision of rural financial markets. Economics and Sociology Occasional Paper 2062, Ohio State University, Rural Finance Programme, Columbus.

Goyal, M., and Jai Prakash. 2011. Women entrepreneurship in India—problems and prospects. *International Journal of Multidisciplinary Research* 1(5). ISSN: 2231-5780

Hulme, D., and P. Mosley. 1996. *Finance against poverty Vol. 1 and 2.* London: Routledge Publications.

IFC. 2014. International Finance Corporation (World Bank Group) Report, 2014: Improving Access to Finance for Women-owned Businesses in India, 2014.

ILO. 2004. Economic security for a better world. *International Labour Organisation*, 2004, Geneva.

Kollan, B., and Indira J. Parikh. 2005. A reflection of the Indian women in entrepreneurial world. Working Paper No.: 2005-08-07, August, 2005, IIM, Ahmedabad.

Khandker, S.R. 1999. *Fighting poverty with microcredit: Experience in Bangladesh.* Dhaka, Bangladesh: The University Press Limited.

Khanka, S.S. 2012. *Entrepreneurial development.* S. Chand & Company Ltd.

Ledgerwood, J. 1999. *Microfinance handbook: An institutional and financial perspective, sustainable banking with the poor.* Washington, D.C.: The World Bank.

Mahajan, S. 2013. Women entrepreneurship in India. *Global Journal of Management and Business Studies* 3(10): 1143–1148. ISSN: 2248-9878.

Mitra, R. 2002. The growth patterns of women run enterprises: An empirical study in India. *Journal of Developmental Entrepreneurship* 7(2): 217–237.

NABARD. 1992. Guidelines for Pilot project for linking banks with SHGs. *National Bank for Agricultural and Rural Development*, 1992, Bombay.

NABARD. 2001. Report of the expert committee on rural credit (Chairman V. S. Vyas), National Bank for Agricultural and Rural Development, Mumbai.

NABARD. 2002. *Ten years of SHG-bank linkage: 1992–2002.* Mumbai: NABARD and Microfinance.

NABARD. 2016. *Annual Report 2015–2016.* Mumbai: National Bank for Agricultural and Rural Development.

Nair, T.S. 2001. Institutionalising microfinance in India: An overview of strategic issues. *Economic and Political Weekly*, 27 Jan 2001.

RBI. 1996. *Linking of self-help groups with banks: Working group on NGOs and SHGs—recommendations—follow up.* Mumbai: Reserve Bank of India.

Robinson, S.M. 2001. *The microfinance revolution: Sustainable finance for the poor.* Washington, D.C.: The World Bank.

Schumpeter, J. 1950. *Capitalism, socialism and democracy.* New York: Harper and Row.

Satish, P. 2005. Mainstreaming of Indian Microfinance. *Economic and Political Weekly* XL(17).

Siddiqui, A.B. 2012. Problems encountered by women entrepreneurs in India. *International Journal of Applied Research and Studies* 1(II), Sept–Nov, 2012. ISSN: 2278–9480.

Sriram, M.S. 2005. Microfinance and the State: Exploring areas and Structures of Collaboration. *Economic and Political Weekly* XL(17).

Von Pischke, J.D. 1992. *Finance at the frontier—debt capacity and the role of credit in the private economy.* The World Bank, Washington, D.C., U.S.A (EDI Seminar Series).

Vossenberg, S. 2013. Women entrepreneurship promotion in developing countries: What explains the gender gap in entrepreneurship and how to close it? Working Paper No: 2013/08, Netherlands: Maastricht School of Management.

World Bank. 1996. Bangladesh: Poverty alleviation microfinance project. Staff Appraisal Report, South Asia Region, Country Department I, Private Sector Development and Finance Division, Washington, D.C.

Yaron, J., M. Benjamin, and G.L. Piprek. 1997. *Rural finance: Issues, design and best practices, ESD Monograph 14.* Washington, D.C.: World Bank.

Yunus, M. 1999. *Banker to the poor—micro-lending and the battle against world poverty.* New York: Pacific Affairs.

Websites

(i) www.epw.org.
(ii) www.nabard.org.
(iii) www.rbi.org.
(iv) www.worldbank.org.
(v) www.msme.gov.in.
(vi) www.dcmsme.gov.in.
(vii) www.ifc.org.

Part III
Microfinance and Women Entrepreneurship

Going Through the New Avenue of Life: A Study on Factors Working Behind Entrepreneurship Development Through Self-Help Group

Kallol Das

1 Introduction

The role of women as the backbone of the family and society is greatly acknowledged, but when it comes to power, participation, access, and reward, she is discriminated and her voice is suppressed. Since independence, women's development has undergone a significant transition from welfare to development to empowerment through various five-year plans. Policy makers understand that, unless and until women are involved in the development activities, the ultimate objectives of the program will not be fulfilled. In patriarchal culture, women are being denied access to social and economic decision making in the family and community. Particularly, the aspect of economic decision making is the domain area of the male members of the family, and women are being considered as indoor beings. Hence, women constitute the most vulnerable group of the society affected by poverty and other social discrimination. In this context, SHGs are envisaged as an important tool to alleviate poverty and also improve the quality of life on 'self-reliant' basis.

Self-help group (SHG) is an important mechanism for grassroots programs that try to bring about positive change by working directly with the poor women. Essentially, SHG is a socially and economically homogenous group of 10–20 poor people coming together to bring a positive change in their life by solving the problems through their collective strength. Mainly, it has three-faced objectives, namely social empowerment, political empowerment, and financial empowerment. It has emerged as the most effective teamwork strategy, working closely with the community and people. SHGs can be considered as the agents of diffusion of innovation through awareness creation and capacity building of the members. Awareness creation is an essential component of behavior change, which leads to sustainable development.

K. Das (✉)
Ambuja Cement Foundation, Howrah, West Bengal, India
e-mail: kallolpck@gmail.com

© Springer Nature Singapore Pte Ltd. 2017
C. Neogi et al. (eds.), *Women's Entrepreneurship and Microfinance*,
DOI 10.1007/978-981-10-4268-3_9

Until recently, the development agencies focused on the 'top-down' approach to sort out the problems of the poor but were unable to achieve the goal, and therefore, replaced it with the 'bottom-up' approach, which means, to give importance to the people and their ideas, values, and experiences by involving them as stakeholders of the development process right from the beginning. It serves the purpose of making women self-confident and empowered by involving them through SHG. It boosts the confidence of the members and makes them capable of taking economic opportunity through utilization of local resources in a productive manner. Hence, SHG is giving them a platform to raise their voice and come to the forefront of the society through their activities.

It is a fact that initially most of the SHG members did not know the objectives of formation of groups. External agencies and resource persons came and motivated them to be a member of the group by saying that they can lead a better life if they get involved in the SHGs. However, due to lack of education and communication they did not understand what the benefits are and how they will get the benefits. As a result, at times it was found that numbers of groups broke away for several reasons. Nevertheless, few groups have been running very smoothly and gradually these existing SHGs are taking a right turn toward income-generating path and earning money by taking up different income-generating activities. On the other hand, few groups are unable to run their businesses due to several reasons: inadequate managerial skills, inability to identify the potential of the members, lack of education, lack of trust, and so on.

Hence, considering the ground facts, specific objectives of this study are to see the factors behind successfully running businesses and also try to understand the factors that hinder other groups to smoothly run their businesses. Another objective of this chapter is to see how SHGs help members change their life in a positive manner.

2 Study Area and Methods

To carry out this study, six SHGs have been taken purposively from Labpur block of Birbhum district, West Bengal. Labpur village is a semi-urban area which is considered as the business center of Labpur block, having immense opportunity of growth and development. Hence, Labpur block has been taken for study. For the purpose of this study, six SHGs who have been involved in the microentrepreneurial activities have been taken, of which four groups are successfully running their business and the other two groups have either stopped their business, or are gasping for breath. A total of 74 women members are taken for study from these six groups. Among these women under the study, 52.70% belong to the unscheduled or upper caste category, called general category (GC), and 47.30% are from other than GC caste communities. Moreover, 77% of the members live below poverty line.

Women face several kinds of a hindrances, starting from their own families. In a patriarchal society, male members are supreme power holders and take all necessary decisions regarding family and economy, as well as those related to the movement of the women members of the families. More recently, it is observed that despite several kinds of obstructions, women do go out and participate in the development activities. Therefore, keeping in view the importance of the study on women empowerment, this study focuses on how women are going out and what are the factors working behind their getting involved in the microentrepreneurial activities and running their businesses successfully. For this purpose, primary data have been collected from SHG members and other stakeholders through interviews, focused group discussions, key informants' interviews, and participatory observation. Apart from the primary sources, the secondary data have been collected from various reports and government offices.

3 Entrepreneurship Development Through Self-Help Groups

SHGs show a unique way to financial intermediation. The approach combines access of local resources through low-cost financial services with a process of skill development and self-management of the SHG members. It promotes the quality of life by reducing rural poverty as well as exploring the female human capital. Status of an individual is directly related to income-generating capacities of that individual; as women are low-paid labors or are unpaid workers in their family, their activities are considered as unproductive. As a result, their status is inferior compared to male members of the society. In these circumstances, SHGs are giving them an opportunity to become economically independent and enhance their knowledge and skills for further development. Entrepreneurship on a small scale is the solution to the problems of unemployment and ensures economic growth and development in a balanced manner. Hence, encouragement of small-scale business has been recognized as an important strategy for economic empowerment of women. It helps to boost up women's confidence, skills, and socioeconomic status. As a result, gradually they are gaining a higher value with in their family and in the society (Basin 2000).

It is found that women are comparatively more emotionally attached to their families; hence, they are more responsible and better connected with their families. Due to lack of opportunities in rural areas, it is observed that most of the husbands either give a small amount of money to their wives for maintaining their families or squander their earned money on alcohol and gambling. Hence, it becomes very difficult for women to maintain their families and to rear their children. In these circumstances, women's earning through involvement in the microentrepreneurial activities shows them a ray of hope to lead a better life. It is also observed that most of the women members who earn money through microenterprise have to complete their

160   K. Das

Table 1 Information related to financial activities run by the SHG members

SHG		Types of business	Buyers
Successful SHGs	SHG-1	*Bori* making (globule), *Papad* making, and *Archar* making (pickle)	Villagers and peddlers
	SHG-2	Spices processing, poultry keeping	Villagers, retailers, and brokers
	SHG-3	Puffed rice making and supply food to the block hospital (lunch and dinner)	Villagers, retailers, and government hospital
	SHG-4	Poultry keeping, embroidery, and tailoring (especially school dressmaking)	Brokers and local schools
Unsuccessful SHGs	SHG-5	Rice making	Producing on demand
	SHG-6	Embroidery and *dhoopkathi* making (incense sticks making)	Not producing round the year

Source Primary data collected from the members

familial responsibilities, such as cooking, washing utensils, cleaning the house, maintaining their children, and caring the older persons, before they are allowed to go out for their business. Therefore, these women are efficient managers; they balance their dual role, managing their life as housewives and as business women (Table 1).

4   Results and Discussions

As stated earlier, among the studied SHGs, four SHGs are running their businesses very successfully, and the other two are unable to run their enterprises. It is found that successful SHGs choose such kind of business for which raw material is locally available and has a demand for the whole year. On the other hand, unsuccessful SHGs are producing such kind of things that do not have demand in the local market. This is also noticed that all four successful SHGs are producing more than one product; if one product has a lack of demand, another product will compensate the loss from first product. However, in the case of unsuccessful SHGs, it is found that they are producing or involved in only one kind of business. It is also observed that successful SHGs make a profit-and-loss statement every month, and take a portion of the profits out and keep it separately for emergency purposes before divide the rest of the profit among the members.

It is found from Table 2 that the average age of the successful SHGs is comparatively lower than unsuccessful SHGs. It is also critically observed that in the first four groups, the strength of GC members more in comparison with the last two groups, whereas in the last two groups, majority of the members belong to castes other than GC. It is also depicted in the table that a high percentage of members come from nuclear families in case of successful SHGs, whereas in the case of unsuccessful SHGs, most of the members are from joint families.

Going Through the New Avenue of Life …

Table 2 Demographic information of the members

SHGs		Number of members	Average age of the members (years)	Marital status (%)		Social identity (%)		Children below 5 years in the family (%)	Family type (%)	
				Married	Unmarried	GC	Other than GC		Nuclear	Joint
Successful SHGs	SHG-1	11	30.82	100	0	63.64	36.36	18.18	60	40
	SHG-2	12	34.58	100	0	75.00	25.00	16.67	66.67	33.33
	SHG-3	12	32.58	91.67	8.33	66.66	33.34	8.33	66.67	33.33
	SHG-4	11	36.73	100	0	72.73	27.27	0	63.64	36.36
Unsuccessful SHGs	SHG-5	13	48.85	92.31	7.69	23.08	76.92	53.85	23.08	76.92
	SHG-6	15	46.93	100	0	26.67	73.33	66.67	27.28	72.72

Source Primary data collected from the members

Table 3 depicts that educational level is high among the members of successful SHGs, which is also reflected on the educational level of the officials, whereas educational level is lower among the members of unsuccessful SHGs. It is found that employment status is high among the members of unsuccessful SHGs, whereas instead of being educated, most of the members from successful SHGs are housewives; apparently, these women have the urge to do something and help her family. It also reveals the fact that successful SHG members have more leisure time to give for their businesses, but the members of unsuccessful SHGs are engaged as wage earner, and apparently that is why they do not have enough time to give for their businesses.

5 Factors Behind the Successfully Running of Business by SHG Members

Entrepreneurship development through SHGs is a way to give an opportunity to the women to become financially independent by exploring their skills and knowledge. They use their indigenous knowledge and personal experience to develop and manage their business. Therefore, this platform has given them an opportunity for all-round development. There are several factors working in the successful development and running of business. These factors are discussed in the following sections (Bhatia 2000).

5.1 Education

Education is an important factor in determining the success of any profession. It helps to understand a critical thing in an easy way. It was found that educated persons easily embrace new technologies and other technical aspects of the business, whereas illiterates are unable to adopt new technologies. It is also noticed that education helps an individual to think in a critical way and can they take a rational decision (Chinnadurai 2005). It enhances the communication skills of an individual, which is useful to communicate with the outer world. Hence, in a word we can say that it enhances the quality of an individual.

It is found from Table 3 that 2.17% of SHG members are illiterate among all members of the successful SHGs, whereas unsuccessful SHGs have 39.29% illiterate members. It is also depicted in the table that 15.22% members of successful SHGs have an education of secondary school level and above, while not even a single member has the education even up to secondary level among the unsuccessful SHGs. Therefore, it is evident that education plays an important role in running a business successfully.

Table 3 Other information of the members

SHGs		Educational level of the members				Employment status (%)		Education level of the SHG officials	Average family income (monthly)
		Illiterate	Up to class IV	Up to class X	Above class X	Employed as wage labor	Only housewife		
Successful SHGs	SHG-1	0	2	7	2	36.36	63.64	Graduate	2900
	SHG-2	0	4	5	3	25	75	Higher secondary	2750
	SHG-3	1	5	4	2	16.67	83.33	Higher secondary	3100
	SHG-4	0	4	7	0	18.18	81.82	Secondary	3000
Unsuccessful SHGs	SHG-5	5	7	1	0	69.23	30.77	Class VII	2550
	SHG-6	6	7	2	0	73.33	26.67	Class VIII	2800

Source Primary data collected from the members

5.2 Consensus Building

SHG is an association of people. They form this association to achieve a common goal and solving their problems by sharing their personal experience. Hence, SHGs are dependent on the centric theme of consensus building. Whenever the groups take up any kind of work, first of all members need to make a consensus on certain things and through continued friction and consensus building the groups take the forward step toward success (Choudhary 2005).

It is found from the study that, before starting the business, these SHGs conducted meetings several times among the members and with other facilitators regarding various issues related to the business. In the case of successful SHGs, on an average seven times the members met and discussed various issues related to their business achieving agreement of 95.65% members upon the decision to start a business. However, in the case of unsuccessful SHGs, members met on an average only three times before starting their business and only 46.43% members agreed to start the business while other members had a different view.

5.3 Meeting on Regular Basis

Meeting is an important factor to sort out any problem and to update the members regarding the recent developments related to their association. In the case of SHG, regular meeting enhances the mutual trust among the members. It is also a tool for monitoring the progress of their activities. Through the meeting, members can identify the problems and solve them by sharing their ideas.

The study revealed that successful SHGs conducted regular members meetings and shared their experiences. It is observed that, they conduct at least two meetings with their members every month, whereas in the case of unsuccessful SHGs, members seldom met; the problem which arose was solved by the officials of the groups, mostly by the Secretary. Moreover, it is also found that successful SHGs prepare their business plan, credit plan, and payment schedules at their monthly meetings, whereas no such activities were found in the case of unsuccessful SHGs. Hence, it seems that a positive association persists through regular meetings and successful running of the businesses.

5.4 Maintaining Proper Documentation

Documentation is an important task of any activity, especially where finances are involved. Proper documentation not only enhances the reliability of the work that is very important for the funding agencies and other stakeholders but also enhances the trust among the members.

Going Through the New Avenue of Life ...

It is observed during the field visits that successful SHGs maintain their handbook, passbook, credits book, meeting book, business activity book, and profit-and-loss book very well. Officials of the groups maintain these books and submit these documents in their monthly meetings for approval of other members, while unsuccessful groups did not maintain proper records of their activities. It is also found that officials of both the unsuccessful groups did not know the importance of proper documentation and they also lacked interest to do so. In the absence of proper documentation, a distrustful environment develops among members.

5.5 Age

Age is an important factor to take up a new activity. In the lower age group, an individual carries a more enthusiastic character and vigorous mind to under take risk-bearing activities. Age becomes a more prominent factor in the case of taking of a risk. In the lower age group, one can do more hard work to achieve the SHG's goal. Therefore, in the lower age group, people have the courage to take the risk.

It is depicted in Table 2 that the average age of the members in successful SHGs is 30.82, 34.58, 32.58, and 36.73 years, respectively, for SHG-1, SHG-2, SHG-3, and SHG-4, whereas in the case of unsuccessful SHGs, average age of the members is 48.85 and 46.93 years, respectively, for SHG-5 and SHG-6. It is also observed during the group discussions with the members of all groups that successful SHG members show more interest to run their business, and all of them are willing to take up new activities, whereas 67.86% members from unsuccessful SHGs either want to stop their business or show a lack of interest to run a business. It is observed that most of the members from unsuccessful groups said that they could not run here and there for their business purposes. However, researcher saw a different picture on the other side of the coin that members of successful SHGs are ready to do anything to run their business. Moreover, they can work hard and can go anywhere to take training or for exposure visits. Hence, age is a strong determinant factor of successfully running the business in case of the SHG members.

5.6 Identifying Skill, Interest, and Potential

Before initiating any business, it is essential to identify the interest of the individuals and also identify the available skills that persons have. It is also needed to analyze the viability of that business. The chances of success will be high if a person identifies his skills, interest, and potentials. Therefore, these are the essential things that need to be found out before the start of any business (Das 2000).

It is revealed from the group discussions that, in the case of successful SHGs, before they start their business they conducted meeting several times to discuss their interest, to identify the skills that they have, and the possibilities of that business.

Analysis is needed to conduct skill resource mapping and training, and members of these successful SHGs took help from the service providers. On the other hand, unsuccessful SHGs also conducted the meeting, but they had never included these issues on their meeting agenda (Nachimuthu and Gunatharan 2012).

5.7 Identification of Resources

Identification of resources is an important determinant of success in the microentrepreneurial activities. It is observed that successful SHGs arranged funds from external sources, mainly loans from banks or grants given by NGOs. Moreover, it is also seen that these successful SHGs selected such kinds of businesses for which raw material is locally available at a cheaper cost and there is a good demand for their product in the local market. On the other hand, in the case of unsuccessful SHGs, arranging fund was not easy for them because their communication skills are very weak and they have selected such kind of business that had lesser demand in the local market. Therefore, identification of resources regarding funds and raw material is essential to get success in the business (Dwivedi 2008).

5.8 Market Survey and Marketing of Products

Before starting microentrepreneurial activities, market survey is essential. A prior assumption can be made by this survey regarding the trend and demand of the market for the product that a group or an individual wishes to produce.

The successful SHG members had conducted the market survey before they started their business. It helped them understand the demand of that product that they are going to produce. Moreover, these members formulated a strategy for marketing their product. They decided to have stalls in the all local *Melas* (fairs) in the name of their group for advertising their product. On the other hand, unsuccessful SHG members never had a market survey and had not formulated any strategy for marketing their product; as such, very limited persons know about them and their product (Srinivastav 2006).

5.9 Managerial Skills and Leadership Quality

Each group has a leader, who represents the group in various platforms. To be a successful entrepreneur a person must have some special qualities, such as ability to undertake risk, the introduction of innovation, the ability to control the administration, and the ability to give effective leadership in all aspects related to SHGs. It is found that 71.74% of the members from all four successful SHGs got training on

Going Through the New Avenue of Life ...

group management, microplanning, and documentation. It is also found that these four groups are running on rotational leadership pattern, which means to give the opportunity to everyone to lead the group and to give some innovative thoughts and do better for her group by introducing her ideas (Mungi 2011). On the other hand, in the case of unsuccessful SHGs, it is observed that only 21.43% members got training on group management and preparation of documents. Members of these two group never followed rotational leadership pattern. From the group discussion, it came out that other members of these two groups did not want to lead their group. It is also explored from the group discussions that there are conflicts among the members, and they do not have trust in their leaders. Moreover, the leader of these two groups did not maintain proper documentation and was unable to sort out the conflicts among the members. As a result, these two groups are not running well. Hence, it can be concluded that good leadership quality and success in running a business are closely associated.

5.10 Efficient Service Provider

The service provider has been playing an important role in successful running of the SHGs. All the successful groups acknowledged that unless and until service providers showed them the way, they would not start their business. These successful SHGs got help from service provides at various levels; at village level these groups got help from an NGO; and at the block level, they got help from the women development officer, bank officials, and other resource persons. However, due to lack of communication and lack of interest, the unsuccessful groups did not get any help from NGO or other resource persons. These service providers, particularly NGOs, who are working at the grassroots level, know everything about these groups (Prasad 2003). During the discussions with a service provider, it comes out that they know the potentials of these groups and their strength and weakness, and accordingly, they give their valuable suggestions to these SHGs. Whenever these successful groups faced some problem, they made contact with their service providers to get some suggestions. The unsuccessful SHGs seldom made any contact with their service providers to solve their problems. Therefore, the service providers play an important role in the successful running of the microentrepreneurial activities.

5.11 Supportive Family Members

Family members have an important role in success of SHG business. The successful SHG members have to complete their familial responsibilities before they go out to run their business. In the case of successful SHGs, 80.44% members said that their husbands support them all the time and 19.56% members said that sometimes their husbands misbehaved with them when return late. On the other hand, 75%

members of unsuccessful groups said that their family members did not support their activities and suggested them to stay at home and perform their familial responsibilities. Hence, in the case of successful SHGs, support from their family enhanced the confidence, and they realized a support system was working behind them. Therefore, they can run their business with the fearless mind. This is another secret of success of these SHGs.

5.12 Drawback of the Unsuccessful SHGs

In this section of the study, an attempt has been made to point out all the drawbacks of the unsuccessful SHGs to run their business. Lack of education is the main drawback of these members to run their business. Lack of education means lack of ideas, lack of communication, and lack of confidence. Lack of communication hinders them from exploiting opportunities. Moreover, it is difficult for these members to adopt new technologies, and also, they are unable to understand the critical issues of the business. Hence, they are lagging behind day by day. Good leadership is an important factor to get success in any work. However, in the case of these two groups, leaders are not capable of motivating their members to do something beyond their routine work. The leader is considered as an engine of a group; the leader can provide a directional change among the members, but in these cases, leaders are unable to do so. It is also found that these two groups did not maintain the proper documentation and this led to distrust among the members, which, in turn, created conflicts among them. Moreover, these groups did not survey the market before they started their business. Hence, they did not have any idea related to the trend and demand of their product. Apart from that, they did not identify the local resources and skills they have, which would have been their strength if they had started their business according to their strength. Moreover, family members of these women are not supportive; they do not want to let their women go out for business, rather they suggest them to stay at home and perform their domestic responsibilities. Age is another handicap for them. The average ages of the members of these two groups are high—48.85 and 46.93 years, respectively. Several types of research show that older people seek more secure life rather than taking the risk; here, also, the member women did not have motivation to take the risk. There are several such reasons that accumulate and hinder them from running their business in a successful manner (Table 4).

An attempt has been made through tabulation to see how microentrepreneurial activities have changed the life of women. It is found that successful SHG members earn on average INR 600 to 900 per month. Most of these women spend their earnings on food, education of the children, and petty expenses of their families. Among these members, 69.57% said that mainly they employ their earnings for their children's education because they understand the importance of education. Moreover, 89.13% members said that their husbands are very happy with them and they always support their activities. Rama Saha is a member of the third group; she

Going Through the New Avenue of Life … 169

Table 4 Benefits of women entrepreneurship

Benefits of entrepreneurship	Empowerment	Impact
Increase in economic status	Increase in income Increase in expenditure Increase in consumption Control over resources	Impact on individual (self) Impact on children education Increase in material product of the family Impact on food culture of the family
Self-confidence	To be proactive Can take risk Motivate others Enhance communication skills	Impact of individual Impact on family
Self-worth	Develop leadership ability Ability to work in group To resolve conflict Opportunities to take decision	Impact on self and others Impact on group of people Greater impact on self-confidence
Social status	Positive image Gender equality Involving in community works Involving in local politics To be a model for others	Impact on self-confidence Impact on family Impact on community Impact on other women

Source Calculated from the earlier analysis, based on Geetha Sulur and Barani Gunatharam's model

bought a bicycle for her husband and her husband uses the bicycle for selling fish in the villages and earn money. She is proud to have helped her husband. Pooja Mondal is leading a better life after being involved in these microentrepreneurial activities. Earlier, she was a victim of violence; whenever she demanded small sum, her husband would beat and humiliate her. But now, she is independent economy and need not beg her husband, rather she is helping her husband when necessary. Thus, her group helps her to sort out her domestic problems and lead a better life. It is evident that SHGs help the poor and destitute women to lead a better life by involving them in the microentrepreneurial activities.

6 Conclusion

Women's entrepreneurship contributes to the economic well-being of the family and communities. It reduces poverty and also helps them to secure a good status in family and community. It is well-known that development of the society is directly related to the income generation capacity of its members. Therefore, an attempt has been made by the government to raise the status of women by involving them in the SHGs. It has given them the opportunity to become economically independent by developing microenterprise. The SHG movement in India has been working in the right direction in empowering women and eradicating poverty and unemployment by developing microentrepreneurial activities. Therefore, the number of women enterprises has grown over a period through SHGs to empower women and enhance their position in the society. As such, it is an important mechanism of grassroots programs that tries to bring positive change by working directly with the poor women. Yet, the tragic aspect of this intiative is that due to several reasons most of the SHGs are not working well and many of them stop their activities. However, few groups are running very well and earning profits by taking up various income-generating activities. Therefore, keeping in view the importance of the research work on women empowerment, this study aimed at discussing some important factors working behind the successful running of the microentrepreneurial activities and also tried to find out the reasons because of which other SHGs are unable to run their businesses successfully. Moreover, another objective of this study was to see how SHGs help the members change their lives for the better. To carry out this study, six SHGs, involved in the microentrepreneurial activities, were considered from the Labpur block of Birbhum district of West Bengal. It was observed from the study that the microentrepreneurial activities have provided the women an opportunity to raise their social status by contributing to the family. However, it also comes out from the study that, unless and until the women members have some special qualities, they would not be able to run a business. Some special qualities come to them by birth and some qualities they acquire by learning. The most important factor that encourages women to start their enterprise is their urge to do something independently. Hence, it provides meaningful opportunities to the poor and disadvantaged women to come forward to achieve sustained social and economic development by involving themselves in the economic activities.

References

Basin, Kamal. 2000. *Women's Empowerment: Perspectives and Approaches*. New Delhi: Kali for Women.

Bhatia, Anju. 2000. *Women Development and NGOs*. Research paper on Micro Small and Medium Enterprises (MSME) and Economic Development of Odisha by Dr Krupasindhu Pradhan, 45–70. Rawat Publication, New Delhi.

Choudhary, Sunil. 2005. Self help group formation through frequently asked question. *Kurukshetra, Ministry of Rural Development* 53 (3).

Das, Mallika. 2000. Women entrepreneurs from India: Problems, motivations and success factors. *Journal of Small Business and Entrepreneurship* 15 (4): 67–84 (winter 2000–2001).

Chinnadurai, R. 2005. Women entrepreneurship and service sector. *Kurukshetra—A Journal on Rural Development* 54 (1).

Dwivedi, Archana. 2008. SHGs and micro-credit. *Yojana—A Development Monthly* 52.

Mungi, Ram, A. (2011). Entrepreneurship development of rural women through SHGs. *Indian Streams Research Journal* 1 (4).

Nachimuthu, G.S., and B. Gunatharan. 2012. Empowering women through entrepreneurship: A study in Tamil Nadu, India. *International Journal of Trade, Economics and Finance* 3 (2): 143–147.

Prasad, R.R. 2003. Social mobilization, concept, meaning and approach. *Kurukshetra*.

Srinivastav, Alka. 2006. Women self help groups in the process of rural development. In *Women in Rural Development: Contemporary Social Policy and Practice*, ed. Kiran Prasad, 81–100. India: The Women Press, Delhi.

Access to Finance, Entrepreneurship, and Empowerment: A Case Study

Sudipto Ghosh and Chiranjib Neogi

1 Introduction

Microfinance program organized by the nongovernment organizations (NGOs) is considered as an effective instrument of addressing rural poverty. Access to credit is an important determinant to facilitate the choice of livelihood among rural households. With the dwindling employment opportunities in agriculture, the majority of the rural people are left with an inadequate resource base to sustain their livelihood. In the absence of social security support, a large section of rural population is forced to depend on moneylenders for credit and become victim of their exploitation. During the last couple of decades, there has been a tremendous growth in microfinance, benefiting the poor, particularly women. Between 1997 and 2005, the number of people receiving microcredit increased from 13.5 to 113.3 million with 84% of them being women (Daley-Harris 2006). It is argued that lending to women is safer due to the fact that they are less likely to default, less likely to misuse the loan, and more likely to share the benefits with other family members in their household, especially with their children. In addition to the economic benefits, it is argued that the increasing importance of women's role in the household economy will lead to their empowerment. Empirical studies have widely accepted that lending to women does improve household incomes and is also linked with other associated benefits, such as increased livelihood diversification, more labor market activity, more education, and better health (Hulme and Mosley 1996; Khandkar 1998; Murdoch and Haley 2002; Mosley and Rock 2004; Todd 1996; Zaman 2004). Some find that microcredit has helped women to increase their

---

S. Ghosh (✉)
Urban Planner, Government of West Bengal, Kalyani, West Bengal, India
e-mail: sudipto_g123@rediffmail.com

C. Neogi
Indian Statistical Institute, Kolkata, India
e-mail: cneogi@yahoo.co.uk

© Springer Nature Singapore Pte Ltd. 2017
C. Neogi et al. (eds.), *Women's Entrepreneurship and Microfinance*,
DOI 10.1007/978-981-10-4268-3_10

income-earning capabilities, leading to greater confidence, and ability to overcome cultural asymmetries (Hashemi et al. 1996). The majority of the studies show the empowerment potential of such schemes.

This chapter focuses on the impact of access to financial services on enhancing the quality of life of the beneficiaries of microfinance institutions (MFIs). Can microfinance linkage empower the women socially and economically? To address this question, this chapter draws on a recent case study on Sreema Mahila Samity of Nadia district of West Bengal. The organization is pioneer in the field of women empowerment, strengthening self-help groups (SHGs) through microfinance programs, and SHG-MFI linkage program from the perspective of economic well-being and sociopolitical awareness of the members.

2 Self-Employment Program of Sreema Mahila Samity

Sreema Mahila Samity started the journey of Community Development and Women Empowerment program in 1972 from Baranberia, a remote village of Nadia district, West Bengal. In 1974, the organization launched an ambitious government-sponsored project aimed at emancipating village women in Nadia district of West Bengal. This self-employment program involved imparting vocational training to women. Loan facilities were extended to the rural women at a competitive rate of interest. The year 1975 saw the introduction of adult literacy programs along with awareness programs aimed at educating the village folks on the dangers associated with domestic violence.

The concept of 'Group Activity' was introduced in the year 1980 where both men and women participated as members and women were given an exclusive leadership role. The highlight of the 'Group Activity' aimed at the betterment of existing living condition. The year 1978 was an eventful one for the organization as it spread its branches in the district of North 24 Parganas. The Tagore Society of Rural Development was involved, and the financial support was provided by the 'Bread for the World' organization. Participating women have developed an attitude toward entrepreneurship and leadership over the years. Sreema Mahila Samity as an organization has been acting as an agent of financial development, the emancipation of rural women, and has also been providing women with the role of leadership. The organization has played a pivotal role in eradicating caste discrimination and superstitious beliefs as well. Awareness on health and hygiene among rural women has been promoted. Rural women have been provided with education and made aware of the environment and their resources. Cultural sensitization of such women was also enhanced. Consequently, the rural women had indeed become more enlightened.

In the day-to-day running of the organization, the organization had laid stress on governance, skill development, liaison with different organizations, and the effective utilization of time. As far as resource utilization is concerned, the organization had laid stress on both human and natural resources. In the case of human resource, proper training, awareness building, and appropriate exposure to the outer world,

Access to Finance, Entrepreneurship, and Empowerment ...

particularly that to the matter of government linkage, were provided. The organization was involved in conducting workshop and training programs in cases of natural resources and those of government linkage, along with the speedy implementation of different projects.

Over the past three decades, the organization has spread its branches across 1500 villages, spread over four districts of West Bengal, and has made rapid strides as far as health, education, and family counseling are concerned. A noteworthy feature of the organization has been the eradication of domestic violence. Knowledge on disaster management has been imparted among women. Awareness on killer diseases, such as AIDS, cancer, and tuberculosis has been generated. Sreema Mahila Samity as an organization prides itself for its achievements, particularly in empowering women through SHGs, generation of employment through microfinance, and poverty alleviation. Basic primary education has also been extended to more than 1500 village children.

As an MFI, the organization has followed a distinctively different path from other MFIs. This ensured a qualitative dimension: The relationship between the organization and borrower is different. The organization is in fact not just a lender, but also a provider of advice and technical assistance and mentor. Self-employment or microenterprise creation requires capital, advice, and training. Every year the organization used to provide different aspects of leadership training, an awareness campaign on various issues, and conducted entrepreneurship development program for the SHG members.

SHG is considered as a fulcrum on which the organization stands and works. SHGs are gradually transforming themselves into building blocks of participatory development. Here, the organization acts as a catalyst for the promotion and formation of SHGs. A separate microfinance department was set up to cater to the growing needs of the poor households who are the members of SHGs, and who are not able to handle the formalities of banks when they are in need of credit.

The organization acted as an MFI to the rural poor and provided credit (or extended credit) after the fulfillment of certain formalities. It came into existence at a time when the locality was witnessing domestic violence against women, failed marriages, caste discrimination, and the pitiable condition of the minorities and scheduled castes and scheduled tribes communities.

The organization started operating in the village households dependent on agriculture; some engaged as daily wage earners. It moved forward as a well-managed organization and sustained its growth in the following manner:

(i) In the first decade of its existence, the organization primarily focused on mobilizing women as a means of alleviating poverty through vocational training.

(ii) Conducting awareness programs on various aspects of health, livelihood, and so on.

(iii) Establishing linkage with financial institutions, such as banks, cooperatives, and the concerned government departments.

To build the infrastructure of the organization, mobilization of village women was very vital. A committee was formed that conducted regular meetings to meet the objectives. In the day-to-day running of the organization, it had laid stress on governance, skill development, liaison with different organizations, and the effective utilization of time. As far as resource utilization is concerned, the organization had laid stress on both human resource and natural resources.

3 Operational Aspects of Sreema Mahila Samity (SMS) as an MFI

Microfinance has two components: microsavings and microcredit. The savings habit promoted by microfinance program is resulting in the accumulation of the fund for entrepreneurial activities. Microsavings are further divided into two parts, mandatory and voluntary. Savings habit can help to reduce the vulnerability of the poor. Low-income people have volatile savings or very small savings and often do not have access to banks. The volume of saving of the people is too small to deposit in the banks. MFIs, however, can provide them the scope for depositing their savings. Both MFI and their clients are benefited from the habit of savings. Savings can also help in acquiring livestock or business assets, which can help in creating a new source of income or can increase the existing income. Savings which are mandatory are called compulsory savings. When the clients can deposit any amount any time with the MFI, these are called voluntary savings. In compulsory savings, the frequency of saving could be weekly or monthly depending upon the frequency of group meetings. Also in compulsory savings, the money is non-withdrawable during the term of the loans.

The organization started the formation of groups during the 1980s. They were mixed groups of poor women and men. The idea behind this composition was collective action, which would empower them to have access to economic and social opportunities. The organization made it mandatory for the members and the groups to save money to build a common fund. This fund was created to meet the emergencies. The malfunctioning and internal rifts within these mixed groups compelled the organization to adopt new strategies to form separate groups for female and male members. Gradually, the apex body of rural bank—National Bank for Agriculture and Rural Development (NABARD)—initiated the program—SHG and bank linkage—in the year 1992. The organization partnered with the nationalized banks under the bank-NGO-SHG linkage program of NABARD.

The organization formed groups under the leadership of women with group savings approach. In this decade, a Central Government program Training of Rural Youth for Self-Employment (TRYSEM) started with skill-based training programs in tailoring, nursing, carpentry, spice grinding, wool knitting, mat knitting, and so on. This decade saw a mixed activity of other such programs, namely Child in Need Institute (CINI)-health program, TRYSEM Program, Children and Communities Program, and other such programs related to social development.

Access to Finance, Entrepreneurship, and Empowerment ... 177

4 Functional Aspects

SHG forms the basic constituent unit of the microfinance. An SHG is a group of a few individuals, usually poor women who pool their savings into a fund from which they can borrow as and when necessary. The group members have to save regularly and hold regular group meetings, that is, twice a month. Fulfilling these two conditions at least for two months enables them to get loans from the organization.

The SHG activities with Savings and Credit (S&C) are (1) to reach the economically weak (who are otherwise resourceful on many accounts) where formal banking never reaches and (2) to provide timely credit through easily comprehensive procedure helping group members to utilize loan to avoid defaults and ensure recovery of loans. The operational mechanism is that members pull savings and lend within the group on a need basis. Democratic mechanism normally characterizes SHGs. Other than S&C activities, the group members also organize activities such as literacy campaigns, running women development centers, health services, child care and education, and movements against dowry and child marriage. Therefore, microfinance is not to be confined to its savings and credit operations only, but the mechanism followed to make this financial operation successful must be recognized as an essential component of it. The process throws open enormous potential of a change; that is, the process is more important for those who demand empowerment of the poor. In this study, the findings are based upon the ambit of this understanding.

An SHG consists of five to twenty persons, usually all from different families in the neighborhood. Each group has a leader and an assistant leader elected by the group members. The members decide among themselves the amount of deposit they have to make individually to the group amount. The starting monthly individual deposit level is usually low—INR 10 or 20. On the basis of resolutions adopted and signed by all members of the group, the supervisor or field workers help to open a group savings account in any one of their nearest branches of the organization. The savings are collected from group members at a fixed date and deposited in the group's account with the organization.

Innovative strategies adopted by the organization for implementation of microfinance program are as follows:

(a) Every group has to pass through few stages; pregroup formation, group formation, saving and thrift operation, group stabilization, growth and expansion, bank linkage, and economic activity.
(b) Every group family depends on the commitment and capability of the concerned facilitation, especially during its nascent stage.
(c) A supervisor monitors every group, and a meeting is held every month.
(d) SHGs have been clustered to form a federation, which is their collective strength.

Structure of SMS from APEX to SHG level is depicted in the following diagram:

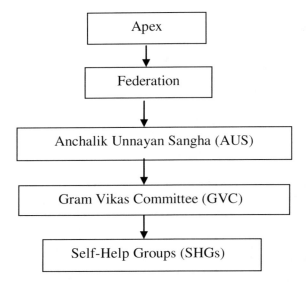

The federal structure of the SHGs works at the grassroots level; GVC (Gram Vikas Committee) at electoral booth level; Anchalik Unnayan Sangha (AUS) at Gram Panchayat level; Federation at the block level; and Apex at the central level.

For policy-level interventions, the governing body provides the necessary support by taking up strategic planning. In the case of operational problems, the Micro Finance Department (MFD) team utilizes the SHG-GVC-AUS-Federation networks to track the loan portfolios through close interaction with the SHGs and the community (social capital) that ensured a high level of loan repayment.

Peer pressure and imposed discipline induce regular repayment of loans. The group members are aware of the flat and reducing balance method of interest. The loan does not involve any collateral security, and this, in turn, induces greater acceptability among the beneficiaries.

The representatives of GVC form the AUS committee. The representatives of SHGs form each GVC committee. SHG is the lowest unit in the microfinance structure.

4.1 *Group Norms and Rules*

A member has to follow the rules as framed by the organization:

(i) Group meetings are usually held twice a month.
(ii) All financial transactions, such as lending, borrowing, repayment of dues, and so on, have to be done in the presence of all members.

Access to Finance, Entrepreneurship, and Empowerment ... 179

(iii) Records are maintained with the help of field workers, supervisors, or office staff.
(iv) Leaders are responsible for conducting meetings, writing resolutions, keeping records, savings, and repayments of the loan amount, interests, and so on.
(v) All kinds of financial or non-financial decisions are taken by consensus, and group responsibility is ensured.
(vi) Leaders are also responsible for discussing other members' problems and helping to solve them.
(vii) SHGs select their leaders through common consensus. A member with personal integrity, honesty, and education is usually given due weight to be accepted as a leader.

Savings is considered as the first criteria, and credit is assumed to be the second. Access to credit is the most important part of the institution. It aims at easy access to credit to improve the economic condition of families and reducing indebtedness to moneylenders. Credit is considered to expand the clientele base and to increase the amount of loan per borrower.

4.2 Agenda for Female Empowerment

Access to finance may contribute to a long-lasting increase in income by means of a rise in investments in income-generating activities and a possible diversification of sources of income; it may contribute to an accumulation of assets; it may ensure a smoother consumption for all; it may reduce the vulnerability due to illness, drought, and crop failures; and it may contribute to the availability of better education, health, and housing facilities of the borrower. Access to finance may also bring about in the improvement of the social and economic status of women. Therefore, microfinance may have positive effects that outperform the monetary and social change of the beneficiary in the following ways:

(i) by bringing about changes that enhance women's well-being at the household, in the community and other social aspects;
(ii) through the development components, such as health, education, earning opportunities, and gender equality;
(iii) by participation in the planning process and political aspects;
(iv) by having an equal say in the decision-making process in the family;
(v) through access to social and legal justice;
(vi) by becoming more independent in financial aspects.

A typical SHG consists of five to twenty persons, which belong to different households. A group has its own name and has a leader and assistant leader, elected by the group members. It is the group member who decides the amount to be deposited to the group account. The starting monthly individual deposit level is as low as INR 10. On the basis of resolutions adopted, the FW/supervisor of the organization opens a savings account with its branch. The savings are collected on a particular date (after the 10th of the month) from individual and deposited in the branch (MFD).

5 Survey Design, Sample Selection, and Methodology

The primary data was collected from surveying the sample of 397 women involved in SHGs located in 41 villages in two districts—Nadia and North 24 Parganas of West Bengal. The rationale behind the selection of SHGs promoted by Sreema Mahila Samity was that the organization has been working in those districts for more than a decade and has extensive experience in the promotion of SHGs under the microfinance program in West Bengal. In addition, it was the largest NGO-MFI functioning in the microfinance field reaching the poor at the remotest of villages and also regarding the amount of disbursed loan. The organization provided non-financial services too, through literacy programs, awareness camps, health care, and sanitation facilities.

In the first stage, two districts, Nadia and North 24 Parganas, were identified because Sreema Mahila Samity is working in these areas for a long period. These two districts are the oldest operational areas of the organization that have the highest cumulative number of SHGs up to the time of the survey. In the second stage, SHGs were selected from 41 villages of Nadia and North 24 Parganas. SHGs were selected based on the criteria that they are at least 1 year old and are involved in microcredit operations. The SHGs were randomly selected from the group list provided. The data were collected from 397 SHGs where the microfinance is in operation in 41 villages. The sample SHGs were selected by using random sampling method.

5.1 The Status of Livelihood Activities in the Selected Villages

The study revealed that the primary occupation of the group members is agriculture. More and more households gradually shifted to other occupations, such as animal husbandry and small business (basically trading activities) over the years after microfinance linkage came into being. Microfinance linkage helps members to purchase agricultural inputs, such as seeds and fertilizers along with dairy animals, cows and goats, that result in diversification of activities. Agricultural purpose means taking land on lease for cultivation, purchasing agri-inputs (such as seeds, saplings, and chemicals/fertilizers), cultivating lands, and so on. Family members are engaged in agri-work, as wage laborers, in animal husbandry, and are also involved in petty trading/income-related activities. They substantially contributed to their family income too by financing their husbands.

Access to Finance, Entrepreneurship, and Empowerment ... 181

6 Results and Discussion

6.1 Socioeconomic profile of group members

Socioeconomic profile of the respondents reveals that majority of the participants failed to complete secondary education level. From the survey data, it is observed that in the SHG in the age group of 1–3 years it is only 9.09%, while 17.39% in the age group of 4–6 years, and it is only 13.45% in the age group of 7 years and above. The maximum average households in the sample belong to scheduled caste (SC) community having 48.66% followed by upper class (general category) which constitutes 25.85% of the population. Scheduled tribe (ST) community constitutes 4.22% of the total samples, while the percentage of other backward communities (OBCs) group is 5.86%. It is observed that there is an increasing trend of participations in SHG from the SC community. The participation of the general community almost remains stagnant in 3 years age group. The populations who do not disclose their caste constitute only 6.3% in the age group of 7 years and above, but in the age group of 4–6 years, it is 21.74%, while in 1–3 years age group, it is 18.18%. The average family size of SHG age groups upto four members is 53.4% of the total sample size, while that of five members is 23.68% and for six members and above the figure is 22.92%.

The 70.28% household members belong to 31–45 years age group, followed by 27.71% in the age group of 18–30 years and 2.02% in the age group of 46–55 years. The proportion of members according to the age of SHGs is 63.64% for 1–3 years, 66.96% for 4–6 years, and 73.11% for 7 years and above. An interesting observation is that the proportion of SHG members in the age group of 46–55 years shows that with advancing age, old people tend to leave the SHGs.

Most of the members belonging to the SHG of age group of 7 years and above are engaged in agriculture. Others are engaged in different economic activities. The survey data show on average agricultural activity constitutes the major share of 57.93%. Business activities are observed in 8.31% households. The income after joining the group increases for most of the members irrespective of the time of their joining. Quite naturally, those who have a longer attachment with the group show a higher percentage of members who can increase their income compared to the other groups with shorter attachment.

Regarding possession of fixed assets of households who belong to SHG, the table shows that there is a definite increase in the percentage of asset holdings of the group members. It is observed that the members having longer durations of associations with the SHGs can increase their asset size in the forms of land and house. There is a definite decline of the members having no assets as the years of association with SHGs increases. The figure dropped from 70.45% to 38.66%. It has been observed that the members associated with the SHGs for 7 years and above can build some forms of assets, most of which can be categorized under building houses. It is found that of the members in SHG age groups, 42.86% in 7 years and above, 26.3% belonging to 4–6 years, and 20.45% in 1–3 years possess houses.

It is observed from the table that average monthly income of most of the group members is between INR 100 and INR 500. It is quite natural that these members are neither very efficient nor is it feasible to utilize their loans to earn a large income. However, interestingly, as the members are experienced, over time they can earn higher income compared to the earlier stages.

6.2 Group Dynamics of SHGs

It is observed that majority of the groups are comprised of 9–12 group members. As far as the relationship between age of group and size of group is concerned, the age of the group is positively related to its size. In the sample, the majority of the SHGs (238) are operating for more than 7 years, while the numbers of SHGs operating between 1 and 3 years are 44. This indicates that the formation of SHGs has reached a saturation level, and new SHGs are being formed at a slower pace.

An important indicator of SHGs functioning is conducting regular meetings of group members. Meetings are utilized for financial transaction, which comprise collection of savings and loan disbursements. From the survey data it is observed that most of the SHGs (93.86%) conduct meetings twice a month, which enhances a good coordination between the members and helps maintain the rules and regulations.

The saving behavior of the SHG members reveals that majority of women (91.69%) on average deposit or save their hard-earned money only with the organization. This shows the trust of members in the organization. The amount of savings per member varies across the groups depending on their capacity to save and the age of the SHGs. The SHG member can save from the least amount of INR 10 to a high amount of INR 40 per month. The sample data shows that 66.75% of the SHG member save INR 10 per month, while 21.9% save INR 20 per month, 9.57% of the sample save INR 30 per month, and 4.53% save INR 40 per month. It reveals that SHG members are maintaining the discipline of the organization.

Within the group, it is also observed that 63.98% of the group leaders from the sample taken can maintain accounts and 36.02% of the group leaders depend on their fieldworkers or supervisor for maintaining their group accounts. It can be observed that 71.85% of the 7 years and above group can maintain their group accounts. The quality of bookkeeping and accounts maintenance is one of the positive indicators of group dynamics, and it also determines the inherent strength of SHGs for future sustainability.

There is a positive association between the age of SHG and the mean level of income. Moreover, the same association is found in the case of the savings of the household of SHG members. It is observed from the coefficient of variation of income that as the age of the SHG increases, the income of the household members tends to become more homogeneous. It may be depicted that the household members can generate more money through their livelihood activities by taking a loan.

6.3 Utilization of Loans

As far as utilization of loans is concerned, the survey data show that 53.58% of SHG age group of 1–3 years take loans for agriculture and 39.28% for business; 68.66% of SHG age group of 4–6 years take loans for agriculture and 25.37% for business; 60.74% of SHG age group of 7 years and above take loans for agriculture and 30.89% for business. On an average, 60.99% of three SHG age groups usually take loans for agriculture purpose and 31.85% for business.

It has been found that regarding savings, there is a rise in the percentage of savings with an increase of the tenure of the SHG members who can save money. Members of SHG age group 1–3 years who can save their money are 60.87%, while this figure is 68.18% for the age group 4–6 years and 85.71% for the age group 7 years and above. The average of three SHG age groups shows that 76.57% can save their money.

The survey data also show that 38.79% of the average of three SHG age groups are agricultural labor (own) and 46.60% are wage labor. It is also observed that the average percentage of SHG members involved in own business is very low, only 14.61%. Most of the members of SHGs belong to the category either of agricultural labor or wage labor. It is basically due to the predominance of agricultural activities in rural Bengal. The own business primarily indicates ownership of small petty shops in the village and the investment in these shops; small household businesses are not very large to depend on loans. However, there may be other reasons behind the small figures in this category. Members usually get a high amount of agricultural loan against their application, which is easy to procure.

6.4 Social Empowerment

Social empowerment of women is a long and difficult process as it requires a change in the mind-set of the people. Rural women of India get less priority in education, are deprived of adequate food, and often have no access to health care. Empowerment, as we understand it in the social aspect, is an increase in self-confidence, increased participation in the decision-making process and bargaining power, and increase in access to resources. In the context of self-confidence, we consider several indicators that are discussed as follows.

Here, self-confidence means to take action in one's life confidently. Confidence in oneself can enhance knowledge, which may facilitate more earnings from livelihood-related activities. Table 1 depicts the percentage of members who give an answer in favor of self-confidence increase from 34.09% of the group with 1–3 years of involvement to 56.30% of the group with an involvement of 7 years and above. There is a rising trend all through the years of involvement. The average of three groups shows that 57.18% of the respondents are self-confident.

According to an increased awareness level about nutrition values, the group members are reported to incur expenses on their food budget. In case of long-time members of the groups, i.e., 4–6 years age group and seven years and above, the households spend a considerable amount on food. Such group members are more conscious about food value.

There is a marginal increase in the level of education expense for the members who are engaged in SHG 7 years or more. According to the figures, of the members who are engaged in SHG for less than 6 years less than 5% spend more than INR 1000 per month on education, while for the last group it is around 10%. Hence, there is a marginal improvement in the expenditure on education among those who are in SHG for a longer period.

The survey data reveal that on average of 44.08% of women of SHG age group have knowledge about child vaccines. It is 66.09% in the age group of 4–6 years and 52.27% in the age group of 1–3 years. The data show that women nowadays are more conscious about their health-related issues. About 51% members of all SHG age group have knowledge on the importance of breastfeeding. It is 56.82% in the age group of 1–3 years and 60.00% in the age group of 4–6 years have the knowledge about the importance of breastfeeding.

The data also show that 47.13% members of all SHG age group have awareness on the necessity of doctor's checkup of pregnant women. 47.73% in the age group of 1–3 years, 48.70% in the age group of 4–6 years, and 44.96% in the age group of 7 years and above have awareness on the necessity of doctor's checkup of pregnant women.

On average, 31.42% members of all SHG age group have correct and proper information about the legal age of marriage and 68.58% have no awareness level. It is 43.18% in the age group of 1–3 years who are aware of the legal age of marriage. A majority of members comprising 81.09% SHG age group of 7 years and above cannot tell about the correct legal age of boys and girls eligible for marriage.

The survey data also indicate that 74.49% of members on average cannot tell properly the minimum government wage rate and only 25.51% have a clear idea about it; 27.27% in the age group of 1–3 years and 27.83% in the age group of 4–6 years have awareness on the minimum wage rate. On the contrary, 78.57% in the age group of 7 years and above have no awareness of minimum wage rate.

Regarding the awareness on different schemes, the survey found that 13.64% in the age group of 1–3 years, 22.61% in the age group of 4–6 years, and 17.65% in the age group of 7 years and above are aware of different government schemes. On average, 17.97% of all SHG age group are aware of various government schemes for the poor.

As far as other social issues are concerned, it is observed from the survey that 9.09% in 1–3 years age group, 20.00% in 4–6 years age group, and 13.03% in 7 years and above age group are aware of women trafficking. A majority of 85.39% members have no idea on women trafficking. Only 14.61% members have knowledge about it. It reveals that the organization cannot intervene in this matter in a significant manner.

Access to Finance, Entrepreneurship, and Empowerment …

Table 1 Descriptive statistics

	SHG age groups								
	1–3 years			4–6 years			7 years and above		
	HH income per month	Savings per month	Average age	HH income per month	Savings per month	Average age	HH income per month	Savings per month	Average age
Mean (INR)	2916.7	101.89	34.66	3090.79	163.35	34.11	3297.97	798.38	34.65
Standard deviation	1430.67	286.19	4.28	1917.16	545.38	4.93	2343.14	615.98	5.85
Coefficient V	49.05	280.88	12.35	62.03	333.87	14.45	71.05	77.15	16.88
Number of sample	44			115			238		

Table 2 T test of savings/month between two SHG age groups

	Between group 1 and group 2	Between group 1 and group 3	Between group 2 and group 3
Mean difference	61.46	696.49*	635.03*
t-statistics	0.92	11.85	9.82*
Significant level	Not significant	Significant	Significant

*Implies significance at 1%

As observed from Table 1 that there is a positive association between the age of SHG and mean level of income. The same association is found in the case of the savings of the household of SHG members. It is observed from the coefficient of variation of income that as the age of the SHG increases the income of the household members tend to become less homogeneous.

It has been found from Table 2 that regarding savings, as t was not significant, there was no difference between the SHG age groups of 1–3 and 4–6 years. Table 2 depicts that as t is significant at 1% level, there is a significant difference in savings/month of the SHG groups 1–3 and 7 years and above. Since the savings/month of 7 years and above are better than those of 1–3 years, it signifies that savings increase with the member staying more years in the SHG. Table 2 reveals that as t is significant at 1% level, there is a significant difference in savings/month of the SHG groups 4–6 and 7 years and above. Since the savings/month of 7 years and above groups is better than those for 4–6 years age group, it signifies that savings increase with the member staying more years in the SHG.

6.5 Entrepreneurship

Women entrepreneurship is perceived as an important tool for empowerment that effectively increases women participation in intra-household decision making and allows them to access information. The ownership and control of various assets enable her to take decisions that make a woman entrepreneur more powerful. Economic independence provides automatic empowerment to women, enabling self-employed women to attain better status and take a decision in family matters.

Entrepreneurship development can be considered as a possible approach to economic empowerment of women. Women can successfully play the role of an entrepreneur as well as a worker. It is because the woman as an entrepreneur has control over assets as well as the freedom to take decisions on her own.

Entrepreneurship in rural areas is community based and faces hurdles created by the following factors:

- Government policies, such as licensing, taxes, and tariff.
- Marketing of goods becomes difficult day by day due to the escalating cost of transport, storage, and advertising.

Access to Finance, Entrepreneurship, and Empowerment ... 187

- Limited access to information on prices and technology.
- Lack of awareness on processing technology.

In the findings, we have identified few successful entrepreneurs who have taken big loans for starting their own business. The main reasons for the entrepreneurs for taking loans are the following:

- The infrastructure at their place is very poor.
- The society having unfavorable attitudes toward them.
- Unfavorable economic factors and environment.
- Limited profit opportunities and limited market.
- MFIs unable to find/identify potential entrepreneurs to lend capital/funds needed to start a new venture.
- There is no lucrative offer for new entrepreneurs from the government.

The role of the organization is now changing with the growing/emerging demands of SHG members. It has been able to understand that their organization greatly depends on the degree of networking in which it operates. Now, the organization has been restructured for better delivery mechanisms.

6.6 Features of Weak Groups

Members of the weak groups do not have adequate knowledge of their work, lack communication skills, self dependency, and maintenance, have no idea of rules, do not submit group accounts correctly, avoid their meetings and often quit after getting loans from the group, do not have the ability to work independently, do not repay their loans, and do not know the value of time. Thus, such SHGs lag behind and become 'D' graded groups. Weak group means the members do not attend the meeting, do not take loans, lack awareness, lack literacy, and do not come forward to help each other. A weak group does not have any social and economic awareness, does not check its accounts, and does not appreciate the value of teamwork, and are not aware of the perspectives of all the members of the group.

Progressive SHGs means timely repayment of their group loan, positive attitude of members, transparency of the accounts, sense of cleanliness, economic change of the members of the family, regularity in savings, good relationship with each other, teamwork in a friendly atmosphere, sharing ideas of their work, timely communication with each other, unambiguous allocation of work to be done, and each and every member following the groups' decision. Members of the group must attend to all their village-level work responsibilities and must monitor progress.

7 Conclusions

In this study, it was observed that women not only repay their loans on time, but also have better saving habits and are willing to work in groups to collect savings, which in turn decreases the costs of loans. Women make a decent employment similar to men, take proper family decisions, have control over assets, can utilize bigger credits to sustain their livelihoods, and are considered positively good clients. They can accumulate substantial savings that could be ranged into insurance and other financial products. They can also pay for services that benefit them. There is a positive impact of microfinance on women's livelihood, which in turn leads them to involve in better reproductive role and ensure better health, nutrition, and educational status of the household members. Apart from this, access to finance among women entrepreneurs helps them to improve productivity, improve status within the family, enhance their self-confidence, and generate valuable resources to the households.

Here, the study is focused on the change in the women's social lifestyle and economic activity after the microfinance program–SHG linkage. There is a behavioral change among the SHG members by associating them with the microfinance program linkage. Based on the empirical evidence, it clearly indicates a general increase in women empowerment for the members of SHG, where a majority of groups are linked with the help of NGOs, which provide support in financial services and specialized training, and have a greater ability to make a positive impact on women empowerment. However, not all women who joined the SHG program were empowered to the same degree. Nevertheless, microfinance is a tool that benefited rural women immensely to uplift economically. In this study, it was observed that despite the significant efforts, the organization failed to encourage entrepreneurship to a satisfactory level among the women.

In this study, it is observed from the characteristics of SHGs from Sreema Mahila Samity, that an SHG is a voluntary organization that gives equal opportunity to their members, which means, to strengthen their group, to enable them to attend their meetings, to stand independently, to repay their own loans timely, to change leadership in time, to develop their social, economic, and education status, abolishing superstition, and to look after all the works of life. SHG programs tend to develop the backward classes and poor people, and to improve the rural lifestyle.

In our society, SHGs are required for poor and backward women to change their lifestyle for the better through economic and social development, such as education, health, and general awareness, to be self-sufficient and to be able to work with unity. They are required to remove superstition and economic inequality from our society, for which proper education is required, as also to protect their rights and to help them increase their small saving deposits and property, to strengthen and build their self-confidence, to help them break free from the hands of the mahajans, and to become financially independent. Putting it in a nutshell, to ensure their security, SHGs are essential.

Microfinance program is seen as an opportunity for the SHG members, and the program has helped to drive business, agricultural activities, and meeting basic needs, such as food, children's education, medical expenses, and loan repayments. The program benefited women enabling them to grow their business or household agricultural activities, empowering them, and giving them a voice in decision making.

References

Daley-Harris, S. 2006. *State of the Microcredit Summit Campaign Report 2006*. Washington DC: Microcredit Summit Campaign.

Hashemi, S.M., S. Schuler, and A.P. Riley. 1996. Rural credit programs and women's empowerment in Bangladesh. *World Development* 24 (4): 635–653.

Hulme, D., and P. Mosley. 1996. Finance Against Poverty, vols. 1 & 2. London: Routledge.

Khandkar, S.R. 1998. *Fighting poverty with microcredit: Experience in Bangladesh*. Washington D.C.: World Bank.

Mosley, P., and J. Rock. 2004. Microfinance, labour markets and poverty in Africa: A study of six institutions. *The Journal of International Development* 16 (3): 467–500.

Murdoch, Jonathon, and Barbara Haley. 2002. Analysis of the effects of microfinance on poverty reduction. NYU Wagner Working Paper No. 1014. http://www.nyu.edu/wagner/public_html/cgibin/workingPapers/wp1014.pdf.

Todd, H. 1996. *Women at the centre: Grameen bank borrowers after one decade*. Colorado: Westview Press.

Zaman, H. 2004. The scaling-up of microfinance in Bangladesh: Determinants, impacts and lessons.

Access to Credit and Microentrepreneurship: A Gender Comparison

Rabin Mazumder, Subham Dastidar and Amit Kumar Bhandari

1 Introduction

Women-led enterprises play an important role in economic development of a nation which has not achieved full potential in many parts of the world. Participation of the women in small- and medium-scale enterprises creates employment opportunities and avenues for women's economic independence. According to the World Bank data, about 25–33% of private businesses are owned or operated by women globally (Ernst and Young 2009). Worldwide, the rates of women entrepreneurs are increasing at a faster rate than men (Global Partnership for Financial Inclusion, GPFI 2011). According to the Global Entrepreneurship Monitor (GEM) report (2013), about 126 million women in 67 countries have started their new business in addition to 98 million established businesses around the world. In the USA, the women-owned firms grew by 23% as compared to 9% men-owned firms; while in Canada, 47% of small enterprises and about 70% new business start-ups in 2004 were registered in the name of women (GPFI 2011). In developing countries, women-owned enterprises are growing at a significant rate and contributing toward economic growth and development. In 2008, Thailand experienced only 0.3% annual growth in men-owned business, while their women counterparts grew at

---

R. Mazumder
Institute of Engineering and Management, Kolkata, India
e-mail: rabin.mazumder@gmail.com

S. Dastidar
Faculty, Department of Commerce, RBC Evening College, North 24 Parganas,
Naihati, West Bengal, India
e-mail: subham2585@gmail.com

A.K. Bhandari (✉)
Department of Economics, RBC Evening College, North 24 Parganas,
Naihati, West Bengal, India
e-mail: amit.kumar.bhandari@gmail.com

© Springer Nature Singapore Pte Ltd. 2017
C. Neogi et al. (eds.), *Women's Entrepreneurship and Microfinance*,
DOI 10.1007/978-981-10-4268-3_11

2.3% (GPFI 2011). The report depicts that the annual growth rate of women-owned enterprises (10%) in Malaysia is higher than its men counterparts (7%).

In India, women-owned enterprises are making a significant contribution to the growth of the economy. Indian economy has increasing number of participation of the women entrepreneurs in micro-, small, and medium enterprises (MSMEs). However, the number of women-owned enterprises is still less than the men-owned enterprises. It was reported in 2014 that about 3 million women enjoyed either full or partial ownership in MSMEs, which comprised only 10% of all the MSMEs in the economy (International Finance Corporation 2014). The contribution of women-owned businesses in industrial output is 3.09%, and the level of employment generated by them is over 8 million people (International Finance Corporation 2014). It is observed that about 78% of women-owned enterprises belong to the service sector, and about 98% of microenterprises are owned by women (International Finance Corporation 2014). Inadequate access to formal credit in the MSME sector is one of the major impediments to the growth of women entrepreneurs.

Credit is an indispensable instrument facilitating the growth of women entrepreneurs, which helps to remove poverty and various social obstacles. About 80% enterprises run by women are self-financed, while 4.4% receive financial assistance from institutional sources. Lack of institutional financing to women microenterprises led to imbalanced entrepreneurial society. The formal financial institutions in India have a negative perception toward women entrepreneurs. Often, they show doubt toward the creditworthiness of women. Financial institutions are often skeptical about the entrepreneurial abilities of women; they often lack the motivation to venture into the male-dominated market. Most of the enterprises started by women are small and self-financed. Despite evidence that women loan repayment rates are higher than men's, women still face more difficulties in obtaining credit due to discriminatory attitude of financial institutions. It is also noticed that of the women who take loan for income-generating activities, only a minuscule percentage have autonomous control over the loan money. In maximum cases, a male member of the family enjoys the control of the proceeds of loans.

There are differences in an entrepreneurial initiative based on gender, particularly in rural areas. The determinants that lead a person into entrepreneurship can be classified into micro- and macrolevels. By microlevel determinants, we understand individual characteristics, such as age, sex, education qualification, credit availability, asset-ownership, and social capital, which enables an individual to take part in different entrepreneurial opportunities, while the macrolevel determinants are mainly concerned with the business environment, policies, and other location-specific variables, which affect the growth of entrepreneurship. Given this backdrop, this chapter investigates the determinants of access to formal credit among rural microentrepreneurs in rural West Bengal, the underlying determinants that lead to an imbalance in entrepreneurship initiative with respect to gender.

Access to Credit and Microentrepreneurship: A Gender Comparison

The rest of the chapter is organized as follows. Section 2 describes the literature review of the study. Section 3 presents the credit accessibility of rural households in India. This is followed by data used in the study, which explains the study areas, sampling techniques, and methodology in Sect. 4. Section 5 presents the results of the study. The final section presents the summary of the research with concluding remarks.

2 Literature Review

Credit can often act as a catalyst for the development of the business and enhance earnings. In developing countries, discrimination against women entrepreneurs in access to formal credit is highlighted in many instances (Mckee 1989; Otero and Downing 1989; Fletscher and Kenney 2011; Hansen and Rand 2014). The problem is worse for rural areas where the financial sector is dominated by male (Abor and Biekpe 2006). In both developing and underdeveloped countries, women have lower access to resources as compared to men. They have no or low access to ownership of land, house, education, and training facilities (Katepa 1999). Accessibility of formal credit by women entrepreneurs is limited because lending institutions demand collateral from borrowers rather than the viability of the project (Thuranira 2009). Collateral plays an important role in the banking business and helps in understanding the creditworthiness of the borrowers (Klein, Meyer, Hanning, Burnett and Fiebig 1999). In the rural financial system, formal lending institutions face difficulties in obtaining information about potential borrower's creditworthiness. Consequently, formal and informal lenders might find lending to be risky and prefer not to offer credit at all (Fletschner 2009). The formal institutions are rigid on the matter of collateral. Lending the money to the resource-less poor involves high risk as high transaction cost involved with these unsecured loans (Xia et al. 2011). The result of asymmetric information leads to moral hazard and adverse selection in the credit market (Khoi et al. 2013). The problem of moral hazard is a more likely event once the loans are authorized to the buyers. Apart from the lack of proper information about borrowers, rural entrepreneurs also face other problems, such as lesser number of bank branches in their locality. Thus, borrowers have to cover a long distance to get access to financial services. On the other hand, banks are often unable to monitor the post-credit phases of the borrowers; that is, where, when, and how the borrowers will make the investment. Thus, lack of financing acts as a barrier to growth and success of women entrepreneurs. Limited financial awareness and understanding of financial products or services are areas of concern of women entrepreneurs in India. It makes disinclination for access to finance from formal channels (International Finance Corporation 2014). The experimental study of Cole et al. (2009) on India and

Indonesia reveals that financial literacy is a significant predictor for availing the financial services. Low levels of training among women entrepreneurs make the situation more difficult to access the formal credit. In addition to that, women have a double burden of domestic responsibilities; cultural constraints related to behaviors of women, and lack of decision-making power restrain them from taking up the challenge of entrepreneurship role (Kumari 2013). Gender inequality in the society is perceptual, and it has different forms. Sen (2001) classifies different types of gender inequality. The majority of the discrimination against women is multidimensional. Economically, they are excluded from property rights (Rao 2002); socially, they are excluded to begin economic activities outside the home (Jaiswal 1993); culturally, their work at home is not recognizable as an economic activity because activity at home is not marketable (Tinker 1990; Bardhan 1985). This is a universal truth for almost every country with different intensity. Discrimination against women entrepreneurs in Indian society has been focused in various literature. About 50% of India's population is women, yet economically, socially, and culturally dominated by male. Soundarpandian (1999) depicts that women entrepreneurs face financial constraint, technical difficulties, lack of family support, and hard competition from male entrepreneurs.

The women entrepreneurs respond that they could not get a loan from banks, as they do not have collateral property to show to banks. A study conducted by Vinze (1987) with 50 women entrepreneurs in Delhi also supports the findings of the present study to some extent. Vinze expresses that stringent documentation and formalities need to be more flexible to access the formal credit. Discrimination shoots from the low value attached to women's work. In Indian society, the role of household maintenance and care activities is predominantly assigned to women (Bhatia 2002; Hirway 2002). Consequently, women entrepreneurs need to manage both family and entrepreneurship, which often restricts their ability to grow their businesses and perpetuates in their limited access to credit. Rural women face discriminatory attitudes from lending institutions. They also get inadequate support from family members at operating level (Manimekalai and Rajeswari 2002). According to GEM (2007) report, the share of early-stage entrepreneurial activities for women (7.49%) is slightly less than men (9.51%), but for owned, established businesses, the gap is more wide (8.69%). Female-headed rural households are among the poorest of the poor, and rural women entrepreneurship in India is still at a nascent stage. In rural areas, women are particularly engaged in agriculture and agro-based industries along with their male counterpart. Women are particularly involved with food preservation, bakery, dairy, poultry, and forest-based weaving and handloom business. It is observed that women face difficulties in terms of arranging the raw materials, lack of technical skills, poor infrastructure, and lack of access to market that challenge them to get success in their businesses (Manimekalai and Rajeswari 2002; Rajendran 2003). According to United Nations Industrial Development Organization (UNIDO 1995), loan repayment performance of women is better than men, although they face a lot of difficulties to access credit from the formal channel.

3 Access to Credit Among Rural Households in India

In India, the credit market is fragmented, which consists of the combination of formal, semi-formal, and non-formal segments. Formal sources of credit consist of national and state banks, private banks, regional rural banks, and cooperative banks. Microfinance institutions (MFIs) and self-help groups (SHGs) are considered as semi-formal sources of finance, whereas informal sources include relatives, friends, and private moneylenders. Formal credit is not so easily available to the rural households. Many borrowers belong to low-income households, landless laborers, peasants, and artisans. They do not have access to formal sources of credit because of lack of collateral and unavailability of procedural documents required for sanctioning the loan. Poor rural households are ignorant about the basics of sound money management (Rao and Priyadarshini 2013). Since independence, the availability of formal and semi-formal sources of credit has improved, but still, the availability of rural credit lags far behind the actual needs of finance by the farmers across the country (Basu 2006).

The commercial banks have been successfully enhancing the flow of rural credit since 2003. However, unfortunately, such increase in credit has not benefited the poor, especially the small and marginal farmers and tenants, as credit availability continues to remain low due to poor banking support. As a result, poor household depends on informal credit which comes with an exorbitant rate of interest. They continue to suffer under excessive indebtedness. Contribution to the rural household debt by the institutional credit sources reduced from 64% in 1991 to 57.1% in 2002, whereas, at the same time, loans provided by the non-institutional credit sources have increased from 36% to 42.9%. The share of moneylenders in rural household debt made a significant jump from 15.7% in 1991 to 29.6% in 2002. The share of commercial banks in total dues, during 1991–2002, remained at 35%, although the number of scheduled commercial bank (SCB) branches in rural sector has fallen from 33,089 in 1996 to 30,625 in 2007 (RBI, Handbook of Statistics of Indian Economy 2011–2012).

For years, several efforts have been made by various organizations to provide adequate credit to the rural poor. However, the greatest initiative was taken by National Bank for Agriculture and Rural Development (NABARD), which is responsible for disbursing agricultural credit to provide financial assistance to the state banks, cooperative banks, RRBs, microcredit institutions, and other money-lending agencies and promotion of various developmental activities in village areas. Percentage distribution of NABARD's financial assistance and disbursement per rural household of states and national level during 1996–1997 to 2006–2007 reveals the adverse distribution of credit to agriculture. Financial assistance provided by NABARD to the eastern region is much lower as compared to the other states of India.

The presence of MFIs is a significant landmark in the field of the rural credit market. The primary objective of MFIs is to provide financial services to the poor households. These services include savings, loans, and insurance (Wrenn 2005). Services are provided by the MFIs to those poor who are deprived of getting such services from the formal financial institutions. MFIs initially started as a non-government organization (NGO) movement to form SHGs, and later led to the emergence of the financial institutions. The poor in India are mainly self-employed, do not possess any expertise skill, and do not restrict themselves to any particular occupation. These small-scale enterprises face limitations regarding capital, physical assets, labor, and so on. The microenterprises operate in areas with low entry barriers and high competition. Moreover, due to continuous low production, their income level becomes low, which further augments poverty of the rural people.

Informal sources of credit provided by the private moneylenders have played a major role in rural credit market since 1950s. Moneylenders provide credit for consumption and investment, and during emergent needs. The interest charged by the informal lenders is nearly 48% per annum. Moneylenders keep a close contact with their clients, and hence, they not only know about their clients, but are also aware of their repayment capacity, something that formal credit institutions are not. Thus, they find easier to offer many flexible services to their clients (Basu 2006).

4 Data and Methodology

4.1 Study area

The data were collected from five districts of West Bengal, namely Howrah, Hooghly, North 24 Parganas, South 24 Parganas, and Bankura. Howrah district is bounded by the Hooghly River and is surrounded by North and South 24 Parganas districts in the east, Hooghly in the north, Purbo Midnapore in the south, and Ghatal subdivision of Paschim Midnapore in the west. Hooghly district is surrounded by Nadia in the east, Burdwan in the north, Bankura in the west, and Paschim Midnapore in the south. North 24 Parganas district is bounded to the Nadia district, South 24 Parganas in the south, and Bangladesh in the east and keeps the Hooghly district, the river Hooghly, and Kolkata at the west. South 24 Parganas located in the southern part of the state. The district is bounded by the river Hooghly in the west, Bay of Bengal in the south, and Kolkata and North 24 Parganas in the north, and eastern boundary is demarcated by Bangladesh and Bidya and Matla rivers. The fifth district Bankura is bounded by Burdwan in the north, Hooghly in the southeast, and Paschim Midnapore in the south and Purulia in the west.

4.2 Sampling

The study is based primarily on data obtained from field survey. After the selection of five districts, the household sample was drawn through multistage random sampling procedure. Every district consists of several subdivisions which in turn

Access to Credit and Microentrepreneurship: A Gender Comparison

comprise several municipalities and community development (CD) blocks. As the study was centered in rural areas, CD blocks were given importance for gathering relevant data. From every district, two CD blocks were selected. Then, from each CD block, two villages were selected. Hence, from every district, total four villages were selected. In this way, from 5 districts, 20 villages were selected for the study. By the low order of penetration of commercial banks in the villages, a group of four villages was formed in every district where all forms of credit organizations, such as formal, informal, and semi-formal are operating. The formal institutions comprise SCBs, RRBs, and primary agriculture cooperative society (PACS). Apart from this, informal sources consist of moneylenders, friends, relatives, shopkeepers, merchants, traders, and so on. The semi-formal sector, similarly, comprises SHGs and MFIs. Based on the borrower's list obtained from Panchayat Pradhan, group leader of the SHGs, personal connection with relatives and local information, sample households were chosen randomly. A total of 209 borrowers were chosen to participate in the interview. These sample households either accessed formal, informal, or semi-formal credit.

The dependent variable of the study is whether the respondent has access to credit from formal financial institutions. The response takes the form of yes and no, which can be modeled with logit regression.

The logistic regression model presented here shows the probability of accessing formal credit (Y) and is estimated on the explanatory variables (X).

The dependent variable of the model is presented as

$Y = 1$ borrower's access to formal credit
$= 0$ borrower does not have access to formal credit

In order to perform the analysis, we use logistic regression with the following model:

$$L_i = \ln\left[\frac{P_i}{1 - P_i}\right] = \alpha + \beta_i X_i \tag{1}$$

where L_i is the log of the odds ratio called the logit or log-odds, which are a linear function of the explanatory variables. P_i is the probability of accessing formal credit of the ith borrower; the vector X_i contains attributes of socioeconomic and household characteristics; and β is the unknown regression coefficients to be estimated. The probability P_i ranges between 0 and 1 and is nonlinearly related to the X_i attributes.

The cumulative logistic distribution function in (1) can be represented as:

$$P_i(Y_i = 1) = \frac{1}{1 + e^{-(\alpha + \beta X_i)}} \tag{2}$$

If P_i is the probability of accessing formal credit, then $(1-P_i)$ is the probability of not accessing:

$$1 - P_i = \frac{1}{1 + e^{(\alpha + \beta X_i)}} \tag{3}$$

The odds ratio is defined as:

$$\frac{P_i}{1 - P_i} = \frac{1 + e^{(\alpha + \beta X_i)}}{1 + e^{-(\alpha + \beta X_i)}} = e^{(\alpha + \beta X_i)} \tag{4}$$

The odds ratio is the ratio of favorable to unfavorable cases of accessibility. This preference depends on the values of the explanatory variables. By taking the natural log of Eq. (4), we get Eq. (1).

If the error term (μ) is taken into account, the logit model becomes

$$L_i = \alpha + \beta_i X_i + \mu \tag{5}$$

To find out the relation between types of states and access to formal credit, we use chi-square test.

5 Results

5.1 Sample Profile

The personal information of the rural entrepreneurs includes age, education, and income, while business-related characteristics include business experience, holding a savings bank account, financial literacy, agricultural land, and other assets. About 77% of the entrepreneurs belong to the 31–50 age group, while 15% of the respondents are above 50 years and 7.8% below 30 years age group. As for the respondents' education level, the majority have up to higher secondary education (55.6%), followed by graduate and above (22.4%), and 17.6% up to primary education. Regarding income, the respondents' household income is considered, rather than their personal income, because entrepreneurial initiative among rural folks depends not only on their personal income but also on the income of other family members. In the sample, 18.3% of respondents' household income was below INR 5000, while 49% fell into the INR 5001–10,000 income bracket, and the remaining 32.7% had an income level more than INR 10,000.

Genderwise distribution in credit accessibility reveals that 64.7% male entrepreneurs have access to formal credit, while 39.3% female entrepreneurs have accessed the same. Respondents were asked whether they hold any savings account in banks. 75.8% male and 51.8% female respondents have a savings bank account.

Distance from the nearest bank branch is categorized into two categories, namely less than 4 km and more than 4 km; 78.4% male and 80.4% female respondent's nearest bank branch is located less than 4 km from their residence. Regarding financial literacy of the respondents, it is observed that male respondents (85.6%) are more financially literate than female respondents (75.0%). As far as household assets are concerned, about 67% respondents have agricultural land for both male and female respondents. Regarding other assets, 88.2% male respondents have other assets compared to 85.7% female respondents (Table 1).

Table 1 Percentage distribution of the rural microentrepreneurs according to different parameters

	Male (%)	Female (%)
Age		
Below 30 years	7.8	14.3
31–50 years	77.2	76.8
Above 50 years	15.0	8.9
Education		
Up to primary level	17.6	33.9
Less than higher secondary	55.6	60.7
Graduate and above	26.8	5.4
Income		
Up to INR 5000	18.3	28.6
INR 5001–10,000	49.0	48.2
Above INR 10,000	32.7	23.2
Access to formal credit	64.7	39.3
Business experience		
Less than 5 years	30.1	51.8
More than 5 years	69.9	48.2
Bank account		
Yes	75.8	51.8
No	24.2	48.2
Distance to bank		
Less than 4 km	78.4	80.4
More than 4 km	21.6	19.6
Financial literacy		
Yes	85.6	75.0
No	14.4	25.0
Agricultural land		
Yes	67.3	67.9
No	32.7	32.1
Other assets		
Yes	88.2	85.7
No	11.8	14.3

Source Primary survey

5.2 Analysis of Access to Credit

Table 2 provides an analysis of the relationship between household access to credit and socioeconomic and business-related factors. About 64.7% of male and 39.3% female respondents have access to formal credit, indicating huge gender gap in access to credit with respect to gender. Chi-square test of independence showed that the relationship between access to formal credit and gender is not independent implying that there is a statistically significant relationship between the two variables, $\chi^2 = 10.867$ and $p < 0.001$. Access to credit with respect to gender reveals that below 30 age group respondents have greater access to credit (65%) compared to 31–50 years (57.8%) and above 50 years (53.6%) age group respondents. However, chi-square test shows no significant association between the variables. About education, those who have completed their higher education and graduation have the higher accessibility of credit compared to the low level of education. Significant relation is found between household income and access to formal credit. The study reveals access to credit increases with successive higher income level, and chi-square test of independence exhibits a statistically significant relationship between the two variables, $\chi^2 = 27.516$ and $p < 0.001$. Access to credit significantly increases with business experience. Respondents with more than 5 years of experience have 67.1% access to credit, while business experiences of less than 5 years have 41.3% access to credit. In line with expectation, a person having a bank account has higher access to credit. As revealed by the empirical investigation, 67.2% respondents access to credit have a savings bank account, while 41.3% have accessed to credit with no bank account, and chi-square test of independence exhibits a statistically significant relationship between the two variables, $\chi^2 = 44.931$ and $p < 0.001$. Having financial literacy does improve accessed only formal credit; 66.5% respondents access to finance with basic financial knowledge, while only 16.7% respondents have accessed with no financial knowledge in financial matters. Asset position of households (not agricultural land) significantly improved respondents' access to credit. Chi-square test of independence showed that access to formal credit and the bank account was statistically significant, $\chi^2 = 11.685$, $p < 0.001$.

The factors that affect accessibility to formal credit are described as follows. We consider variables that have a significant association with the access to formal credit as observed from the chi-square test. Based on the results found in Table 2, three socioeconomic and household characteristics and four variables in the business environment have been selected for further analysis.

Gender: Male entrepreneurs are likely to take more risk compared to the females. In the Indian society, headship of the family member is claimed by male members, where they take the major financial decisions. Acute gender discrimination prevails in rural India. A comprehensive study from Latin America, South Asia, and Sub-Saharan Africa found that rural women are more deprived of accessing credit than men under equivalent socioeconomic conditions (Fletschner 2009 and Diagne et al. 2000). Evidence from primary data reveals that male entrepreneurs have greater access to formal credit compared to female entrepreneurs.

Access to Credit and Microentrepreneurship: A Gender Comparison

Table 2 Relationship between credit accessibility and socioeconomic and business-related factors

	Access to formal credit (%)	Calculated χ^2
Gender		
Male	64.7	10.867*
Female	39.3	0.000
Age		
Below 30 years	65.0	0.630
31–50 years	57.8	0.730
Above 50 years	53.6	
Education		
Up to primary level	39.1	27.516*
Less than higher secondary	52.9	0.000
Graduate and above	90.9	
Income		
Up to INR 5000	47.7	5.929**
INR 5001–10,000	54.9	0.052
Above INR 10,000	69.8	
Business experience		
Less than 5 years	41.3	13.162*
More than 5 years	67.1	0.000
Bank account		
Yes	67.2	44.931*
No	41.3	0.000
Distance to bank		
Less than 4 km	57.6	0.33
More than 4 km	59.1	0.499
Financial literacy		
Yes	66.5	30.326*
No	16.7	0.000
Agricultural land		
Yes	56.0	0.619
No	62.0	0.458
Other assets		
Yes	62.30	11.685*
No	26.90	0.000

Source Primary survey
*Significance level at 1%
**Significance level at 5%

Education: With higher education, an individual understands intricate information, maintains business records, conducts cash flow analysis, and also makes right business decisions (Roslan and Karim 2009). In West Bengal, it is observed that people with higher education are more likely to get institutional credit (Mazumder 2013). As shown in Table 3, the percentage of sample respondents who have access to credit increased with the level of education. Hence, it is hypothesized that level of education has a positive effect on formal credit accessibility.

Households income: Findings of the study in rural West Bengal revealed that as income of the rural households increases, the probability of getting institutional credit also increases (Mazumder 2013). The percentage of male entrepreneurs' access to finance increases with the successive higher income group, while the percentage of the female respondent who has access to financing increases with income but not proportionately with a male counterpart (Table 3). Therefore, the

Table 3 Relationship between credit accessibility and explanatory variables

	Access to formal credit (%)	
	Male	Female
Age		
Below 30 years	83.3	37.5
31–50 years	64.4	39.5
Above 50 years	56.5	40.0
Education		
Up to primary level	33.3	47.4
Less than higher secondary	61.2	32.4
Graduate and above	92.7	66.7
Income		
Up to INR 5000	57.1	31.3
INR 5001–10,000	60.0	40.7
Above INR 10,000	76.0	46.2
Business experience		
Less than 5 years	43.4	37.9
More than 5 years	73.8	40.7
Bank account		
Yes	16.2	44.8
No	80.2	33.3
Distance to bank		
Less than 4 km	65.0	37.8
More than 4 km	63.6	45.5
Financial literacy		
Yes	74.8	40.5
No	4.5	35.7
Agricultural land		
Yes	61.2	42.1
No	72.0	33.3
Other assets		
Yes	69.6	41.7
No	27.8	25.0

Source Primary survey

income of the households and accessibility of formal credit is expected to be positively related.

Experience in business: Borrowers having more experience in their business are more successful, and hence have high repayment rate (Roslan and Karim 2009). Therefore, we may hypothesize that loan repayment performance is positively related to borrower's experience. As per research studies, besides age and education, factors, such as business experience, family business history, industry knowledge, training, and so on, also determine credit accessibility (Kimuyu and Omiti 2000; Zeller 1993; Lore 2007). Women often find it difficult to access loans from formal sources due to lack of education and experience. Those who are literate are not that confident about obtaining loans, particularly when there exists an absence of past credit experience (Kurwijila and Due 1991; Weidemann 1992).

Financial literacy: Financial literacy, as defined by the Organisation for Economic Co-operation and Development (OECD), is 'a combination of awareness, knowledge, skills, attitude and behavior necessary to make sound financial decisions and ultimately achieve individual financial well-being' (OECD, INFC 2011). Financial literacy has a predominant influence on financial inclusion and protection of customer. Every player in the economy needs to have financial literacy (Chakrabarty 2013). It may be expected that financial literacy and credit accessibility have a positive relationship. In this study, financial literacy of borrowers includes awareness and knowledge about formal sources of credit such as loan schemes for poor sections of people, the interest rate on agricultural credit, and insurance facility provided by the formal credit sources.

Bank account: It is noticed that a large section of the rural people in India does not avail banking services. Hence, they are excluded from getting the facility of the electronic benefit transfer to the bank accounts. Electronic transfer facilitates to reduce the number of intermediaries and corruption. Bank account helps to avail the formal credit. According to Bhaskar (2013), the bank account enables holder to access all financial services. Hence, we may hypothesize that the facility of bank account ensures greater access to formal credit at reasonable cost. Although formal credit institutions have emerged lately, still many villages in India do not have a bank branch. While more than 70% of the population resides in rural areas, only 10% or even lesser enjoy the commercial bank credit. RBI data show that of 84,640,867 villages, only 46,126 were covered by banks in March 2014. Therefore, the necessity of financial inclusion is beyond question (Lok Sabha Secretariat, India 2014). Presently, it is found that most Indians depend on moneylenders for their credit needs and on the parallel, informal banking for savings, such as Saradha group and Sahara group. Saving in these informal banks is highly unsafe. Owning bank accounts might resolve this difficulty. It is important that the facility of a bank account is made available to ensure greater access to credit at reasonable cost. Consequently, the government will be able to provide social growth and development benefits as well as subsidies to the bank accounts of beneficiaries, thereby removing the lacunas in the social welfare schemes. Easy and quick access to the banking system (and freedom from scam-artists and moneylenders) will ultimately lift the country's economic prosperity.

Assets of the household: In our study, we consider assets owned by a household except for agricultural land. The size of landholding is directly proportional to the credit borrowed by a household (Duy 2011). Landownership plays a significant role in increasing the chances of accessibility to credit as formal creditors demand ownership certificates for giving loans or because the families possessing more land can borrow more (Quach et al. 2005). As shown in Table 3, the percentages of male and female sample respondents are higher for households possessing other assets. It is hypothesized that formal credit accessibility enhances with the assets of households.

5.3 Results of Logit Regression

A logistic regression model is used to investigate the impact of the determinants of the access to formal credit by rural entrepreneurs. Respondents who had successfully acquired credit from a formal financial institution are deemed to have accessing credit, while those whose applications were turned down or not applied for formal credit are deemed as not accessing to formal credit. The results of the logistic regression model are depicted in Table 4. Overall, the model fitted the data relatively well, and most of the regression coefficients are statistically significant to have expected signs and significance levels. Hosmer and Lemeshow's (H&L) R^2 measures how much the badness of fit improves as a result of the inclusion of the predictor variables (Field 2005). Its range is $0 \leq R^2 \leq 1$. $R^2 = 0$ indicates that the predictors

Table 4 Results of estimated credit accessibility among rural entrepreneurs

Variables	Coefficient	Odds ratio
Constant	−3.859* (0.803)	0.201
Gender (male)	0.352** (0.394)	1.422
Education		
Class VI to XII	0.048 (0.048)	1.049
Graduate and above	1.447* (0.692)	4.252
Households income		
INR 5001–10,000	0.013 (0.478)	1.002
Above INR 10,000	0.272* (0.536)	1.312
Business experience	0.840* (0.519)	2.317
Bank account	1.508* (0.393)	4.517
Financial literacy	1.450* (0.519)	4.263
Other assets	0.946* (0.590)	2.575
H&L's R^2	0.558	
Number of observations	209	

Dependent variable Access to formal credit (1 = access credit; 0 = otherwise)

Source Primary survey

*Significance level at 1%

**Significance level at 5%

are useless at predicting the outcome variable, whereas $R^2 = 1$ means that the predictors are perfect at predicting the outcome variable. In Table 4, H&L's R^2 was 0.558, so the predictors such as gender, educational level, income, and constraint for accessing formal credit are good enough to predict the outcome variable. Bank accounts, business experiences, financial literacy, and asset position of households are proficient in predicting the outcome variable for supply-related factors.

The coefficient of gender is positive and significant. The odds ratio for the predictor is 1.422, implying males are 1.422 times higher odds of credit accessibility compared to females. They are willing to start their own business if they have sufficient amount of capital, whereas a large proportion of the females are engaged in household-related activities. In addition to that, male members head the family in Indian society, therefore, they have responsibility of their family, which induces them to demand credit more than female members.

The education has positive effect on the probability of access to credit from formal institutions. This is because highly educated people can comprehend information on credit terms and conditions, and have the ability to complete loan application formalities properly. The result of the study also reflected that the odds of credit accessibility increases by 4.25 times, for those who have completed their study up to graduation compared to other lower education categories.

Household income of the respondents with more than INR 10,000 per month has a significant positive impact on formal credit accessibility compared to other lower income categories. High income indicates the higher capability of repayments. Hence, they are more inclined to access formal credit. For low-income households, high transaction costs of credit from formal sources discourage them from taking loans. Rather, they resort to informal sources, especially from friends and relatives, because they are less expensive as compared to formal credits.

Bank account is seen as a gateway to mainstream financial products and services. The result indicates that having a bank account in a household has a positive and significant impact on access to formal credit. Owning a bank account gives the poor households a sense of financial security and growth and encourages the habit of saving among the people so as to enhance the accessibility of credit from formal financial institutions.

Business experience is an important determining factor of credit accessibility. The results suggest a significant impact of business experience on credit accessibility. The odds in favor of accessing to formal credit increases by a factor of 2.317 as compared to the business experience of less than 5 years. A household having more business experiences has better credit management skills. Hence, institutional lenders have more trust on them compared to the inexperienced or less experienced borrowers.

In the second step, we calculate the predicted probability of credit accessibility. The market for formal credit for rural microentrepreneurs can be segmented on the basis of their socioeconomic and business environments. From the coefficients of logistic regression, we have calculated the individual respondents predicted access to credit with respect to gender and categorized them according to different parameters considered for logistic regression (Table 5). Identification of gender biases with respect to different parameters is important in framing appropriate policies for reducing the gender gap. As calculated from the logistic regression, male microentrepreneurs enjoy 25.5% more probability to receive credit from formal sources than female counterpart. The level of education of the male entrepreneurs increases the probability to access to credit compared to female entrepreneurs. Predicted access to credit with respect to education reveals that probability of access credit is higher for male entrepreneurs in all three education categories. The highest probability is seen among graduates and higher education levels, where the predicted probability is 92.2% for male and 72.9% for female entrepreneurs. Thus, enhancing women education helps women to access more formal credit. The predicted probability is higher among microentrepreneurs who belong to higher income groups. Male entrepreneurs enjoy greater access to credit among all income categories compared to female. The gender gap in predicted access to credit is highest (28.5%) among INR 5001–10,000 income group as indicated earlier; experience in doing business is a significant predictor of access to credit. The estimated predicted probability is higher for both male and female

Table 5 Gender difference in access to credit according to predicted probability of the characteristics

Variables	Male	Female	Gender gap (male—female)
Access to credit	0.647	0.392	0.255
Education			
Up to primary level	0.413	0.360	0.053
Less than higher secondary	0.588	0.381	0.207
Graduate and above	0.922	0.729	0.193
Income			
Up to INR 5000	0.524	0.393	0.131
INR 5001–10,000	0.624	0.339	0.285
Above INR 10,000	0.749	0.502	0.247
Business experience			
Less than 5 years	0.484	0.299	0.185
More than 5 years	0.716	0.492	0.224
Bank account			
Yes	0.773	0.560	0.213
No	0.249	0.212	0.037
Financial literacy			
Yes	0.726	0.472	0.254
No	0.175	0.152	0.023
Household assets			
Yes	0.694	0.421	0.273
No	0.290	0.222	0.068

Source Primary survey

entrepreneurs with business experience of more than 5 years. However, the gap between male and female entrepreneurs is 22.4% higher in this category, while 18.5% gap is found for those whose business experience is less than 5 years. Entrepreneurs with savings bank account significantly improve access to credit, 21.3% higher for a male. The gender gap is also noticed with respect to financial literacy. Male entrepreneurs with basic financial literacy enjoy 25.4% more probability than female. Not much difference in access to credit is observed between male and female entrepreneurs without any bank account, with no financial literacy and without assets of households. The gender gap in predicted probability is large (27.3%) for entrepreneurs holding different assets.

6 Summary and Conclusion

Women-led entrepreneurship is regarded as an untapped source of economic growth and development, which has largely been neglected in Indian society. The majority of the women entrepreneurs are urban based, while entrepreneurship among women in rural areas is very limited. Lack of entrepreneurial initiatives by women is due to the combination of individual, social, and business environment. This chapter analyzed the factors underlying credit accessibility of rural households among rural microentrepreneurs. Using the data from five districts of West Bengal, the study investigated the factors affecting access to formal credit and the discrimination against women entrepreneurs in credit accessibility.

The result shows that gender of the entrepreneur has a dominant and significant impact on access to credit, indicating gender discrimination in access to credit where male respondents were more favored in accessing formal credit than females. Education of the households is another stimulating factor for enhancing institutional credit accessibility. For entrepreneurs with higher levels of education, particularly graduate and above, their chance of accessing institutional credit increases. Household income is another significant determinant, where higher income group households enjoy greater access to credit. The results from factors related to business environment observed that possessing of a bank account is the largest influence on access to credit, followed by financial literacy, other assets, and experience in doing business.

The study also estimated gender gap in access to credit. Among socioeconomic factors, the gender gap is higher among higher education and income levels. Highest gender difference in access to finance is noticed among the respondents holding different household assets, which might help them to access institutional sources of credit. The gender difference is also noticed among respondents with a bank account, financial literacy, and experience of more than 5 years in doing the business.

The results of this study are relevant for policy makers to reduce the gender gap in credit accessibility to promote women-led microentrepreneurs in the country. The gender difference in access to formal credit among microentrepreneurs demands further theoretical and empirical work to investigate the source of the discrimination.

References

Abor, J., and N. Biekpe 2006. SME's access to debt finance: A comparison between male-owned and female-owned business in Ghana. *The International Journal of Entrepreneurship and 66 Innovation* 7 (2): 105–112.

Bardhan, K. 1985. Women's work, welfare and status: Forces of tradition and change in India. *Economic and Political Weekly* 20 (51): 2261–2269.

Basu, P., 2006. *Improving access to finance for india's rural poor*. Washington, D. C., New York: The World Bank. Paper No. 36448, 20–40.

Bhaskar, P.V. 2013. Financial inclusion in India—An assessment, reserve bank of India at the MFIN and access-assist summit organised in New Delhi. Retrieved from https://www.rbi.org. in/scripts/BS_SpeechesView.aspx?Id=862.

Bhatia, R. 2002. Measuring gender disparity using time-use statistics. *Economic and Political Weekly* 37 (33): 3464–3469.

Chakrabarty, K.C. 2013. Address by Dr. K.C. Chakrabarty, Deputy Governor, Reserve Bank of India at the Stakeholders Workshop on Financial Literacy organized jointly by the UNDP, NABARD and MicroSave at Mumbai on February 4. Retrieved from http://www.rbi.org.in/scripts/BS_SpeechesView.aspx?Id=779.

Cole, S., T. Sampson, and B. Zia. 2009. Financial literacy, financial decisions, and the demand for financial services: evidence from India and Indonesia. Working Paper 09–117. Cambridge, MA, Harvard Business School, 3–19.

Diagne, A., M. Zeller, and M. Sharma. 2000. Empirical measurements of households access to credit and credit constraints in developing countries. Washington, D.C.: International Food Policy Research Institute. FCND Discussion. International Food Policy Research Institute. Paper No. 90.

Duy, V.Q. 2011. Factors affecting on access to formal credit of households in the Mekong Delta, Vietnam. Retrieved from http://papers.ssrn.com/sol3/papers.cfm?abstract_id=1972944.

Ernst and Young. 2009. Scaling up: Why women-owned businesses can recharge the global economy, 3. Retrieved from http://www.ey.com/Publication/vwLUAssets/Scaling_up_-_Why_womenowned_businesses_can_recharge_the_global_economy_new/$FILE/Scaling_up_whywomen_owned_businesses_can_recharge_the_global_economy.pdf. p. 3.

Field, A. 2005. *Discovering statistics using SPSS*, 2nd ed. London: Sage publication.

Fletscher, D. and L. Kenney. 2011. Rural women's access to financial services: Credit, savings and insurance. ESA Working Paper No. 11–07.

Fletschner, D. 2009. Rural women's access to credit: Market imperfections and intrahousehold dynamics. *World Development* 37 (3): 618–631.

Global Entrepreneurship Monitor (GEM). 2007, *Executive Report* 2007, Global Entrepreneurship Monitor, Babson College, London Business School and Global Entrepreneurship Research Consortium (GERA), 12.

Global Entrepreneurship Monitor (GEM). 2013. *Global Entrepreneurship Monitor* 2012 *Women's Report*, 2. Retrieved from http://www.babson.edu/Academics/centers/blank-center/global-research/gem/Documents/GEM%202012%20Womens%20Report.pdf. p. 2.

GPFI, IFC. 2011. *Strengthening access to finance for women-owned SMEs in developing countries*. International Finance Corporation. Washington, DC.

Hansen, H., and J. Rand. 2014. The myth of female credit discrimination in african manufacturing. *The Journal of Development Studies* 50 (1): 81–96.

Hirway, I. 2002. Employment and unemployment situation in the nineties: How good are the NSS data?, *Indian Journal of Labour Economics* 31 (43): WS87–96.

International Finance Corporation. 2014. Micro, small and medium enterprise finance; improving access to finance for women-owned businesses in India. A research report on opportunities, challenges and the way forward, New Delhi 9–25.

Jaiswal, R.P. 1993. *Professional status of women: A comparative study of women and men in science and technology*. Jaipur: Rawat Publications.

Katepa-Kalala, P. 1999. *Assessment report on: women and poverty and economic empowerment of women*.

Khoi, P.D., C. Gan, G.V. Nartea, and D.A. Cohen. 2013. Formal and informal rural credit in the Mekong river delta of Vietnam: interaction and accessibility. *Journal of Asian Economics* 26: 1–13.

Kimuyu, P. and J. Omiti. (2000). Institutional impediments to access to credit by micro and small scale enterprises in Kenya. *IPAR Discussion* Paper No. 026/2000. IPAR. Nairobi.

Klein, B., R. Meyer, A. Hannig, J. Burnett, and M. Fiebig. 1999. *Better Practices in Agricultural Lending FAO/GTZ*. Rome: Italy.

Kumari, N. 2013. The role of NGOs in promoting women entrepreneurship in India. Ph.D. thesis: University of Trento, 30–70.

Kurwijila, R., and J.M. Due. 1991. Credit for women's income generation: A tanzanian case study. Unpublished manuscript.

LokSabha Secretariat, India 2014. Parliament Library and Reference, Research, Documentation and Information Service (LARRDIS) Pradhan Mantri Jan-Dhan Yojana (PMJDY). Reference Note, No 7. Retrieved from http://164.100.47.134/intranet/PRADHAN%20MANTRI.pdf.

Lore, M. 2007. *An evaluation of human capital factors that can enhance access to credit among retailers in Nairobi*. Nairobi: Unpublished Project Report Submitted to United states International University-Africa.

Manimekalai, N., and G. Rajeswari. 2002. Grassroots entrepreneurship through self help groups (SHGs). *SEDMI Journal* 29: p2.

Mazumder, R. 2013. Vicious circle of financial exclusion: An empirical study in West Bengal. *Indian Journal of Finance* 7 (12): 38–46.

McKee, K. 1989. Micro-level strategies for supporting livelihoods, employment, and income generation of poor women in the world: The challenge of significance, in Jacob Levitsky (ed.), World Development, 17 (7): 993–1006.

OECD, INFE. 2011. *Measuring financial literacy: Questionnaire and guidance notes for conducting an internationally comparable survey of financial literacy*. Paris: OECD.

Otero, M. and D. Jean, 1989. Meeting women's financial needs: Lessons for formal financial institutions. In: *Paper presented at the seminar on informal financial markets in development*, Washington, D.C. 18–20.

Quach, M.H., A.W. Mullineux, and V. Murinde. 2005. Access to credit and household poverty reduction in rural Vietnam: A cross-sectional study. Retrieved from http://www.grips.ac.jp/vietnam/VDFTokyo/Doc/1stConf18Jun05/OPP01QuachPP R.pdf.

Rajendran, N. 2003. Problems and prospects of women entrepreneurs, SEDME Journal 30 (4): 39–42.

Rao, P.S., and Y.J. Priyadarshini. 2013. Credit options to the rural poor: Microfinance as a source of rural credit in India. *International Journal of Management and Social Sciences Research* 2 (4): 8–21.

Rao, P. 2002. *Entrepreneurship and economics development*. New Delhi: Kaniska Publishers.

RBI. 2011–2012. *Handbook of statistics of indian economy*. Retrieved from https://rbidocs.rbi.org.in/rdocs/Publications/PDFs/00HB130912LF.pdf.

Roslan, A.H., and M.Z.A. Karim. 2009. Determinants of microcredit repayment in Malaysia: The case of Agrobank. *Humanity and Social Sciences Journal* 4 (1): 45–52.

Sen, A. 2001. An inauguration lecture for the new Radcliffe Institute at Harvard University. Retrieved from http://www.hindu.com/fline/fl1822/18220040.htm. Accessed on September 09, 2016.

Soundarapandian, M. 1999. *Women entrepreneurship*. New Delhi: Kanishka Publishers.

Thuranira, C.A. 2009. Retrieved from http://thuraniracharlesatayacurriculumvitae.blogspot.com/2009/10/factors-affecting-accessibility-of.html, accessed on September 11, 2016.

Tinker, I. (ed.). 1990. *Persistent inequalities: Women and world development*. New Delhi: Oxford University Press.

UNIDO. 1995. *Integration of women in industrial development unit, participation of women in manufacturing: Patterns*. Regional Analysis, ECA Region, Final Report, Vienna: Determinants and Future Trends.

Vinze, M.D. 1987. *Women Entrepreneurship in India: A socio-economic study of Delhi, 1975–85*. New Delhi: Mittal Publications.

Weidemann, C.J. 1992. *Financial services for women*. GEMINI: Tools for Microenterprise Programs.

Wrenn, E. 2005. Microfinance-literature review. Retrieved from www.dochas.ie/documents/MicroFinance_literature_review.pdf.

Xia, L., G. Christopher, and H. Baiding. 2011. Accessibility to microcredit by Chinese rural households. *Journal of Asian Economics* 22 (3): 235–238.

Zeller, M. 1993. *Participation of rural households in informal and formal credit markets in Madagascar*. Washington, D.C.: IFPRI.

Printed in the United States
By Bookmasters